Congress and the War on Terror

Congress and the War on Terror

Making Policy for the Long War

Darren A. Wheeler

Conflict and Today's Congress

An Imprint of ABC-CLIO, LLC
Santa Barbara, California • Denver, Colorado

Copyright © 2018 by Darren A. Wheeler

All rights reserved. No part of this publication may be reproduced, stored in a retrieval system, or transmitted, in any form or by any means, electronic, mechanical, photocopying, recording, or otherwise, except for the inclusion of brief quotations in a review, without prior permission in writing from the publisher.

Library of Congress Cataloging-in-Publication Data

Names: Wheeler, Darren A.
Title: Congress and the War on Terror : making policy for the long war / Darren A. Wheeler.
Description: Santa Barbara, California : Praeger, [2018] | Series: Conflict and today's Congress | Includes bibliographical references and index.
Identifiers: LCCN 2018018222 (print) | LCCN 2018021765 (ebook) | ISBN 9781440857096 (ebook) | ISBN 9781440857089 (alk. paper)
Subjects: LCSH: War and emergency legislation—United States. | United States. Congress—Powers and duties. | Legislative power—United States. | Terrorism—Prevention—Law and legislation—United States.
Classification: LCC KF7225 (ebook) | LCC KF7225 .W48 2018 (print) | DDC 363.325/170973—dc23
LC record available at https://lccn.loc.gov/2018018222

ISBN: 978-1-4408-5708-9 (print)
      978-1-4408-5709-6 (ebook)

22 21 20 19 18   1 2 3 4 5

This book is also available as an eBook.

Praeger
An Imprint of ABC-CLIO, LLC

ABC-CLIO, LLC
130 Cremona Drive, P.O. Box 1911
Santa Barbara, California 93116-1911
www.abc-clio.com

This book is printed on acid-free paper ∞

Manufactured in the United States of America

*To
Augustus Jones Jr.
Mentor and Friend*

Contents

Preface ix

Abbreviations xi

Chapter 1 Introduction 1
Chapter 2 Electronic Surveillance and National Security 21
Chapter 3 Interrogation and Torture 59
Chapter 4 Military Tribunals 95
Chapter 5 Drones and Targeted Killing 127
Chapter 6 Making Policy for the Long War 159

Notes 173

Bibliography 191

Index 215

Preface

A considerable amount has been written about the American government's response to the 9/11 terror attacks. It was one of those moments in history when people remember where they were at the time. It has shaped, and will continue to shape, national security policy for years to come. I have been studying the government reaction to 9/11 now for 17 years—primarily as a judicial politics scholar who also has an interest in the presidency. However, as time has passed, it has become clearer to me that terrorism policy is really the result of all three branches of government working together. Much of the literature in this area ignores or downplays the role of Congress and consequently underestimates an important actor in the process.

I am not the first scholar to conceptualize what we are in as a "Long War," but I agree with that premise and think that recognition is an important step in making terrorism policy. Each chapter in this book begins with a historical examination of policy prior to 9/11. This is important because political actors after 9/11 were not writing on a blank slate, but rather simply continuing to develop and change policy as they had done before the attacks. To be sure, 9/11 did mark some significant shifts in policy making in some areas; but even here, there was a history, a history in which Congress played an important role.

If nothing else, I hope this book serves as a reminder that the U.S. Congress—contrary to presidential power narratives—will play an important role in developing terrorism policy as the years pass in the Long War. Only in this way can we develop policies that promote national security, while also providing accountability and transparency, hallmarks of our republican form of government.

A book-length project is always a marathon rather than a sprint, and it is never accomplished alone. I would like to thank Ball State University and the Department of Political Science for supporting a well-timed sabbatical that allowed for the completion of this book in a timely fashion. I would also like to thank Lydia Kotowski for her research assistance on this project. Her help was invaluable. Significant portions of this book were presented at numerous political science conferences around the country. I would like to thank all the panelists and reviewers for their thoughtful comments and suggestions. While I'm thankful for all the input from others that made this a better project, any errors remain mine alone.

Abbreviations

ACLU	American Civil Liberties Union
AQAP	Al Qaeda Arabian Peninsula
AUMF	Authorization to Use Military Force
CIA	Central Intelligence Agency
CIPA	Classified Intelligence Procedures Act
CSRT	Combat Status Review Tribunal
DNI	Director of National Intelligence
DOJ	Department of Justice
FBI	Federal Bureau of Investigation
FDR	Franklin Delano Roosevelt
FISA	Foreign Intelligence Surveillance Act
FISC	Foreign Intelligence Surveillance Court
FISCR	Foreign Intelligence Surveillance Court of Review
FOIA	Freedom of Information Act
ISIL	Islamic State of Iraq and the Levant
KSM	Khalid Sheikh Mohammed
MCA	Military Commissions Act
MST	Material Support for Terrorism
MTCR	Missile Technology Control Regime
NATO	North Atlantic Treaty Organization
NGO	Nongovernmental Organization
NSA	National Security Agency
OIG	Office of Inspector General

OLC	Office of Legal Counsel
RPV	Remotely Piloted Vehicle
TSP	Terrorist Surveillance Program
UAV	Unmanned Aerial Vehicle
UCMJ	Uniform Code of Military Justice
WMD	Weapons of Mass Destruction
WOT	War on Terror

CHAPTER ONE

Introduction

> The accumulation of all powers, legislative, executive, and judiciary, in the same hands, whether of one, a few, or many, and whether hereditary, self appointed, or elective, may justly be pronounced the very definition of tyranny.
>
> James Madison—*Federalist #47*

The 9/11 terrorist attacks are arguably the most significant political event of the 21st century. Americans still remember where they were when they heard the news and watched the twin towers fall. The impact these attacks had on American social, military, political, and economic policies is incalculable. Their legacy will influence public policy for decades.

The American response to these attacks was swift and forceful. "We're at war," President George W. Bush was quoted as saying that day. With those words, the War on Terror (WOT) commenced. President Bush was not just using the word "war" in the figurative sense like the "War on Drugs" or the "War on Poverty," but rather a war comparable to military conflicts such as World War I and World War II which—according to the Bush administration— required extraordinary military powers for the president. This idea that the United States is at war against terrorists has been redefined and reinterpreted by succeeding presidential administrations, but no subsequent president has rejected the idea that the United States is in a state of war against Al Qaeda and associated terrorist forces. Not only does the United States remain at war, but the struggle has even been expanded in some ways over the course of three presidencies.

All wars evoke heated passions and controversy, and the WOT is no exception. It is an unconventional struggle against an unconventional enemy that presents a variety of unique challenges. Controversies exist at two levels. The first involves the policies the United States has devised to fight this war against terrorists. Issues like warrantless electronic surveillance, the use of military tribunals, armed drones, and "enhanced" interrogation have all sparked fierce debates about how the United States should combat terrorism—what works and how these policy choices reflect American values. These are debates where the answers are unclear and many questions remain.

The procedures used to design and implement government policies in these areas have been just as contentious. Following 9/11, government policies designed to counter terrorist threats were often hastily conceived and applied in a secretive, unilateral, ad hoc manner due to the fear that more attacks were imminent. The ongoing threat of terrorism requires a more open and searching government response. Some commentators have begun referring to the WOT as "the Long War,"[1] and a long war requires long-term policy-making solutions.

This book shows how Congress—an often-overlooked actor in this policy-making area—has played a key role in laying the foundation for many post-9/11 programs in areas such as electronic surveillance, military tribunals, and the detention/interrogation of suspected terrorists. It is predicated on the belief that Congress will continue to have a vital role to play in the development, implementation, and oversight of national security policy in the WOT. A prolonged struggle of this nature requires a legal and statutory regime that is built on a solid foundation rather than a series of highly changeable and often opaque executive orders. Only by working together with the president and the judiciary can Congress develop transparent and effective long-term policies that protect national security, while maintaining democratic accountability and protecting civil liberties.

Congress and the War on Terror

The first question one might ask when discussing the WOT is: "Why Congress?" Since 9/11, all presidents have consistently repeated the refrain that it is the job of the president to protect the people of the United States almost as if the job were personally done by one individual alone. Congress can help, the narrative goes, by doing what the president directs it to do.

There is no shortage of critics when it comes to taking the measure of Congress in the WOT. In fact, even supporters of Congress lament its failures to check executive power and exercise its own constitutional powers. One critic concluded that the "legislative record has been desultory, reactive, and unimaginative,"[2] while another referred to its impact as "indirect and relatively insubstantial."[3]

The reasons for this critical view of Congress are almost as numerous as the list of criticisms themselves. There are many who argue the executive branch has simply run roughshod over Congress. In 2003, Representative David Obey (D-WI) declared, "This administration thinks that Article I of the Constitution was a fundamental mistake."[4] Even Republicans joined in periodic criticism of the Bush administration's extraordinarily broad interpretation of its own war powers. Senator Chuck Hagel (R-NE) lamented that the administration treated Congress as "an appendage, a Constitutional nuisance."[5]

Others conclude Congress has not so much been "run over as it has lain supine."[6] Many members of Congress adopt the view articulated by former House Majority Whip Roy Blunt (R-MO) when he said that "the truth is that in time of war . . . there is not a whole lot for members of Congress to do."[7] They firmly believe the prosecution of any war is almost exclusively the prerogative of the president and the executive branch of government.

However, it would be a gross exaggeration to say Congress has done nothing. Congress has passed legislation that includes the Authorization to Use Military Force (AUMF), the Patriot Act, the Detainee Treatment Act, the Military Commissions Act of 2006, the REAL ID Act of 2005, the Transportation Security Act, and the USA Freedom Act just to name a few. It also passed legislation creating the Department of Homeland Security, the largest executive branch reorganization since the Great Depression. This record leads some scholars to conclude congressional efforts in this area have been underappreciated. Others are not so sanguine about the impact and importance this legislative record.[8]

Can Congress do more in the fight against terrorist extremism? The answer is a resounding yes. If the United States is going to continue to fight the WOT, continued congressional input is absolutely necessarry. Benjamin Wittes, a journalist and Fellow at the Brookings Institution, has written extensively on this very topic. He captures the essence of how important this question is when he writes: "Congress can offer something priceless: actions that, unlike unilateral presidential acts, can build comprehensive legal systems and do so in the name of the political system as a whole."[9]

Like Wittes, this book argues Congress has an important role to play in the WOT going forward, a role grounded in this country's Constitution and its history. The chapters in this book will show how Congress has historically been involved in these controversial policy areas in the WOT, from electronic surveillance to military tribunals. These histories are important because they refute the idea that these policy areas are the exclusive prerogative of the executive branch. Congress is constitutionally imbued with a variety of war and foreign affairs powers that, if exercised vigorously, can serve as a foundation for an increased role in the design and implementation of policy going forward in the WOT.

It is important to note at the outset that Wittes recognizes the difficulty in both advocating this position and in eventually making it a reality. He admits that very few are really calling for an increase in the congressional role in the WOT. There may even be more who oppose than support the idea. He also adds, "Nothing Congress has done to date justifies particular faith" that it will step up and play a larger role in the design, implementation, and review of policy in these controversial policy areas.[10] In spite of this, he argues that Congress should at least try since it represents the best way forward in the Long War.

This book will examine how, both historically and constitutionally, Congress has played an important role in areas that are of key interest today: electronic surveillance, military tribunals, armed drones, and interrogation of detainees. These serve as a springboard for future congressional involvement. This does not mean Congress will replace the president as the primary actor in the WOT, but it illustrates what roles Congress can play going forward.

National Security and War Powers

Ensuring the security of any state is arguably the most fundamentally important task a government has. Governments of all stripes are often given extraordinary powers in this area. If one listens to the rhetoric of any elected official—the president or members of Congress—it is punctuated with references to keeping the American people safe. It is that underlying rationale that is used to validate just about any action taken in the name of fighting terrorism since 9/11.

The question is not whether national security is an appropriate goal or something that deserves support, but rather how it is best achieved. Its importance, and the severity of the consequences for getting it wrong, usually means that debates about how to best achieve national security are vital and often controversial. There are at least two levels of discussion. The first deals with defining the roles of political institutions and political actors. At this level, it is important to know what role Congress should play. What are its constitutional powers, and what are its responsibilities in the American political system?

The second level deals with the design and implementation of terrorism policies themselves. How does terrorism legislation work its way through Congress, and how much should it compromise with the executive branch? What role should the courts play? These questions serve as the foundation for discussions of particular policies. The first step toward answering these questions requires an examination of the constitutional and historical foundations of war powers in the American political system.

Introduction 5

Presidential War Powers

There is a general consensus among observers that the scope of presidential war powers has grown over time despite the fact there have been no formal constitutional changes that have expanded the president's authority in this area. Some have argued that this is a good thing. Others characterize it as executive usurpation of power contrary to the intention of the founding fathers and the Constitution.[11]

While there is little disagreement that the traditional British model of war powers lodged them exclusively with the king, scholars disagree about the lessons the founding fathers took from this system. The king had the exclusive power to raise and direct armies, declare war, and determine peace. By the time the framers were drafting the Constitution, the ascendant British Parliament had established the power of the purse as a check on the king's war powers.

John Yoo, an influential architect of the Bush administration's antiterror policies and staunch academic defender of broad executive prerogatives, argues the framers intentionally adopted much of the British model of war powers, agreeing with influential theorists such as Locke, Blackstone, and Montesquieu that the war power was inherently executive in nature.[12] This means there are few checks on executive war powers. They should be read expansively, subject only to the specifically enumerated checks placed in the Constitution. Silences or points of contention should be read in a manner most favorable to the president.[13] Other scholars reject this conclusion. They argue that the framers quite consciously rejected the British model of war powers. This is foremost evident in the fact that Congress was explicitly given a host of enumerated war powers including the power to declare war.

The Constitution gives the president a number of enumerated war/foreign affairs powers. Article II states: "The President shall be Commander in Chief of the Army and Navy of the United States, and of the militia of the several states, when called into the actual service."[14] While the Constitution does not specifically detail what actions the president may take as commander in chief, it can, at a minimum, be safely described as the ability to make war. The president was also given the power to negotiate treaties on behalf of the United States with the advice and consent of the Senate. The president is also required to "take care that the laws [of the United States] be faithfully executed." He is also solely endowed with the "executive power" of the United States. Some scholars have interpreted these latter two powers to mean the president has inherent executive powers as noted earlier. Included in these inherent powers is a broadly defined ability to wage war on behalf of the country, a power subject to few political and institutional checks.[15]

During the 19th century, presidential military excursions were generally limited in scope and duration. Presidents such as Abraham Lincoln and James Polk who used military force decisively were the exception rather than the rule. People sometimes point to Lincoln as a good example of a forceful commander in chief, but it is important to remember even Lincoln enacted many of his unilateral military policies while Congress was not in session. When it reconvened, Lincoln laid his actions before it for retroactive approval.

Some scholars point to the Korean conflict as a turning point in how presidents—not Congress—would take the lead in initiating military conflict.[16] It is certainly true that after World War II the United States defined its national interests in a more global fashion than it had before the war. The emerging Cold War with the Soviet Union would facilitate and accelerate this trend. Twin U.S. foreign policy goals of fighting communism and promoting democracy prompted dozens of presidentially initiated military actions in such diverse countries as Korea, Vietnam, Panama, Libya, Lebanon, Grenada, Bosnia, and Iraq. The scope of these military operations also varied considerably from enforcing no-fly zones to larger military campaigns involving hundreds of thousands of troops. No longer did presidents consider it necessary to obtain congressional approval to initiate military hostilities. United Nations resolutions, North Atlantic Treaty Organization (NATO) treaty obligations, the president's own commander in chief power, and open-ended congressional resolutions served as substitutes.[17]

By the time Al Qaeda terrorists struck the twin towers on 9/11, presidential ascendency in the area of war/foreign affairs powers was virtually complete and institutionalized. While the weight of academic criticism may have cautioned against the confluence of war powers in the presidency, historical practice had left presidents with good reason to think they could largely define their own powers in this area. Indeed, while many argued the Bush administration's interpretation of its Article II war powers were outrageously expansive, the Obama administration did not reject many of these claims, and there is little to suggest that President Trump will either.

Congressional War Powers

Despite recent claims that the framers intended to imbue the presidency with plenary power in the area of war powers and foreign affairs,[18] Congress clearly has some role in this policy area. Even a cursory reading of the Constitution confirms this. Article I, Section 8 of the Constitution includes the following express congressional powers:

"To define and punish Piracies and Felonies committed on the high Seas, and offenses against the Law of Nations;

To declare War, grant Letters of Marque and Reprisal, and make Rules concerning Captures on Land and Water;

To raise and support Armies, but no Appropriation of Money to that Use shall be for a longer Term than two Years;

To provide and maintain a Navy;

To make rules for the Government and Regulation of the land and naval forces;

To provide for the calling forth the Militia to execute the Laws of the Union, suppress Insurrections, and repel Invasions;

To provide for the organizing, arming, and disciplining the Militia . . ."[19]

The U.S. Senate also has the power and responsibility to advise and consent in the selection of executive branch officials and for the ratification of treaties to which the United States is a party.

This is a long list, especially when juxtaposed with the president's express war powers in Article II. It also lends credence to Professor David Gray Adler's contention that the framers intended for Congress to have "senior status" in its partnership with the president in the area of foreign affairs.[20]

Constitutional author James Madison strongly argued the war power was legislative in nature rather than an executive prerogative.[21] As early as 1801, Chief Justice John Marshall wrote that the "whole powers of war [are] by the Constitution of the United States, vested in Congress."[22] The president is also constitutionally obligated, argues Louis Henkin, to take care that the laws are faithfully executed. This includes laws related to the war powers where the president was designed to be "a loyal agent of Congress to enforce its laws."[23]

However, when presidents and Congress have clashed in struggles over war and foreign affairs powers—especially in the 20th century—presidents have usually emerged on top. Why does Congress often come out on the losing end of struggles with the president over war powers? A number of factors facilitate and perpetuate presidential advantages in this area. Some are institutional, while others are political. The president has his own reservoir of war and foreign affairs powers upon which to draw and, constitutional powers aside, Congress has to have the willingness to act. It is important to briefly note these historical trends as they help to set the context for congressional action in the WOT.

Members of Congress frequently express the opinion that war powers and foreign affairs powers are the responsibility of the president. This type of thinking has fed a congressional culture of acquiescence to broad claims of executive war power. Military crises tend to breed an urgency that feeds presidential desires to test the limits of their war powers. To the degree others (e.g., Congress) do not push back, presidential war powers slowly expand over time serving as precedents for even further expansion in the future. This ratcheting effect almost invariably works up, never down.

Second, congressional leaders are often at cross-purposes. Some see themselves primarily as presidential supporters first and agents of a legislative body second. Instead of offering meaningful critiques and alternatives to executive policies, they view themselves as presidential foot soldiers whose primary goal is to make sure the president's agenda makes it through Congress unscathed.[24] This phenomenon has coincided with the rise of hyperpartisanship in Washington, D.C., where party loyalty becomes the standard by which all things are measured.

This criticism was on full display at the outset of the WOT when a Republican Congress was very reluctant to engage in any oversight that might make a Republican president look bad or question his policies. Republican congressman Ray LaHood (R-IL) was simply being candid at the time when he said, "Our party controls the levers of government. We're not about to go out and look beneath a bunch of rocks and try to cause heartburn."[25] As will become clear in the succeeding chapters, it is a charge to which both parties are guilty.

Third, Congress is decentralized, and congressional efforts to legislate on war powers issues face a number of obstacles. Any legislation that limits the president's war powers will almost certainly have to have the support of a supermajority to overcome a presidential veto. When Congress does legislate in war powers matters, it has often given broad powers to the president. Both the Gulf of Tonkin Resolution in 1964 and the AUMF in 2001 are prime examples of such delegations. While wide-ranging delegations of power to the executive are at some level necessary, presidents have not hesitated to stretch their powers to the limit under these types of authorizations. Even without broad delegations of power, presidents have been inclined to interpret existing statutes in very broad ways so as to maximize their war powers.[26]

Fourth, presidents often enjoy what some scholars refer to as the "first mover advantage."[27] When it comes to war powers matters, presidents often seize the initiative and act first using the formal unilateral powers of their office. These results can be very difficult for others to "undo." An example of this includes presidents moving troops into active combat zones or places where combat is likely to occur. Countering this is difficult due in part to the fact any legislation would need to have the support of a veto-proof majority, something increasingly difficult to obtain in this partisan era.

Finally, some scholars argue members of Congress generally lack the political will to take the responsibility and blame that can be associated with war powers decisions.[28] Instead, they defer, increasingly delegating war powers responsibilities to the president. They can say that they supported the president's military initiatives if they are successful. They can also step back and assign blame to the president if things go poorly.

Aside from the list of war powers outlined earlier, perhaps the biggest direct threat to unilateral presidential action in war powers matters is the appropriations power.[29] Congress has used this power on numerous occasions to bring military actions to conclusion in such diverse places as Vietnam, Angola, Nicaragua, and Somalia.[30] Still, the appropriations power is an unwieldy tool. It is often difficult for members of Congress to withstand charges that they are "abandoning" troops abroad when they vote to withhold funding for presidential military excursions. The appropriations power can be a powerful tool, but it is often one that takes incredible political will for Congress to wield with respect to war policies.

There is considerable constitutional, scholarly, and historical foundation to advance the proposition that Congress has a significant role to play in foreign affairs, war powers, and national security decisions. There is also considerable evidence to show there are a variety of challenges to the exercise of this power. These are difficult challenges, but they can be overcome.

Courts and War Powers

Perhaps the most oft-quoted phrase on the subject of courts and war powers is *Inter arma silent leges*, loosely translated as "In time of war, the law is silent."[31] While many readers may be disheartened at the thought that law may wholly cease to exist during times of war, American history clearly demonstrates there is at least some truth to this maxim. It is not difficult to find scholars who are highly critical of the role the Supreme Court has played in protecting civil liberties during times of war.[32] The Constitution confers no specific foreign affairs or war powers to the judiciary. In the area of foreign affairs and war powers, this judicial duty has largely become one where the courts are tasked with judging the proper scope of presidential war powers actions.[33]

The scholarly consensus is that the courts are generally deferential to presidential war powers claims.[34] The courts either go out of their way to avoid ruling on the merits of the question or, absent that, they often rule in favor of the president. This is not to say the judiciary *cannot* act as a check on presidential war power, but rather that it has—historically speaking—not often done so.

In fairness to the judiciary, attempting to determine the constitutional scope of the president's commander in chief powers is not an easy task. As Justice Jackson noted in the Steel Seizure Case, the commander in chief is "something more than an empty title," but it is not the "power to do anything, anywhere, that can be done with an army or navy."[35] This question becomes even more difficult to answer when a nation is at war. Courts understandably are reluctant to decide major constitutional issues regarding the scope of presidential war power while the country is fighting a war. Questions of constitutionality often take a backseat to the survival of a nation.

Scholars and judges have offered a variety of reasons to explain why the judiciary has adopted this generalized deference to presidential war power. First, arguably the best way for a president to obtain favorable decisions from judges on war powers cases is to appoint "pro-executive power" judges to the bench.[36] Some judges appear to be of the opinion that presidents possess plenary power in the area of foreign affairs. Such a belief would certainly cause judges to provide a great degree of deference.

Modern origins of this viewpoint are often traced to the Supreme Court's majority opinion in *U.S. v. Curtiss-Wright* (1936). Justice Sutherland spoke of "the very delicate, plenary and exclusive power of the President as sole organ of the federal government in the field of international relations—a power which does not require as a basis for its exercise an act of Congress."[37] This "sole organ" doctrine has achieved what one scholar called a "talismanic" status leaving a "powerful, albeit unfortunate legacy," one judges use to defer to expansive claims of presidential war power.[38]

Another tactic the modern judiciary often employs is to find a reason not to even hear cases involving challenges to presidential power. Sometimes this is done simply out of a view that judges are not capable of making informed, intelligent decisions in such cases.[39] In the Japanese internment case *Korematsu v. U.S.* (1944), Justice Robert Jackson concluded:

> In the very nature of things, military decisions are not susceptible of intelligent judicial appraisal. They do not pretend to rest on evidence, but are made on information that often would not be admissible and on assumptions that could not be proved. . . . Hence courts can never have any real alternative to accepting the mere declaration of the authorities that issued the order that it was reasonably necessary from a military viewpoint.[40]

The courts also use threshold questions to either avoid ruling on the merits of a war powers case or to rule in favor of the president. In recent years, courts have often used standing, ripeness, and mootness arguments to uphold the general pattern of judicial deference to presidents in war powers matters.[41] Finally, courts often fear the embarrassment, confusion, or chaos that might ensue if the judiciary was to rule against the president on an important war powers question during a time of conflict.[42] This type of decision might not only give support to the president's domestic critics but also make fighting the war more difficult.

Courts do sometimes rule against presidents, and when this happens presidents rarely defy the judiciary outright. In *Youngstown Sheet & Tube v.*

Sawyer (1952), the Supreme Court ordered President Truman to return the steel mills seized by the government to private control and Truman did so. Judges must exercise judicial review carefully because they have no institutional means to enforce their decisions. They are often reliant on the president and other political actors to carry out their decisions. Courts are most likely to rule against presidents on war powers questions when presidents are acting alone without the support of Congress and/or the public.[43] Still, decisions such as *Youngstown* are generally the exception rather than the rule.

This brief summary of presidential, congressional, and judicial war powers is important for several reasons. First, it gives a sense of what institutional war powers looked like when 9/11 occurred. The responses that followed were not political actors and institutions writing on a blank slate but rather ones with defined and evolving histories and roles. Second, these generalizations and trends, which have manifested themselves in the past, are once again on full display after 9/11. They offer some explanation to U.S. government responses after 9/11 and illuminate why certain actions have occurred, while others have not.

Policy Making: Fundamental Concepts

In American government classes across the United States, students are taught the fundamental principles of the American political system. The legislative branch of government is responsible for writing the law, the executive branch is responsible for enforcing the law, and the judicial branch is responsible for ensuring the laws passed by the political branches of government—Congress and the president—are constitutional. The fundamental powers and duties of each branch have been separated, and checks have been built into the system to prevent any particular individual or institution from abusing power and running roughshod over others. Power is separated, balanced, and checked.

While fundamentally correct, scholars realize this depiction of the U.S. government fails to capture the many nuances that exist in the day-to-day world of politics. This disconnect between theory and reality becomes even more pronounced when the nation is at war. In fact, it is almost axiomatic that a state of war changes the practical, if not the constitutional, balance of power between the three branches of government comprising the U.S. political system.

More often than not there is a system characterized by "executive initiative, congressional acquiescence, and judicial tolerance."[44] Executive power increases during conflicts, while Congress and the judiciary often play a secondary role. This occurs despite the fact the Constitution recognizes no emergency powers for any political actor or institution.[45] Powers once separated become concentrated in the executive. Checks and balances often fall by the wayside or prove ineffective. As a result, American history is littered with wartime policies that, in hindsight, are quite regrettable such as the detention of tens of thousands of Japanese-Americans during World War II. It is a pattern that surfaces again and again throughout the nation's history.

Many discussions concerning government policies and the WOT begin (and sometimes end) with a focus on what the president has done. Presidents Bush, Obama, and Trump have been at the center of the action, but it should not be forgotten that Congress has held hearings and passed key pieces of legislation. In similar fashion, the Supreme Court has issued key opinions in cases involving military tribunals, habeas corpus, and indefinite detention of suspected terrorists.[46]

All three branches of government have played a role in designing and implementing government responses to 9/11. What this book emphasizes is that discussions failing to take this into account miss a big part of the government's overall response to the 9/11 attacks. This is not an argument that the roles each institution plays are equal ones or that they necessarily should be. Examining what each institution has done, and considering what roles they might play in the future, is vital to the design and implementation of policy as the U.S. government continues to fight the ongoing threat of international terrorism.

Political scientist Edward Corwin once astutely noted that the Constitution "is an invitation to struggle for the privilege of directing American foreign policy."[47] It is important for those participating in this struggle to remember that their actions and policies need to remain true to long-standing political ideals: separation of powers, transparency in government, and governmental accountability. While these ideals may seem antithetical to the quick, decisive decision making often advocated when a country is at war, this book will argue that they are not. Rather, fidelity to them will produce better policies in the long run that both protect national security and the liberties of the American people.

Separation of Powers

Separation of powers and checks and balances are two fundamental concepts that run throughout the American Constitution. The founding fathers, fearing the concentration of too much power in any single individual or political institution, separated the executive, legislative, and judicial powers into three separate branches of government and then provided a series of checks so the exercise of these powers is almost always subject to review by other political actors and institutions. These were not new concepts. One of the more important influences on the framers, English philosopher John

Locke, argued that "well-framed governments" have arrangements where "Legislative and Executive Power are in distinct hands." Similarly, noted French theorist Montesquieu concluded the only way to maintain liberty was to establish a system of government where "power must check power."[48] Separation of powers was also a well-established principle in many colonial governments by the time the Constitution was written.

While there is no explicit statement on separation of powers in the Constitution, the fact it clearly separated powers far more distinctly than the Articles of Confederation was widely regarded as one of its strengths.[49] James Madison's familiar words in *Federalist #51* capture the spirit of this sentiment:

> If men were angels, no government would be necessary. If angels were to govern men, neither external nor internal controls would be necessary . . . the great difficulty lies in this: you must first enable the government to control the governed; and in the next place oblige it to control itself.[50]

These "controls" are designed to ensure "ambition . . . counteract[s] ambition." How can these controls be designed? Madison answered that question too: "by so contriving the interior structure of the government as that its several constituent parts may, by their mutual relation, be the means of keeping each other in their proper places."[51] Thomas Jefferson also expressed similar sentiments when he wrote that the concentration of power "in the same hands is precisely the definition of despotic government."[52]

Madison also foresaw how difficult in practice separating and checking government power would be on a routine basis. In *Federalist #37*, he concluded:

> Experience has instructed us that no skill in the science of government has yet been able to discriminate and define, with sufficient certainty, its three great provinces—the legislative, executive and judiciary; or even the privileges and powers of the different legislative branches. Questions daily occur in the course of practice which prove the obscurity which reigns in these subjects, and which puzzle the greatest adepts in political science.[53]

These puzzles involving the distribution of government power and checks upon its use are in full display as the American political system seeks the most effective ways to fight terrorism.

Given today's complaints about centralized executive power it is somewhat ironic to note that Madison's primary concern when it came to checking power was reining in the legislature, not the executive. Colonial experience, opined Madison, "had provided a tendency in our governments to throw all power into the Legislative vortex." As a result, the legislature dominated the "more feeble" branches.[54]

The American political system was designed with enough ambiguity and flexibility so as to allow for changes and challenges over time. In the 19th century, Congress was more often the dominant interbranch partner. But this changed in the 20th century. This is perhaps understandable. There is no reason to think that the American political system should necessarily remain static in an ever-changing world.

Institutions can change, grow, and evolve. Supreme Court decisions can also set (or change) the parameters of institutional power. And the Court is not the only one that has a role in defining power. The president, members of Congress, and other political actors also have a say. Today's separation of powers critics tend to focus on the expansion of executive power, particularly since World War II and the Korean conflict, and principally in the area of war and foreign affairs powers.[55]

Separation of powers and the interbranch conflicts they engender are an important backdrop for any discussion of policy making in the WOT. First, much of the literature on warrantless electronic surveillance, military tribunals, and other terror-related issues focuses mainly on presidential action with little or no attention given to the roles that other political institutions are playing in the policy design and implementation process. This type of focus is both misguided and myopic.

Second, presidents have claimed extraordinary unilateral powers, powers that would minimize (or in some cases even eliminate) the roles Congress and the courts play in WOT policy making.[56] Third, the U.S. government is still attempting to devise anti-terror policies years after 9/11. This means rather than making unilateral, ad hoc polices, the government should make greater use of the regular, institutionalized policy making processes already in place and used for over 200 years.

Transparency

The idea of transparency in government is not a new phenomenon. The word itself is Latin for "to shine a light through."[57] Theorists Immanuel Kant and Jeremy Bentham extolled the virtues of transparency though, importantly, they made some exceptions in the area of national security.[58]

The framers were intimately familiar with these arguments as well. In a letter to one of his contemporaries, James Madison wrote: "Knowledge will forever govern ignorance. And a people who mean to be their own governor must arm themselves with the power that knowledge gives. A popular government without popular information or the means for acquiring it is but a prologue to a farce or a tragedy or perhaps both."[59] Patrick Henry, one of the

Introduction

foremost critics of the new Constitution, concluded: "The liberties of a people were, nor ever will be, secure, when the transactions of their rulers may be concealed from them."[60] Clearly, the framers saw an informed populace as one important check on government.

At first blush it might seem the pursuit of national security and transparency in government are antithetical principles. This does not necessarily need to be the case. In fact, one scholar referred to transparency as "an essential homeland security value" because it helps ensure accountability and provide expectations about legal definitions and the scope of power.[61]

The last several presidents have issued conflicting statements about the importance of transparency. President Bush often opposed investigations into his administration's terrorism policies saying that any publicity would inform terrorist groups about U.S. policy and tactics, giving them an advantage against the United States. On the other hand, President Obama boldly asserted that "my administration is committed to creating an unprecedented level of openness in Government."[62] Whether the Obama administration actually achieved this goal is a subject of fierce debate, but it is worth noting the president thought it important. These statements also illustrate one truth about transparency. It is important, but transparency cannot be absolute when it comes to national security. The difficult question is where government officials draw the line.

It is important at the outset to define what is meant by transparency in government. Transparency is "government according to fixed and published rules on the basis of information and procedures that are accessible to the public."[63] Public information is key. It is the only way the people, or their representatives, can make informed decisions in a democratic political system.

The presumption in a democratic society is that information and policy making should be open and informed. The burden should be on the government to keep information secret. The knowledge that their actions will be made public, the theory goes, will encourage government officials to behave scrupulously. "Sunlight," said noted Supreme Court justice Louis Brandeis, "is said to be the best of disinfectants."[64]

Questions of war and peace are not exempt from this premise. There may be times where transparency may be "traded off" when put up against competing values such as national security. But national security should never be a value that always or automatically trumps all other competing values—freedom, transparency, accountability, morality, and others. Many homeland security decisions can and should be made openly. The framers intentionally gave the people's body, Congress, the power to declare war. The idea is that taking a country to war was serious business that should be debated openly and fully by the people's elected representatives.

Advocating transparency and openness does not mean the government is required to divulge sensitive military and diplomatic secrets. Effective national security requires some level of secrecy. Transparency in this context does not mean something like printing the names of the Central Intelligence Agency's (CIA) spies in the newspaper. What it does mean is that major policy decisions—the rules governing how suspected terrorists are interrogated or how government monitors electronic communications—should be the result of informed public debate. People cannot make informed decisions about government polices—policies that are being made in the name of the people—if they do not have information.

Edward Snowden's revelations about the previously unknown scope of the National Security Agency's (NSA) programs are a good example of this. Once many of the government's previously unknown surveillance practices became known, it was possible for the American people to have a more informed conversation about whether these were activities that they wanted their government to perform. Some strongly objected to the NSA's activities, while others were content to let the agency continue its efforts in this area.

Regrettably, some skeptics have observed instances where the public has voluntarily removed itself from many important national security debates. The public's right to know has morphed into "the public's right not to know."[65] There are a variety of reasons for this. For many, foreign affairs and war powers issues are largely divorced from their everyday lives. They have little knowledge and little interest in these types of issues and are content to leave their management to government officials. They trust that their government—the president—will just "do the right thing" and so issues surrounding how and why decisions are made are largely seen as unimportant. Transparency is not demanded.

Presidents have become the de facto keepers of national security information. The national security literature is replete with discussions of the information asymmetry between the president and Congress, and presidents have used this wealth of national security information at their fingertips to their considerable advantage when pressing their policy preferences.[66] Unfortunately, many observers conflate the president's ability to keep information secret with his *right* to do so.[67] Just because presidents can does not mean they should.

Presidents have also become more aggressive in withholding this information from Congress.[68] For some presidential scholars, this development is a good thing primarily because national security information is too important to be widely disseminated even among members of Congress. It is, they argue, a presidential prerogative to decide what information to share and with whom to share it.[69] This leads to what one scholar refers to as the secrecy dilemma: "How can the public be confident that foreign policy programs advocated by the executive will enhance security if that same leader also has the power to selectively reveal and hide relevant information?"[70] It is a

Introduction 17

question that has taken on particular importance since 9/11 as presidents have established and operated secret policies and withheld important information from the other branches of government and the American people.

There are two important points regarding transparency that should be noted. One positive trend for pro-transparency advocates is that technological advances are making information available today at a scope previously thought impossible. With the Internet at their fingertips, citizens today have access to far more government information—including information on national security—than even experts used to have. Second, transparency policies are frequently not codified in statute. They can be readily changed from administration to administration. This is unfortunate because it makes it difficult to know what information is, or should be, available to both policy makers and the public, causing confusion.

Accountability

Accountability is one of the hallmarks of a democratic political system. People have the right to hold those who govern in their name accountable for their actions and the policies they create. One mechanism for this is periodic elections. If people agree with the government's policies, the people can vote to retain that particular set of government actors in office. If not, the people can replace them with a different set of actors. Theorists have long identified public accountability as a strength of democratic political systems.

Transparency and accountability are often linked together, and the former certainly facilitates the latter. When President Obama promised to be the most transparent administration ever, he also noted, "Transparency promotes accountability and provides information for citizens about what their Government is doing."[71] Beth Noveck, the leader of President Obama's Open Government Initiative, echoed the president's sentiment adding, "When the public cannot see how decisions are arrived at, it cannot identify problems and criticize mistakes. Accountability declines and so does government effectiveness."[72]

One of the recurring criticisms leveled at both Republican and Democrat administrations during the WOT is that accountability has been lacking. There are two distinct problems. First, the executive branch has in many instances kept terrorism policies and procedures hidden from view—not just from the public but from Congress and the courts as well. Secrecy, necessity, and national security have been used to prevent a critical examination of controversial terrorism policies. Consequently, executive accountability has declined. In the immediate period following the 9/11 attacks, emergency executive prerogative action was justified in the name of speed and national security. But ultimately, even in situations such as these, the executive must eventually come before the people and justify his actions as Abraham Lincoln did at the outset of the Civil War.

A second—and related—problem involves congressional accountability. As noted earlier, there was a seismic shift in war and foreign affairs powers to the executive branch of government in the latter half of the 20th century. One congressional critic noted "the legislative surrender was a self-interested one: Accountability is pretty frightening stuff."[73] In some instances, Congress has willingly divested itself of these powers. In others, Congress can make the argument that its members should not be held responsible when the executive branch has intentionally engaged in activities and kept them secret. The subsequent chapters will explore ways in which individual members of Congress and Congress as an institution can both act to help make and monitor terrorism policy and help provide more government accountability for its actions in the WOT.

Chapter Outlines

The book will be organized in the following fashion. The first chapter introduces the topic and explains, from a theoretical and practical perspective, why Congress is such an important actor in war powers and foreign affairs decisions. It also introduces the argument that increased congressional involvement and a return to principles such as transparency and accountability is the best way to make long-term policy in the WOT.

Each of the substantive issue chapters will chronicle the historical development of policy in that area with a particular emphasis on how Congress, the president, and the courts have interacted over time to essentially establish a policy baseline that was in effect when 9/11 occurred. These chapters will then examine the Bush and Obama administrations in turn with a particular emphasis on the activity of Congress. Finally, each chapter will examine the outstanding problems and issues in each policy area and explore some of the things Congress can do to help craft successful, long-term terrorism policy.

Chapter 2 will explore the issue of national security and electronic surveillance. Struggles to define the scope of institutional surveillance powers have only intensified with the evolution of new technology in this area. The Bush administration's secret warrantless surveillance program was consistent with a long and often notorious tradition of warrantless executive branch surveillance activities. Historically, Congress and the courts have attempted to place checks on executive surveillance power, but these checks have often proven ineffective.

Introduction

Chapter 3 will chronicle how government interrogation policy has developed over time and note the extent to which the issue of torture has surfaced. The interrogation of detainees plays an important role in both criminal and military schemes, but rules apply in both areas. Discussions about the interrogation and possible torture of military detainees lead to the intersection of constitutional, statutory, and international law. These discussions also touch on issues that reflect the moral compass of the American people.

The treatment of suspected terrorists at the detention center in Guantanamo Bay and Abu Ghraib prison in Iraq put the issue of coercive interrogation and torture on the front pages of the newspapers and made it an important policy issue in the WOT. Still, the answer is not necessarily settled. When lives are on the line, are any interrogation methods acceptable, or are there certain lines that should never be crossed?

One of the first decisions made by the Bush White House following the 9/11 attacks was to design a system of military tribunals to try suspected terrorists. Despite overtures from Congress, the Bush administration insisted the executive branch alone had the power to develop a military tribunal system. Chapter 4 discusses the controversies that have plagued the military tribunal systems put in place by Presidents Bush and Obama. Congress and the courts have also had plenty to say about the composition and constitutionality of using military tribunals to try suspected terrorists. These military tribunals remain in place, even though critics question their value.

The WOT is the first to see an extensive use of weaponized drones. U.S. drones have the capacity to gather intelligence, provide tactical support to military units, and even kill militants directly. However, the rise of this new weapon is not without questions. How should the United States decide whom to target and where? How do constitutional, statutory, and international law limit the use of drones? This chapter will explore how Congress can involve itself more deeply in these vitally important, though controversial, questions.

The conclusion will contain an assessment of congressional progress to date in the WOT. It will also explore how Congress can play an even greater role in making terrorism policy going forward in ways that enhance national security while also promoting transparency and accountability and, ultimately, making more effective and lasting policy for the Long War.

CHAPTER TWO

Electronic Surveillance and National Security

The Fourth Amendment to the U.S. Constitution places a prohibition on unreasonable government searches and seizures. This seemingly simple proscription has been the subject of hundreds of cases where the Supreme Court has attempted to determine what is reasonable and what is not when it comes to government actions. The relentless pace of technology complicates these questions even further. Can government monitor the telephone calls, e-mails, and Internet browsing habits of American citizens in the name of national security and if so, when? The government's terrorism-fighting responses to the 9/11 attacks once again brought these questions into the public eye.

After 9/11, President George W. Bush's administration implemented a host of policies as a part of its War on Terror (WOT). Some, such as military tribunals for suspected terrorists and the use of Guantanamo Bay as a detention facility, were quite public. Others were far less transparent. In December 2005, the *New York Times* reported the Bush administration had been conducting a top secret warrantless electronic surveillance program that gathered information on American citizens.[1] Though the administration was eventually forced to admit it was conducting such a program, it vigorously defended the surveillance in the name of fighting terrorism.

Eight years later another set of explosive disclosures rocked the political landscape when Edward Snowden stole thousands of classified documents from his job at the National Security Agency (NSA). These documents revealed numerous government programs conducted by the Obama administration were surreptitiously gathering staggering amounts of data on millions of people ranging from American citizens to the leaders of foreign countries around the world.[2]

Both programs were exposed by the media rather than being disclosed through official government channels, and both sets of revelations set off extensive public debates about the types of policies that the U.S. government should employ in the fight against terrorists. People wanted to know what the executive branch was actually doing and whether Congress knew and approved of these activities.

This chapter reviews the history and evolution of electronic government surveillance. It reveals a long history marked by aggressive (and often secret) executive branch programs that have occasionally been checked by Congress when abuses became public. It is a pattern that continues in the WOT, one that explains congressional responses to the exposure of both the Bush and Obama administration surveillance programs. The chapter concludes by exploring issues that will confront Congress in this area and how Congress may be able to address them.

The Historical Development of Electronic Surveillance

The importance of communication in warfare has been understood for thousands of years. Communicating with one's own military forces and capturing or monitoring the enemy's communications can provide an invaluable edge in any military conflict. As a result, military commanders have always placed a priority on protecting their own communications while trying to monitor or steal their enemy's communications.

Since the nation's founding—even before intelligence gathering became electronic—political officials recognized the need for government to conduct various types of surveillance and intelligence gathering in the pursuit of national defense. There was also some recognition this would likely be a task performed by more than one government entity. The Continental Congress ran intelligence operations itself through its "Secret Committee" during the Revolutionary War.[3] However, in *Federalist #64*, John Jay noted the president "will be able to manage the business of intelligence in such a manner as prudence may suggest."[4]

The advent of telephone wires only compounded the number of issues associated with government surveillance. In the case of *Olmstead v. U.S.* (1928), the Supreme Court was asked to determine if government wiretaps used to help obtain criminal convictions violated the Fourth Amendment of the U.S. Constitution. In a ruling that set the stage for expanded use of government use of wiretaps, the Court held the interception of telephone communications did not constitute a search under the Fourth Amendment unless there was an actual physical trespass. Writing for the Court, Chief Justice William Howard Taft noted that gathering information via wiretaps might be unethical but that did not mean it was unconstitutional. Congress, he added, had the power to protect the secrecy of telephone conversations and prevent them from being used in judicial proceedings if it wished.[5]

Congress eventually responded to the Supreme Court's *Olmstead* invitation by passing the Federal Communications Act of 1934. Section 605 of the act provided that "no person receiving . . . [or] transmitting . . . any interstate or foreign communication by wire or radio shall divulge or publish the existence, contents, substance, purport, effect, or meaning thereof, except through authorized channels of transmission or reception."[6] The Supreme Court later made clear this statute essentially made wiretapping for law enforcement purposes illegal.[7]

Nevertheless, President Franklin Roosevelt (FDR) felt compelled to continue the practice for national security reasons. In a confidential memorandum, he authorized his attorney general, Robert Jackson, to permit warrantless wiretapping in "grave matters involving the defense of the nation," though Jackson was encouraged to limit its use and direct it primarily at "aliens." FDR justified this continued use of warrantless electronic surveillance on foreign intelligence grounds rather than law enforcement ones.

Even before World War II, FDR authorized the Federal Bureau of Investigation (FBI) to spy on "subversive" organizations. The advent of the war also expanded the use of electronic surveillance dramatically as FBI investigations for espionage cases went from roughly 35 per year in the 1930s to almost 70,000 in 1940.[8] Between 1942 and 1945, over 600 listening devices were installed by the FBI to keep tabs on "domestic subversive targets."[9]

The continuation (and expansion) of government electronic surveillance programs after World War II for the purposes of national security—both foreign and domestic—was a growth industry under Republican and Democrat presidents alike. Programs which may have originally been justified as wartime measures eventually became institutionalized. President Harry Truman followed FDR's lead and expanded electronic surveillance inside the United States in an effort to combat "subversive activity."

More important, Truman's justifications for such programs also began to rest more explicitly on a broad-based conception of executive power rather than statutory authority.[10] What this means is presidents increasingly argued they had the power to engage in surveillance for foreign intelligence collection whether Congress passed legislation to allow for this or not. This focus on inherent executive power as a justification for wiretapping was a precedent upon which future presidents would build.

The Cold War, and particularly the Vietnam era, saw a plethora of executive branch-directed electronic surveillance programs. Executive branch agencies secretly implemented a host of programs designed ostensibly to counter domestic and international threats to U.S. national security. COINTELPRO was a counterintelligence program originally intended to target racist groups, Black Nationalist groups, and Communists. It included illegal eavesdropping, mailing anonymous threats to targets, disinformation, harassment, the fabrication of evidence, and the creation and dissemination of false documents. Operation CHAOS gathered information on political protesters that resulted in over

13,000 computerized files on over 300,000 people. Operation MERRIMAC targeted civil rights and peace organizations. In project SHAMROCK, Western Union and other wire service providers gave intelligence personnel at the NSA access to private messages. Project MINARET was a NSA database that contained computer files on over 75,000 American citizens including members of Congress.[11]

By the late 1960s, almost every intelligence agency in the executive branch was spying in one form or another on nonviolent protesters.[12] Abuses of constitutional rights and liberties were rampant in all of the aforementioned programs. It is worth noting, many officials who were involved subsequently argued they had no malicious or subversive intent when they performed these actions. They, in the words of one FBI official, were acting on the "assumption . . . what we were doing was justified by . . . the greater good, the national security."[13] Whether these individuals had subversive intent or not, it was these widespread abuses that eventually prompted Congress and the courts to respond with increased oversight measures.

It is fair to ask where congressional oversight was during this period. This era was described by one scholar as the "Era of Trust." Reporting was sporadic and limited to a handful of individuals. This was by design. "Congress," related former secretary of defense Clark Clifford, "chose not to be involved and preferred to be uninformed."[14] The common refrain from the intelligence community was that it was almost impossible to get Congress interested in intelligence gathering. It was often a "don't ask, don't tell" mentality. As a result, intelligence oversight was "sporadic, spotty, and essentially uncritical."[15]

Congress and the Courts Respond

In 1967, the Supreme Court began to address some of the issues raised by warrantless electronic surveillance. The Court overturned its long-standing *Olmstead* decision in *Katz v. U.S.* (1968) holding that electronic surveillance does indeed fall under the purview of the Fourth Amendment. However, it specifically declined to address any "national security exception" to its ruling.[16] In a separate case, the Court also noted just because a search is conducted for non-law enforcement purposes does not mean the Fourth Amendment does not apply.[17] This was an important conclusion for the Court to reach since presidents have on occasion advanced the argument that warrantless electronic surveillance for national security purposes might not be subject to Fourth Amendment restrictions at all.

The closest the Supreme Court has come to ruling on presidential power to engage in warrantless electronic surveillance for national security purposes was in *U.S. v. U.S. District Court* (1972), a case often referred to as the Keith Case. In a unanimous decision, the Supreme Court held the Fourth

Amendment required prior judicial approval for the domestic surveillance intelligence used by the government in the case. "Fourth Amendment freedoms," wrote Justice Lewis Powell, "cannot properly be guaranteed if domestic security surveillances may be conducted solely within the discretion of the executive branch. The Fourth Amendment does not contemplate the executive officers of the Government as neutral and disinterested magistrates." The Court concluded that an "extremely limited post-surveillance judicial review" was insufficient to protect the civil liberties of Americans.[18] Congress, said the Court, had the power—if it wished—to develop standards for electronic surveillance in a domestic national security context. These standards might differ from traditional law enforcement standards and still be constitutional.[19]

It was an open invitation for Congress to legislate in this area. It would also appear to be a recognition that Congress, not the president, had the authority to set boundaries in this arena if it desired. The Court did add one important caveat to its opinion. Justice Powell explicitly noted that the case did not address the power of the president to engage in electronic surveillance of *foreign* agents/powers, and that the Court expressed no opinion as to the scope of the president's power in that particular context.[20] Future presidents used the Court's refusal to address this issue as evidence that they possessed inherent constitutional authority to engage in warrantless wiretapping for the purposes of gathering foreign intelligence information.

Spurred in part by these judicial decisions, Congress passed the Omnibus Crime Control and Safe Streets Act of 1968. Title III of the act proscribed how to get warrants for electronic surveillance and essentially criminalized most warrantless wiretapping. Recognizing the occasional need for flexibility, it also contained emergency procedures where electronic surveillance could take place without a warrant for 48 hours if organized crime or national security threats were implicated.[21]

The Church Committee

On December 22, 1974, *New York Times* reporter Seymour Hersh published the first in a series of articles that chronicled the aforementioned Cold War abuses of government surveillance power, such as the COINTELPRO and MERRIMAC programs. Public outrage was swift and widespread. The resulting political firestorm prompted President Gerald Ford to form a presidential commission to investigate the matters in hopes of forestalling a broader congressional investigation. It did not work. On January 27, 1975, the U.S. Senate appointed a select committee led by Idaho senator Frank Church to conduct its own investigation.[22]

When the Church Committee published its report in April 1976, it revealed the staggering depth of executive branch lawlessness in the area of electronic surveillance committed by a string of presidents over several decades, which culminated in the Watergate affair. These events were often justified in the name of "national security" or in fighting "subversives," but the committee concluded these executive branch agencies conducted "illegal, improper or unethical" actions that ran contrary to the ideals of a free and open American society. The committee ultimately made more than 180 recommendations designed to provide increased checks on executive branch surveillance agencies.[23]

The Church Committee's investigation is widely considered to be the most thorough and comprehensive ever conducted into the U.S. intelligence community. It was, perhaps, the high watermark of congressional oversight and influence over executive branch surveillance activities. In its wake, reform was inevitable.

The Foreign Intelligence Surveillance Act (FISA)

Negotiations on a bill to regulate electronic surveillance began in 1976 and eventually resulted in the passage of FISA, which was signed into law by President Jimmy Carter in October 1978.[24] FISA provides a statutory framework that allows the executive branch to gather information for foreign intelligence via electronic surveillance and physical searches. Indeed, the text of FISA "establishes the exclusive means by which [presidentially ordered] surveillance may be conducted."[25]

FISA also created the U.S. Foreign Intelligence Surveillance Court (FISC) and the U.S. Foreign Intelligence Surveillance Court of Review (FISCR). The Chief Justice of the U.S. Supreme Court selects seven federal district court judges to sit on the FISC court (this number was increased to eleven with the passage of the Patriot Act in 2001). The chief justice also designates three federal judges to sit on the FISCR. Judges on both courts serve seven-year, nonrenewable terms.

This judicial oversight is an important component of the FISA statutory scheme. If the executive branch wishes to engage in electronic surveillance for the purposes of collecting foreign intelligence in the United States, it must complete an application and the application must be approved by a FISC judge. Unlike Title III, the government does not have to show probable cause that the target of the electronic surveillance is committing or is about to commit a crime, but rather that there is simply reasonable cause to believe the target is a foreign power or an agent of a foreign power. This is a lower standard of proof and an important difference between the law enforcement and intelligence frameworks.

The FISA warrant process keeps law enforcement officials and FISC judges quite busy. Since the inception of FISA, the FISC has entertained almost 40,000 warrant requests, approving 99 percent of them.[26] While there are many critics who use this data to conclude the FISC is simply a rubber stamp for the executive branch, FISC Chief Judge Royce Lamberth disagreed:

> I think the win-loss record is more a tribute to the superb internal review process created within the Department of Justice, now through several different administrations, than it is (a reflection) on the judges. Indeed, there might be a concern that the Justice Department has been too conservative in what they are presenting to the Court if we're approving everyone.[27]

Since the 9/11 attacks, the number of applications for FISA warrants has increased dramatically. Each FISC judge hears about 150 applications per year, or roughly an application every two-and-a-half days.[28]

There are several important takeaways from these numbers that become important when attempting to assess the role of the FISC in the WOT. First, FISC judges now hear applications for a considerable number of warrants under FISA. This is not something that only happens occasionally, but rather something that happens very frequently. The total volume of applications for these judges, some scholars conclude, almost precludes any meaningful judicial supervision.

Second, the government is almost never denied the warrants it seeks. Only on rare occasions are they denied outright. In other instances, the government is required to modify its applications, but it still ultimately receives the warrant.

There are several reasons for the government's success. One reason is the lower standard of proof required by FISA compared to regular criminal warrants. However, another significant part is related to the fact that proceedings before FISC judges are ex parte, that is, only one party—the government—is represented. In this sense it is unlike most judicial proceedings in America. Finally, FISC judges lack the resources to thoroughly investigate the veracity of the government's assertions in these applications. They are often obliged to take the government's word regarding the reliability of the information contained in the warrant applications. Former FISC Chief Judge Reggie Walton echoed this problem when he noted that "the FISC is forced to rely upon the accuracy of the information that is provided to the Court. . . . The FISC does not have the capacity to investigate issue of noncompliance."[29]

Congressional Oversight after the Church Committee

The Church Committee's investigation and subsequent congressional legislation ushered in a new era of intelligence community-congressional relations. Congress passed a handful of other laws in addition to FISA that were designed to strengthen congressional oversight over the intelligence community including the Intelligence Oversight Act of 1980, the Inspector General Act of 1989, and the Intelligence Oversight Act of 1991.

The intelligence community naturally viewed this new era of increased scrutiny with some degree of suspicion. Some chafed at the new scrutiny faced by intelligence agencies. William Casey, Director of the CIA under President Reagan during the 1980s, went so far as to say, "The job of Congress is to stay the f--- out of my business."[30] While not all intelligence officials were as irascible as Casey, it was clear that the "Era of Trust" was gone.

Newt Gingrich and his new Republican House majority rose to power in 1994. This change in leadership is sometimes identified as another important turning point in congressional oversight of the intelligence community. Gingrich's unabashed and unapologetic partisanship permeated all aspects of the House, including oversight duties.[31] This is a trend that accelerated after 9/11, complicating efforts to obtain meaningful oversight. In fact, just when effective oversight over executive branch intelligence was most needed after 9/11, partisan differences were most evident. This led one long-time observer to conclude the relationship between oversight committees and intelligence agencies had "degenerated into a mutual admiration society for secret agencies," where oversight meant Republicans placing support for a Republican president over institutional prerogatives.[32]

It is important to note this oversight history, particularly when there are so many who are critical of congressional responses to executive policies in the WOT. Issues with congressional oversight existed long before 9/11. Most congressional responses in this area have been of a "fire alarm" nature. Oversight is minimal until a "fire" bursts into flames at which time Congress rushes to respond. Congress then returns to a minimalist oversight posture once the fire is extinguished. Oversight, in the words of one long-time surveillance scholar, "has proven difficult and has often failed."[33]

Pre-9/11 Electronic Surveillance

The pre-9/11 history of electronic surveillance outlined earlier is only a sliver of a much longer story. It does, however, illustrate several basic points, which will inform the analysis of how the subject of warrantless electronic surveillance has been approached in the WOT. First, all presidents since FDR have engaged in warrantless electronic surveillance. Some have done so for law enforcement purposes, and all have done so in the name of "domestic security" or "national security." The fact all presidents have done this has led to an institutionalization of such power at least as far as the executive branch is concerned. This power has also frequently been abused by many presidents, indicating the need for strong oversight.

Second, courts and Congress have periodically asserted themselves. The passage of Title III and FISA reflects a recognition that Congress can constitutionally impose limits on presidentially ordered electronic surveillance. Courts have upheld these limitations. Presidents generally need to obtain a warrant if they're going to use electronic surveillance for law enforcement purposes. They also need to obtain warrants if they are engaging in electronic surveillance for "domestic security" purposes.

Finally, there remains a murky area where both Congress and the courts have shown some reluctance to tread. When it comes to gathering foreign intelligence, are there limitations that either branch can place on the executive, or is this particular realm one reserved exclusively for the executive branch? More important, what happens when law enforcement, domestic security, and national security concerns are interrelated? This becomes one of the central questions in the discussion of electronic surveillance in the WOT.

Electronic Surveillance and the War on Terror: The Bush Administration

After 9/11, defending the country against terrorism became the Bush administration's number one priority. All government agencies were asked to reset their priorities to reflect this change. CIA Director George Tenet approached NSA Director Michael Hayden to ask if there was anything more the NSA could do in the WOT. Hayden reportedly replied that his agency was doing all it could within existing legal authorities. When asked what more the agency could do absent such constraints, Hayden put together an outline of what would later become known as the Terrorist Surveillance Program (TSP).[34]

While the operational details of the TSP remain classified, the subsequent public discussion of the TSP allows some glimpse at the scope and content of the program. The TSP allowed the NSA to engage in warrantless electronic surveillance when one of the parties was suspected of being a member or a supporter of Al Qaeda. This surveillance was limited to calls where one party was overseas. The other party could be in the United States. The program was reauthorized by the president himself every 45 days.[35]

The White House strictly controlled who had knowledge of the warrantless surveillance activities. Even within the executive branch, knowledge of the TSP was closely guarded. It also later became clear that the Bush administration went to great lengths to cloak the program in legality in order to justify its operation. At the outset, the Office of Legal Counsel (OLC), the executive branch office that offers legal opinions to the president on executive branch actions and programs, provided the legal justification for the program. However, it was hardly a standard arrangement.

Assistant Attorney General John Yoo worked directly with the White House and was initially the only Justice Department official with knowledge of the program. Even Yoo's superior at OLC, Jay Bybee, did not know of this arrangement at the time.[36] In a subsequent report, the DOJ's Office of the Inspector General concluded it was "extraordinary and inappropriate" to limit the legal analysis of such an important program to one attorney. When Yoo's legal reasoning for the TSP and other presidential surveillance activities was later reviewed by his OLC colleagues, they concluded there were "deficiencies" in his legal reasoning, which resulted in a legal analysis that was "at a minimum factually flawed."[37]

Bush administration officials did see fit to brief the FISC chief judge on the program, but not the other FISC judges. Both Chief Judge Royce Lamberth and later Colleen Kollar-Kotelly expressed "serious doubts" about the TSP at the time believing it ran a "significant risk" of being declared unconstitutional if ever made public. Nevertheless, they did not reveal the program to the public.

The Terrorist Surveillance Program Goes Public

The public debate over the TSP did not erupt until the publication of a December 2005 *New York Times* article by Eric Lichtblau and James Risen. In this article, the authors revealed the existence the TSP. The NSA originally referred it to as a "special collection program." The program began soon after 9/11 when the CIA began to seize the cell phones and computers of captured Al Qaeda members. The government began to monitor numbers mined from these phones, some of which belonged to American citizens living in the United States.[38] As many as 500 citizens were under NSA surveillance at any given time though fewer than 10 each year generated enough suspicion to justify additional surveillance (with a warrant) of their domestic activities.[39]

Initial congressional responses served as a harbinger of how Congress would all too frequently respond to the executive branch in this area after 9/11. Democrats were outraged. "This is Big Brother run amok," declared long-time senator Ted Kennedy (D-MA). Some Republicans also expressed shock and surprise at the revelations. Senate Judiciary Committee Chairman Arlen Specter (R-PA) was among the foremost critics when he stated, "There is no doubt that this is inappropriate."[40] He immediately vowed to hold hearings on the matter.

Most Republicans rushed to the defense of the administration, emphasizing the national security importance of the Bush administration's program. Representative Dan Burton (R-IN), a defense hawk, reminded the public: "This is war, not a tea party. . . . The President is doing the right thing and we need to support him."[41] Senate Majority Leader Trent Lott (R-MS) asserted, "I want my security first. I'll deal with the details after that."[42]

The Bush administration, fearing public backlash at the revelation of a secret program authorizing the government to engage in warrantless electronic surveillance of American citizens, quickly moved into damage control mode. A few days after the *Times* story broke, the president himself addressed the issue in a press conference. In it, he publicly acknowledged the existence of the TSP. The program, he stressed, was limited to targets "with known links to al Qaeda" enabling the government to "move faster and quicker."[43]

The president also attempted to deflect criticism over the program by blasting the media for revealing its existence saying, "My personal opinion is it [the release of the story] was a shameful act, for someone to disclose this very important program in time of war. The fact that we're discussing this program is helping the enemy." Public hearings about the propriety and legality of the program, he argued, were the last thing that should occur. It would be tantamount to saying, "Here's what they do. Adjust."[44]

Attorney General Alberto Gonzales and NSA Director Michael Hayden held a separate press conference where they also publicly discussed the scope of the TSP. Hayden stated "unequivocally" that the program had been successful in thwarting potential terrorist attacks. Attorney General Gonzales reminded the public that the TSP remained highly classified. He also repeated the president's criticism that any discussion of the program "is really hurting national security."[45]

Did Congress Know?

While the Bush administration feared approaching Congress about the TSP might compromise its effectiveness, administration officials repeatedly provided top secret briefings on the program for a handful of members. Between October 2001 and January 2007 there were a total of 49 congressional briefings. Seventeen of these briefings took place before the program's existence was publicly disclosed at the end of 2005.[46]

NSA director Hayden reported no one from Congress ever suggested during one of these briefings that the NSA stop the program.[47] In other words, the administration asserted it had kept Congress informed. Claims that the administration had spied on Americans without congressional approval were incorrect. Senate Intelligence Chairman Pat Roberts (R-KS) and House Intelligence Chairman Peter Hoekstra (R-MI) agreed with the administration's claims. The chairmen stated a number of Democrats were present at these briefings and had an opportunity to ask questions, though neither Roberts nor Hoekstra recalled them doing so.[48]

Key Democrats who attended these intelligence briefings told a different story. Nancy Pelosi (D-CA) remembered being briefed on the program but considered these briefings merely notifications of what was being done, "not a request for approval." She claimed she voiced strong concerns at the time.[49]

Similarly, Senate Minority Leader Harry Reid (D-NV) agreed that, while some members had been briefed, they had not been asked for advice or consent. "Key details," he said, "about the program were apparently not provided to me. I am surprised and disappointed that the White House would now suggest that none of us informed of this program objected."[50]

The manner in which these briefings were conducted—something no one disputes—surely contributed to these different recollections. Depending on the subject matter, intelligence briefings to Congress are usually limited to only a handful of members. Often this is what is colloquially referred to as the "Gang of 8." It includes the Speaker of the House and the House Minority Leader, the Majority and Minority Leaders in the Senate, and the Chair and Ranking Members of the House and Senate Select Committees on Intelligence.

As a general rule, members are not allowed to bring staff or counsel with them to these briefings, nor are they allowed to take notes, copy documents, or talk about anything they have seen or heard with anyone else (including other members of Congress). As one might imagine, it is extraordinarily difficult to ask thoughtful, probing questions of the executive branch under these conditions. Many critics argue limiting disclosure in this fashion provides cover for the executive branch to say they shared information with Congress, while at the same time avoiding any meaningful oversight.[51]

There is also a record indicating at least one Democrat was uncomfortable with these briefings and their associated restrictions. On July 17, 2003, Senate Select Intelligence Committee Ranking member Jay Rockefeller (D-WV) drafted a handwritten letter to Vice President Dick Cheney. In it he wrote, "[G]iven the security restrictions associated with this information, and my inability to consult staff or counsel on my own, I feel unable to fully evaluate, much less endorse, these activities."[52] Rockefeller never received a reply and notes he was prohibited from sharing his concerns with other members of Congress.

Even some Republican members of Congress publicly questioned these restrictions on information. Representative Heather Wilson (R-NM), the chair of the House subcommittee with jurisdiction over the NSA, called limited briefings "increasingly untenable" since it had the effect of leaving most members of Congress completely in the dark about executive branch activities.[53] How can members be expected to vote on activities about which they have no knowledge?

Some of the TSP's supporters within the Bush administration had reservations about the legality of the program as well. Alberto Gonzales later acknowledged administration lawyers initially concluded the TSP could not legally be squared with FISA but that they decided to "push the envelope."[54]

The Bush administration's Justice Department soon released an extensive 42-page memorandum that outlined legal defense of the program.[55] One of the larger legal questions the administration was forced to address was how the TSP could be reconciled with FISA. FISA clearly states it "shall be the exclusive means" by which the government is permitted to engage in foreign intelligence surveillance.[56] Why did the administration not just request Congress amend FISA to include the activities contained in the TSP? After all, FISA had been amended numerous times in the past and had even been amended several times since 9/11 (in 2001, 2002, 2004, and 2005). The Bush administration had given no public indication these amendments were insufficient.[57]

The answer, revealed Attorney General Gonzalez, was that the administration had been informed by congressional sources it "would be difficult, if not impossible" to get congressional approval for such a program.[58] As a result, the administration just opted to go ahead with the program on its own. Gonzales also emphasized the Bush administration was still using FISA for some things but that it was "not legally required to" in the case of the TSP.[59] Despite the public revelations and criticisms, the Bush administration doggedly contended that the TSP was entirely legal.

Congressional concerns about the TSP were widespread enough that a late December vote on renewing various Patriot Act provisions was postponed. Arlen Specter, the Republican chair of the Senate Judiciary Committee, commenced hearings the following February. As part of its investigation, the committee requested the executive branch legal opinions that supported the TSP. The White House refused, saying everything Congress needed to know about the legal foundation for the TSP was already publicly available.[60]

In those Judiciary Committee hearings, Attorney General Alberto Gonzalez was grilled by senators about the origins and legality of the TSP. Two basic lines of argument were introduced by the administration in defense of the TSP. One was constitutional, the other statutory. Both arguments relied on framing the president's powers and duties in an expansive manner while minimizing the checks placed upon presidential power by the other branches of government.

On the constitutional side of the ledger, the Justice Department first argued the president had "well recognized inherent constitutional authority as Commander in Chief and sole organ for the Nation in foreign affairs to conduct warrantless surveillance of enemy forces for intelligence purposes."[61] This framed the issues in a foreign affairs context, which allowed the administration to advance an expansive vision of the president's commander in chief powers.

Not only did the president have the constitutional authority to engage in warrantless electronic surveillance, the DOJ argued, but FISA could not limit his ability to do so "unless Congress made a clear statement in FISA that it sought to restrict presidential authority to conduct warrantless searches in the national security area—which it has not."[62] Finally, the administration concluded that if FISA really purported to be the "exclusive means" by which electronic surveillance for foreign intelligence is gathered, then it was an unconstitutional infringement on the president's Article II powers.[63]

The second argument made by the DOJ focused on authority granted to the president by statute. As a fallback position, the administration conceded FISA was the statute that governed the collection of electronic foreign surveillance but noted FISA also contained a provision allowing for Congress to authorize, via statute, the collection of electronic foreign intelligence outside of FISA's guidelines.[64] According to the administration, Congress did just this when it passed the Authorization for Use of Military Force (AUMF) shortly after 9/11. The AUMF authorizes the president to "use all necessary and appropriate force" against those who perpetrated the 9/11 attacks in order to prevent "future acts of international terrorism against the United States."[65]

This authorization to use force, argued the administration, should be read broadly. Gathering electronic "signals intelligence" (via electronic surveillance), concluded the DOJ, is certainly incident to the authorized use of force and therefore squarely within the president's war powers.[66] The Bush administration's defense was therefore comprehensive. The president had both the constitutional and statutory authority/permission to engage in warrantless electronic surveillance.

A number of members of Congress pushed back against the Bush administration's perspective on the scope of FISA. Senators as ideologically diverse as Russ Feingold (D-WI) and Lindsey Graham (R-SC) openly scoffed at the idea that the AUMF somehow trumped FISA when it came to electronic surveillance gathering. "When I voted for it [the AUMF]," Senator Graham told Gonzalez in the hearings, "I never envisioned that I was giving this president or any other president the ability to go around FISA carte blanche." Chairman Specter voiced his skepticism as well when he asked, "If he didn't think he could get Congress to act, why does he think Congress intended to give those broad powers in the force resolution?"[67] Despite these skeptical overtures, Gonzalez held fast to the administration's position that the text of the AUMF did allow the executive branch to lawfully implement the TSP.

The hearings did nothing to change the Bush administration's view on the legality of the TSP. Instead, it continued to offer a full-throated defense of the program on several levels. It continued to claim the president had the power to implement the TSP, regardless of what Congress thought. President Bush repeatedly asserted he would use every constitutional means at his disposal to keep the American people safe. Vice President Cheney conveyed the same message leaving no doubt about who he thought was in charge of the WOT. Members of Congress, opined the vice president, "have the right and the responsibility to suggest whatever they want to suggest" when it comes to electronic surveillance, but "we have all the legal authority we need."[68]

Second, the administration painted critics of the program as being weak on national security. "Our enemy is listening," Gonzalez lectured the committee during his testimony, "and I cannot help but wonder if they aren't smiling at the prospect that we might disclose even more, or perhaps unilaterally disarm ourselves of a key tool in the war on terror."[69] Finally, the Bush administration attempted to deflect criticism of the program by focusing instead on those who leaked the information of its existence. These leakers were threatening national security by exposing key national security programs to the enemy.

Pleas for increased oversight, either by Congress or the courts, were also rebuffed by the administration. A resolution to censure President Bush for the TSP offered by Senator Russ Feingold was easily repulsed.[70] In March 2006, Congress overwhelmingly renewed the Patriot Act, once again providing legislative support for executive branch electronic surveillance.

Many influential Republicans backed the administration's position and were able to head off a more comprehensive congressional investigation into the administration's surveillance policies.[71] Senate Intelligence Committee chairman Pat Roberts (R-KS), in a party-line vote, created a new, seven-member subcommittee to oversee the TSP. This move drew criticism from Democrats who accused the Republicans of essentially doing the bidding of the White House rather than engaging in serious oversight. They noted the members of the newly formed subcommittee could not even relate to other members of the Intelligence Committee what the White House told them about the program.[72] Unfortunately for the Bush administration, before this issue even had a chance to subside, a new bombshell broke.

Data Mining

On May 12, 2006, the *USA Today* published a story that revealed the Bush administration had been secretly collecting metadata on over 200 million U.S. phone accounts—over one trillion calls—without warrants or any other judicial supervision.[73] The scope of this claim went far beyond that of the TSP, and once again the administration had decided not to conduct its programs under the auspices of FISA.

The collection of metadata does not involve listening in on the call itself. In other words, the government is not actually hearing the conversations taking place over the phone lines. Metadata refers to information regarding the time and date of the call, the number called, and the length of the call. While the collection of this information may seem innocuous, when collected in bulk it has the capacity to reveal a considerable amount of information about people.

Consider the following example. If the government knows that an individual made a phone call to a local agency that provides abortion or drug counseling services, one would probably not have to listen to the actual call itself to know what the general content of the conversation was. Put enough of these pieces together, and the government would have the capacity to paint a very thorough picture of an individual's life without ever hearing the content of any of that person's calls.

President Bush was once again forced to defend his administration's surveillance programs saying, "We're not mining or trolling through the personal lives of millions of innocent Americans."[74] Yet, it appeared as if that was exactly what the administration was doing. A March 2006 Justice Department inspector general's report found the FBI had secret contracts with telecommunications companies to get phone records of Americans claiming "exigent circumstances" when in many instances none existed.[75] AT&T, Verizon, and Bell South all defended their participation by forcefully claiming they were protecting the privacy of their customers even as they cooperated with the government's surveillance programs.

Republican leadership in Congress once again supported the Bush administration's defense of the program though it had some trouble keeping individual members in line. Chair of the House Intelligence Subcommittee on Technical and Tactical Intelligence Heather Wilson called for full hearings into the new revelations. The White House responded with somewhat extended briefings on the matter. But Peter Hoekstra, the House Intelligence Committee Chair, refused to hold hearings on the matter and Senate Majority Leader Bill Frist (R-TN) called Democrat requests for hearings "stifling partisanship" and "politically motivated."[76] Congress ultimately failed to pass any legislation on the matter prior to the 2006 midterm elections.

The Democrats Take Control

The 2006 midterm elections ushered in a new era of Democratic leadership in Congress. The Democrats picked up 31 seats in the House and 6 seats in the Senate giving them control of both bodies. A Republican-controlled Congress had spent several years deflecting congressional inquiries into the Bush administration's surveillance program, prompting many observers to anticipate a more aggressive approach now that the Democrats were in control.

Perhaps sensitive to this shift in power on Capitol Hill, the Bush administration changed course in January 2007 by suddenly announcing its surveillance programs would now be put under the auspices of the FISC. The administration announced this new approach basing it "on evolving legal interpretations" by DOJ on "foreign surveillance law, changes in the FISA statute, and FISC precedents." It described the arrangement with the FISC as "innovative" but refused to publicly divulge even the contours of it.[77]

One important question for members of Congress was whether this new arrangement still required the executive branch to get FISA warrants on an individual basis or whether it allowed broader "programmatic" applications for warrants. The Bush administration had consistently been pushing for warrants that covered broader groups of people. It preferred this approach rather than to being required to seek a separate warrant for each individual, a more exhaustive and time-consuming task. While this question was never publicly resolved, most observers concluded that the programmatic approach was the one codified by the new arrangement.[78] A few weeks after this announcement, the administration agreed to provide more details about the legal underpinnings of the program to some members of Congress.[79]

Suing Telecommunications Companies

With many Patriot Act provisions still under sunset restrictions, the Bush administration and congressional Democrats attempted to develop a new surveillance bill to address outstanding differences on the nature and scope of executive branch surveillance. One of the key sticking points at this time was the administration's insistence that telecommunications companies— AT&T, Verizon, Qwest, Bell South—receive retroactive immunity against civil lawsuits. Many of these suits had been filed following the TSP's public outing in 2005 by customers who argued these companies violated their expectation of privacy by sharing their metadata information with the government without their consent.

A brief examination of these civil suits against these telecommunications companies illustrates the numerous problems associated with using the judiciary to challenge the legality of executive branch electronic surveillance for national security purposes. While the judiciary might seem like a logical place for individual citizens to pursue legal recourse, it has not, at least historically speaking, been a highly effective one.

One of the biggest hurdles in these lawsuits was the State Secrets Privilege. This is a common-law privilege (i.e., it is not codified in statute, nor is it found in the Constitution), which can be invoked by the government in cases involving sensitive national security information. When using this defense, the government claims it cannot defend against the suit in question without divulging sensitive national security information (e.g., classified information). When the government successfully invokes this defense—a defense to which judges have been extremely deferential—the suit is simply dismissed and the plaintiffs have no further judicial recourse. In this sense, national security trumps the individual's right to justice. The Bush administration invoked this defense frequently in all manner of cases following 9/11 including challenges to its electronic surveillance programs.

The case of *Terkel v. AT&T* (2006) illustrates the state secrets issue nicely. Several individuals alleged AT&T released "massive numbers of domestic telephone calls" to the NSA in violation of federal law, which prohibits companies from disseminating its customers' records except as prescribed by law. The government intervened on AT&T's behalf and requested the lawsuit be dismissed on state secrets grounds. Federal district court judge Matthew Kennelly reviewed classified submissions by the government and was satisfied in the end that the government's invocation of the State Secrets Privilege was appropriate in this case. As a result, the case was dismissed.[80]

In 2006, a group of scholars, media members, and attorneys filed suit in an eastern Michigan federal district court arguing they had a "well-founded belief" they were subject to warrantless surveillance under the Bush administration's TSP in violation of FISA and the U.S. Constitution. District Court Judge Anna Diggs Taylor concluded as an initial matter that the State Secrets Privilege did apply and that the government could use it as a defense, but that the plaintiffs would be allowed to proceed with their case against the government anyway.[81]

Having resolved the standing issue, Judge Taylor proceeded to find in favor the plaintiffs by holding the TSP "obviously" violated the Constitution and federal law.[82] In 2007, a sharply divided Sixth Circuit Court of Appeals panel overruled Judge Taylor's decision and ruled in favor of the government. The panel, by a 2–1 count, vacated Judge Taylor's decision and remanded the case to her with instructions to dismiss the plaintiffs' claims for lack of standing.

The circuit court's wide-ranging opinion concluded the injuries alleged by the media, attorneys, and scholars were, at best, speculative. It reasoned the reluctance of people overseas to communicate with the plaintiffs could be tied to any number of things, not just the TSP. Most important, the plaintiffs could not *prove* they had been subject to warrantless surveillance (and since the State Secrets Privilege was properly invoked here they could not obtain evidence from the government that they had).[83] The U.S. Supreme Court refused, without comment, to review the case effectively ending this particular challenge to the TSP and leaving the constitutional issues in this case unresolved.

A separate case involves the Al-Haramain Foundation. This foundation describes itself as a charitable Islamic group. After 9/11, the U.S. government designated it as a terrorist organization due to its ties with Al Qaeda. As the government was in the process of going through the paperwork to freeze the organization's assets, it accidentally gave the Al-Haramain legal team a top secret document that revealed members of Al-Haramain were subjects of the NSA's warrantless TSP in 2004. Armed with this inadvertent disclosure, the group filed suit in federal court alleging the warrantless electronic surveillance violated FISA. The government moved to dismiss the entire suit on state secrets grounds.[84] *Al-Haramain* and dozens of other TSP challenges continued to move through the judicial system as Congress and the president attempted to fashion new electronic surveillance legislation.

In the fall of 2007, congressional Democrats and the Bush administration reached a temporary agreement on executive branch electronic surveillance. The Protect America Act of 2007 was passed by a Democrat-controlled Congress with no hearings and only four days of discussion. It was designed with sunset provisions that expired after six months. It would also allow the FISC to issue broad warrants, require private companies to comply with government warrant requests, and eliminate the need for a warrant when wholly foreign calls were run through U.S. telecommunications switches.[85]

The fact the agreement was only temporary in nature was a result of ongoing distrust between the Bush administration and congressional Democrats. The Bush administration argued attempts to address even the most simple surveillance issues prompted Congress to seek all sorts of additional and unnecessary restrictions. Democrats countered the Bush administration had repeatedly refused to provide detailed documentation about the administration's surveillance activities and offered incomplete or misleading information to Congress.[86]

The immunity issue remained unresolved. For the administration, it was an essential part of any long-term deal. Many Democrats wanted to conduct further investigations into the Bush administration surveillance and worried providing immunity to telecommunications companies would thwart this effort. A deal had been reached, but no one was happy. Speaker of the House Nancy Pelosi declared portions of the bill "unacceptable" and stated the Congress would not wait six months before "corrective action" was taken.[87]

In the spring, Congress and the White House remained at an impasse on a surveillance bill even as the temporary six-month bill passed the previous year expired. Each side blamed the other. The White House claimed the United States was losing vital intelligence information because private companies were reluctant to cooperate with government surveillance programs. This, according to the administration's rhetoric, increased the likelihood of another terrorist attack. Speaker Pelosi, on the other hand, accused the president of "misrepresenting the facts" in the surveillance debate.[88] Electronic surveillance did not cease with the lapse of the 2007 provisions as existing orders were valid for a period of a year. However, new ones could not be issued. The standoff between Congress and the Bush administration continued.

FISA Amendments Act of 2008

An agreement was finally reached in the summer of 2008. Congress passed the FISA Amendments Act of 2008, a bill regarded as a major victory for the White House. The telecommunications firms were granted retroactive immunity against civil lawsuits. The bill also outlined a procedure where the FISC would oversee executive branch surveillance programs. "Broad warrants" (for groups of suspects) could be used against foreign targets.[89] Republicans hailed it as a victory for the American people and downplayed concerns voiced by civil libertarians. The American people had nothing to fear from this legislation, stated supporter Senator Kit Bond (R-MO) "unless you have Al Qaeda on your speed dial."[90]

While some Democrats such as Jay Rockefeller supported the compromise, many others were disappointed by the new bill. Senator Pat Leahy (D-VT), the Chair of the Senate Judiciary Committee, voiced the thoughts of many when he lamented Congress had essentially become a rubber stamp for the Bush administration's surveillance programs.[91] Senator Barack Obama (D-IL), the Democratic nominee for the presidency in 2008, originally opposed the provision for telecommunications company immunity, going as far as to threaten a filibuster. In the end, he voted for what he described as "an improved but imperfect" bill.[92]

The immunity provision found in the act ultimately put to rest the dozens of pending civil suits against the telecommunications companies. These cases were going through the appeals process when the 2008 act became law. On June 3, 2009, Federal District Court Judge Walker agreed the retroactive immunity provisions in the bill were constitutional and dismissed all claims.[93] As a practical matter this ended all of the lawsuits against the telecommunications industry for whatever complicity they might have had in the Bush administration's TSP.

The abrupt end to these lawsuits highlights the difficulties associated with relying on the judiciary to oversee, or check, the executive branch in the area of electronic surveillance for the purposes of national security. The Bush White House never hesitated to invoke the State Secrets Privilege as a means to avoid adjudicating any cases where objections were raised to its programs. This tactic was often successful, with several lower courts accepting the government's arguments and dismissing cases outright. Even in cases where the courts did not automatically dismiss the case on state secrets grounds, plaintiffs often had difficulty showing they had standing (i.e., that the government had actually eavesdropped on their communications) since the information in question was almost invariably classified.

In this instance, the executive branch had the willing help of Congress, that eventually acceded to the administration's demand that retroactive immunity be given. Once this was secured, it was clear to the judiciary the people's branches had collectively spoken and that their will was to immunize the telecommunications companies. There was little left to do but to dismiss the cases.

In return for immunity and other concessions to the White House, Democrats received a provision acknowledging FISA was the "exclusive" vehicle for

Electronic Surveillance and National Security 41

executive branch wiretapping. The Office of Inspector General was also tasked with reviewing NSA surveillance programs in the future.[94] The most noteworthy of these reviews was released shortly after Barack Obama took office in 2009.

Summary

The pattern of events that unfolded after 9/11 is eerily familiar to those in the past. President Bush authorized multiple secret electronic surveillance programs. Someone from outside the government, in this instance the press, was ultimately responsible for making knowledge of these programs public. Rather than deny their existence, the Bush administration forcefully defended both their necessity and their legality.

While many in Congress expressed shock and outrage at the surveillance revelations, congressional leadership—generally Republicans—often worked with the Bush administration to help prevent meaningful investigations into executive branch surveillance programs. Republicans regularly backed President Bush, sometimes at the expense of their own institutional prerogatives, agreeing it was primarily the responsibility of the president to drive policy in the WOT.

The limits of the congressional oversight scheme in this policy area were painfully on display, particularly the limited scope and nature of what was shared about some of the executive branch surveillance programs. And even this limited information was shared with only a handful of members. Members were technically informed of these surveillance programs, but the problematic nature of the briefings was called into stark relief when made public. Some minor adjustments were made around the edges (e.g., the new subcommittee to monitor the TSP) but no significant oversight reforms were enacted.

Congress did hold hearings and pass legislation, renewing and revising the Patriot Act surveillance provisions multiple times. While some of this legislation enacted additional oversight and reporting requirements, it also codified and provided immunity for any potential legal transgressions committed by private companies that supplied the government with their customer data.

When Democrats gained control of Congress in 2006, there was an increased desire for oversight over Bush administration WOT programs, but even then there were limits on congressional action. George W. Bush completed his second term in office in 2008. Democrat Barack Obama, a senator during the Bush administration, became the new president. The new president also had a Democrat-controlled Congress at his disposal.

Electronic Surveillance in the War on Terror: The Obama Administration

Every morning the president of the United States receives a national security briefing. He has access to information few others in Washington have. Given this, it is perhaps understandable that political officials who are critical of executive branch programs sometimes change their mind when they are the ones sitting in the president's chair.

Senator Barack Obama was critical about many of the Bush administration policies but in the area of electronic surveillance it appears he continued many of those very policies. One of the first significant decisions President Obama faced in this area as president was whether to conduct an investigation of his predecessor's policies. There was a considerable amount of division on this question. Some, now that the Democrats controlled the White House, were eager to call the Bush administration to account on its terrorism policies, while others preferred to focus on the future. Several events shaped the Obama administration's early actions on this question and others in the area of electronic surveillance.

Early Challenges

The FISCR, the FISA review court, was created to review FISC decisions the government wanted to challenge (e.g., the denial of a government warrant application). During its first 20 years of existence, the court heard no cases. However, during the WOT, it issued several important opinions. FISA court opinions are generally not available for public consumption since they often are filled with classified information. While it is theoretically possible for an unhappy litigant to appeal a FISCR decision to the U.S. Supreme Court, it has never happened in practice. This is because, as is the case with the FISC, the FISCR proceedings are also non-adversarial. As a result of this structural arrangement, the FISCR usually has the last word when it comes to the legality and constitutionality of electronic surveillance matters.

Shortly before Obama was sworn into office, a 2008 opinion of the FISCR on the constitutionality of the 2007 Protect America Act was made public. The decision was in response to a telecommunications company's initial refusal to comply with the government's data collection requests. The court held that telecommunications companies must comply and that the act itself was constitutional. In an important passage the court ruled that the Fourth Amendment warrant requirement did not apply to the collection of foreign intelligence involving Americans. In effect, it created a "national security" exception. The court decided that when "serviceable safeguards" are present, the courts should not frustrate national security efforts.[95] This decision was important because it helped provide a legal foundation for the Obama administration's secret bulk metadata collection programs.

In April 2009, the *New York Times* reported that in late 2008 and early 2009 the NSA was systematically over-collecting thousands (perhaps even hundreds of thousands—the exact number is unknown) of e-mails and telephone conversations belonging to American citizens. These collections were wholly domestic (i.e., the senders and recipients were both located in the United States) and done without warrants. The NSA went beyond the parameters established by the FISC in approximately 8–10 orders, but because multiple numbers can be contained in a single warrant the magnitude of the over-collection was very difficult to determine.

This over-collection came to light in the course of a routine review of executive branch intelligence gathering practices mandated by the 2008 FISA Amendments Act. Intelligence agencies reported they were having difficulties complying with the 2008 FISA Amendments due to the technical difficulties in separating foreign communications from wholly domestic ones.[96] When the Obama administration discovered the problem, it quickly moved to rectify the situation, though according to one intelligence official the FISC was none too happy to hear the executive branch was once again having problems complying with the FISA warrant process.[97]

The Bush administration also had its issues providing the FISC with accurate data in warrant applications. At one point in time, the FBI was apparently providing inaccurate data on FISA warrant applications so frequently that Chief Judge Kollar-Kotelly wrote to the Department of Justice to complain about the problem.[98] These difficulties again illustrate the complexity of the law and technology in this area. Sometimes compliance can be difficult even with the best intentions.

The Curtain Pulled Back on Bush Administration Practices

Pursuant to the FISA Amendments Act of 2008, the Office of the Inspectors General (OIG) released a report on electronic surveillance programs during the Bush administration. The unclassified version of the report, released in July 2009, was the result of more than 200 interviews. However, key figures such as former vice president Dick Cheney, Attorney General John Ashcroft, OLC lawyer John Yoo, and CIA director George Tenet all declined to be interviewed for the report. Almost lost in media sensation amid the release was the fact that the report noted there were still other classified surveillance programs about which the public knew nothing.[99]

One of the key criticisms to emerge from the OIG report was related to the OLC analyses prepared by Bush administration attorney John Yoo. These memoranda served as the legal underpinning for the TSP and other Bush administration surveillance programs. The report noted it was "extraordinary and inappropriate" for the administration to rely on a single attorney (without oversight!) in the preparation of these memoranda. Subsequent review of Yoo's memoranda revealed "deficiencies" in both facts and legal reasoning that eventually led the executive branch to repudiate the reasoning they contained.[100]

The report also criticized the Bush administration for its "extraordinary and inappropriate" secrecy surrounding the program. At some level, the report concluded, this extreme secrecy might have impacted the effectiveness of the program. So few people were "read into" the TSP that it was difficult to make effective use of the data.[101]

One of the key points the Bush administration repeatedly asserted in defense of the TSP was its importance as an indispensable tool for fighting terrorism. It had disrupted terrorist plots and, in the words of Vice President Cheney, "saved thousands of lives."[102] This was a claim that, given the classified nature of the information in question, was very difficult to disprove. However, the OIG report released in 2009 (the unclassified version) found little evidence to support these claims. Everyone the OIG talked to agreed the surveillance programs were important and should be maintained, yet no one could point to specific instances where they were instrumental in thwarting a terrorist attack.[103] The report indicated there was perceived political pressure related to the production of threat assessments (sometimes referred to as "scary memos") with lower officials never really knowing why they were generating these memoranda.[104]

The news was not all bad for the Bush administration. Despite all of these issues, the report concluded that there was no intentional misuse of the TSP by the NSA or anyone else associated with the program. It also noted that lawmakers on Capitol Hill had been briefed almost 50 times between 9/11 and January 2007.[105] This supports the administration's claims that Congress had been appropriately informed of the TSP.

This was as far as the Obama administration and Congress were willing to go. Further efforts to bring criminal charges or form investigative commissions to examine the Bush administration's record on electronic surveillance failed to generate any substantial support in Congress. Congress and the president were largely content to let the matter rest.

Shortly after Obama took office in 2009, a group of lawyers, journalists, and nongovernmental organizations filed suit in federal district court challenging provisions found in the FISA Amendments Act of 2008. In *Clapper v. Amnesty International*, these provisions allowing government surveillance were alleged to have an unconstitutional chilling effect on their international communications with clients, sources, and other contacts. These contacts were fearful of engaging in communications out of fear that the U.S. government was illicitly gathering information on them.

The case eventually made its way to the U.S. Supreme Court in 2013 where the justices ruled against the plaintiffs. In a close 5–4 decision, the

Court held the plaintiffs did not have standing. In other words, they had failed to demonstrate they had suffered any concrete injury traceable to the statute itself. Any injury, the Court concluded, was merely speculative. The plaintiffs could not prove they had been the targets of any government surveillance and the case was dismissed. Since the Court ruled the plaintiffs did not have standing, it was not forced to address the underlying constitutional question about the government's authority to collect bulk metadata.[106]

More revelations about the scope of executive branch electronic surveillance were forthcoming. During a debate regarding the renewal of several Patriot Act provisions, two Senate Democrats, Mark Udall (D-CO) and Ron Wyden (D-OR), went to the floor of the Senate to ominously warn there was a considerable amount of important information being withheld from the public. "I want to deliver a warning this afternoon," stated Senator Wyden. "When the American people find out how their government has secretly interpreted the Patriot Act, they will be stunned and they will be angry." Senator Udall seconded the remarks asserting that Americans would be "alarmed" if they really knew how the government was carrying out the act.

The two senators sent a letter to Attorney General Eric Holder, which reiterated these concerns and added:

> As we see it, there is now a significant gap between what most Americans think the law allows and what the government secretly claims the law allows. This is a problem, because it is impossible to have an informed public debate about what the law should say when the public doesn't know what its government thinks the law says.[107]

When questioned about this, the Obama administration responded that congressional committees and the FISC knew and approved of what the administration was doing.[108]

During a March 2013 Senate hearing, Senator Wyden asked Director of National Intelligence (DNI) James Clapper if the NSA collected "any type of data at all on millions or hundreds of millions of Americans." Clapper responded, "No; not wittingly." Less than four months later, the veracity of this response would be called into question with Clapper himself ultimately referring to it as the "least untruthful" answer.[109] It turns out this was exactly what the NSA was doing.

The Snowden Leaks

On June 5, 2013, the British newspaper *The Guardian* revealed the FISC had approved the U.S. government's request to force Verizon to hand over metadata from millions of American phone calls to the NSA and the FBI.[110]

And this revelation was just the tip of the iceberg. Subsequent stories would chronicle a U.S government that was, unbeknownst to its citizens, collecting a staggering amount of information on them and others around the world.

Journalist Glenn Greenwald's source for this information was Edward Snowden, a former Booz Hamilton employee working on contract for the NSA. Snowden is thought to have stolen over 1.5 million files while working for the NSA, many of which contained highly classified information. It was the largest leak of classified information in U.S. history.

In the year following the *Guardian*'s initial disclosures, more stories chronicled the extent of the NSA and allied governments' surveillance activities. Revelations included documents detailing the following NSA activities:

- The agency's goal: Acquire data from "anyone, anytime, anywhere."
- The agency infected over 50,000 computer networks with malware to steal sensitive information.
- It stores billions of foreign cell phone location records.
- It secretly monitored games such as World of Warcraft and Angry Birds to gather user data.
- The agency had backdoors into Google, YouTube, Skype, and Facebook allowing it to gather data on users.
- Documents revealed U.S. drones rely largely on NSA intelligence for targeting, not human intelligence on the ground.
- The agency was also collecting American citizens' e-mail, text, and Internet metadata.
- The NSA broke privacy rules thousands of times a year per an internal audit.
- The agency has the capacity to access user data in most smartphones.
- It has over 250,000 e-mail contact lists from Yahoo and Gmail.
- The NSA built a system capable of recording "100 percent" of a foreign country's phone calls with a voice intercept program called Mystic.[111]

The NSA also conducted extensive surveillance operations abroad. It targeted the foreign embassies/missions of over 38 countries. The phones of over 35 world leaders—including Germany, Italy, Spain, Mexico, and Brazil—were tapped. The agency routinely monitored communications at cultural, political, and economic meetings around the world in an attempt to give the United States various negotiating advantages. The U.S. government even monitored communications from the Vatican and Pope Francis.[112]

Snowden fled the country and eventually ended up seeking political asylum in Russia, where he remains indefinitely. His passport has been cancelled. Less than two weeks after the first *Guardian* story broke, Snowden was charged in U.S. District Court with Theft of Government Property, Unauthorized

Communication of National Defense Information, and Willful Communication of Classified Communications Intelligence Information to an Unauthorized Person.[113] He remains a wanted fugitive from the U.S. government.

Given that punishment was virtually guaranteed to be swift and certain, why did Snowden do what he did? "My sole motive," he said in an interview, "is to inform the public as to that which is done in their name and that which is done against them."[114] He eventually came to realize "these things need to be determined by the public, not by somebody who is merely hired by the government."[115]

If Edward Snowden was seeking a public debate with the release of these classified documents, he achieved his goal. Reactions were immediate and varied tremendously. Senator Dianne Feinstein (D-CA), the Chair of the Senate Intelligence Committee, called Snowden's leaks "treasonous,"[116] while others referred to him as a hero and a patriot for revealing government programs many felt were unethical, if not illegal. Many members of Congress expressed outrage at the Obama administration for conducting operations far beyond the scope of what members thought they were authorizing.

At some level, the aforementioned revelations should come as no surprise. Countries spy on each other all the time and monitoring communications of foreign citizens and governments is fairly routine. What is striking about the Snowden information is the scope of these previously unknown activities, particularly as they relate to the communications of American citizens.

In a defense paradoxically similar to the Bush administration's, the Obama White House moved quickly to assert that the NSA bulk collection metadata program was vital to the national security of the United States. It also asserted that the program was closely monitored to prevent the government from abusing this collection power. The Obama administration quickly released a White Paper defending the constitutionality of bulk data collection under Section 215 of the Patriot Act. On the constitutional side of the ledger, the administration argued the Supreme Court has consistently ruled citizens have no reasonable privacy expectation in their telephone metadata,[117] nor does such surveillance violate any First Amendment rights.

The administration also pointed out its interpretation of Section 215 had been endorsed by FISC judges.[118] The 2008 FISA Act amendments had broadened both the scope of the court's review powers and the definitions of many key terms such as "foreign intelligence information." The FISA courts were also receptive to the government argument that the "special needs doctrine" applied to national security and foreign intelligence-related searches, diminishing Fourth Amendment expectations of privacy.[119] Collectively, these forces inclined the FISA courts to be more receptive to bulk collection requests and given the secretive nature of FISC opinions, did so in a manner that was virtually invisible to policy makers in Congress and the general public. These were the legal interpretations Senators Wyden and

Udall had attempted to warn their colleagues about months earlier on the floor of the Senate.

The Obama administration similarly claimed the program was vital to preventing terrorist plots. On June 18, NSA director Keith Alexander said the NSA metadata surveillance program had helped prevent over 50 terrorist events.[120] Upon closer inspection, it was ultimately revealed the program was helpful only in a handful of cases.[121] The administration also claimed it had kept Congress up to date on these NSA programs, a claim many in Congress again disputed.[122]

Technology companies were also forced to scramble after the Snowden revelations. Some companies argued they had been compelled by the government to participate either by court order (e.g., Verizon) or by threat of fine. It was divulged Yahoo was threatened with a fine of $250,000 per day if it did not comply with the government's information requests. Companies were also frustrated they were not allowed to publicly disclose they were passing their customers' data to the government. The Snowden leaks also had the potential to cost technology companies over $35 billion in foreign business from customers who were now leery that their personal information might surreptitiously wind up in the hands of the U.S. government without their consent.[123]

New Lawsuits

Armed with the Snowden disclosures, new lawsuits were filed challenging the constitutionality of the government's metadata collection practices under Section 215. While the plaintiffs in *Clapper* had only been able to speculate they had been the targets of government surveillance, the documents leaked by Edward Snowden appeared to provide concrete proof about the scope of NSA surveillance under the Patriot Act. Two suits in particular managed to work their way up through the federal judiciary.

Six months after the initial Snowden disclosures, Federal District Court Judge Richard Leon, in *Klayman v. Obama* (2013), granted Klayman's motion for a preliminary injunction calling for a halt to the government's metadata collection. Unlike the *Clapper* case, Judge Leon concluded Klayman did have standing to sue and that the metadata program was likely an unconstitutional infringement on Klayman's Fourth Amendment rights.[124] The case was then appealed to the D.C. Circuit Court of Appeals.

A separate suit filed in the Southern District of New York alleged similar constitutional violations. In *ACLU v. Clapper* (2013), district court judge William Pauley III ruled against the plaintiffs and granted the government's motion to dismiss the case. While he did agree that the plaintiffs had standing to pursue a case, he ultimately concluded that previous Supreme Court precedent indicated that the plaintiffs had no privacy expectation in their telephony metadata so there was no constitutional violation. He also held that the government metadata collection did not significantly burden the plaintiffs' First Amendment rights.[125]

The case was appealed to the Second Circuit Court of appeals where a panel of judges overruled Judge Pauley. The panel agreed that the plaintiffs had standing and went even further. It concluded that Congress never intended to authorize bulk metadata collection when it passed the Patriot Act. The plaintiffs could therefore proceed and press their constitutional issues in district court.[126] As was the case with the Bush administration court cases against the telecommunications companies, Congress would soon pass legislation that would effectively moot these challenges and prevent any authoritative Supreme Court ruling on the constitutionality of bulk metadata collection.

Congress Responds: The USA Freedom Act

Immediately after the Snowden disclosures, many in Congress set about the task of once again writing new surveillance policy legislation. A mere six weeks after the first story broke, conservative congressman Justin Amash (R-MI) and senior liberal John Conyers (D-MI) introduced an amendment to the 2014 National Defense Authorization Act. The amendment would have barred funding for the NSA's metadata collection program under Section 215 of the Patriot Act.[127]

House leadership from both parties and senior Republicans and Democrats on the House Intelligence Committee all strenuously opposed the Amash-Conyers amendment. The Obama administration's NSA director, Keith Alexander, held an emergency four-hour briefing with members of the House imploring them to oppose the amendment. The administration argued that taking away the NSA's bulk collection ability would have severe national security repercussions. Collectively, they urged disaffected members not to rush into anything.

On July 24, 2013, the Amash-Conyers amendment was defeated in an extraordinarily close vote, 217–205. Unlike most terrorism legislation, a remarkable bipartisan coalition came together to support the amendment. Ninety-four Republicans joined 111 Democrats, but it was not enough. A parallel effort, the LIBERT-E Act, also authored by Amash and Conyers, was introduced that June but it died in committee. These early legislative efforts served as a wake-up call for House leadership. The surveillance issue was not just going to quietly go away.

Additional stories about Snowden's leaks continued to make headlines helping increase the call for congressional action of some type. Republican congressman James Sensenbrenner (R-WI), one of the original authors of the Patriot Act, was among the foremost advocates of writing new legislation to ban bulk data collection.[128] The USA Freedom Act was introduced in October 2013. It passed the House of Representatives by a solid margin in May 2014, but many of the act's supporters were disappointed that, in their opinion, the Obama administration and defense hawks watered down some of the more restrictive provisions. The act proceeded to the Senate where security-minded Republicans managed a successful filibuster. The act died when its supporters fell a mere two votes short of ending debate on the matter.[129] Supporters vowed to bring the bill back up for consideration in the near future.

The following May, USA Freedom Act supporters once more attempted to push the bill through Congress. This time the dynamics were somewhat different. Several important surveillance-related sections of the Patriot Act—including Section 215—were set to expire at the end of May. The House passed the Freedom Act by an even larger margin this time around, 338–88. The pressure was on the Senate to either pass the bill or extend the Patriot Act provisions until a compromise could be reached, otherwise the surveillance provisions would lapse.[130]

Once again supporters were unable to break a Senate filibuster. Senate Majority Leader Mitch McConnell (R-KY) introduced a request to extend the Patriot Act provisions for a week, while the Senate continued negotiations but this attempt was blocked by Senator Rand Paul (R-TN), a libertarian-leaning Republican whose long-standing opposition to the Patriot Act was well known.[131] McConnell was frustrated at the impasse and loath to let the Patriot Act provisions expire. "There are," he fumed, "a number of us who feel very strongly that this is a significant weakening of the tools that were put in place in the wake of 9/11 to protect the country."[132] Negotiations eventually extended past the May deadline and the Patriot Act provisions did indeed expire. But not for long. On June 2, 2015, the Senate overwhelmingly, 67–32, passed the USA Freedom Act.

The USA Freedom Act restored the authorizations for roving wiretaps and warrants for "lone wolf" terrorists that had expired under the Patriot Act. The act also specifically ended bulk data collection under Section 215 though this ban would not take effect for 180 days. It was replaced with a more targeted call detail records program, which allowed for metadata collection under particular circumstances:

> Under [the Act], if the government can demonstrate a reasonable, articulable suspicion that a specific selection term is associated with a foreign power or an agent of a foreign power engaged in international terrorism or activities in preparation therefor, the FISC may issue an order for the ongoing, daily production of call detail records held by telephone companies. The prospective collection of call detail records is limited to 180 days.[133]

This abolition of bulk data collection under Section 215 essentially mooted the pending court challenges so the Supreme Court never had a direct opportunity to rule on whether the bulk data collection under that section was constitutional.

Congress also added a host of reporting requirements related to the request and issuance of FISA warrants including a provision that Congress be notified in the event that any FISA warrant is rejected or modified by the FISC. In a nod to corporations that had been frustrated by the fact that they had been forced to comply with government programs yet forbidden from divulging that publicly, the act contained a provision that allowed them (with some restrictions) to publicize what data the government had requested.[134]

In response to those who were unhappy that the FISC and FISCR had issued secret opinions on surveillance measures that played an important role in defining the scope of government surveillance, the new act contained a provision that amici (i.e., a third party) could be consulted to provide technical or legal expertise if either FISA court was being asked to define existing surveillance law in a "novel" or "significant" way. The FISC soon established a panel of six individuals with technical and legal expertise and has consulted them in several cases since 2015.[135] There is also now a mechanism where FISC judges can certify a question of law for the FISCR to review. The DNI was also now instructed to release (or declassify) FISC and FISCR court opinion wherever practicable.[136] All of these provisions are designed to provide more transparency and accountability to the FISA courts' decision-making processes.

Responses to the new legislation varied considerably. Some privacy groups applauded the USA Freedom Act as an important piece of the privacy puzzle, while others were less sanguine about whether the provisions—which might look good on paper—would result in any substantive changes.[137] Perhaps the most widely hailed change was the prohibition of bulk collection under the Patriot Act. Bulk collection was not banned entirely, but from that point on it would, at least in theory, be more difficult for the government to do.

Summary

Despite rhetoric to the contrary as a senator and then a presidential candidate, President Obama found himself engaging in and defending electronic surveillance programs that in many ways looked very much like those seen in the Bush administration. Obama supporters were always quick to point out that their administration placed a greater emphasis on internal checks and separation of powers issues. This was a point that the president continually emphasized as well, but the Snowden leaks called into question how meaningful these changes were in practice.

Once again it took a media leak of classified information to galvanize Congress into action. But once Congress was spurred to action, it did manage to pass significant surveillance reform with the support of both Republicans and Democrats in Congress and the Obama White House. This does not mean that there are no remaining issues to be addressed, but the bipartisan manner in which the USA Freedom Act was passed has given some hope that Congress will be able to address other outstanding issues in this policy area.

The Trump Administration

The issue of electronic surveillance continued to be in the news during the early months of the Trump administration but for different reasons than those that arose under Presidents Bush and Obama. While the issue of mass data collection and surveillance faded from public discussion, the issue of surveillance of government officials was thrust into the spotlight. Two incidents highlight the issue.

On March 4, 2017, President Donald Trump published—with no warning whatsoever—a tweet accusing the Obama administration of secretly wiretapping the Trump campaign during the latter stages of the 2016 presidential election. Calling it a "new low" and Obama a "Bad (or sick) guy," Trump compared these actions to "Nixon/Watergate," the 1970s presidential scandal where secretly taped recordings in the White House played a key role in the resignation of President Richard Nixon.[138] President Trump offered no proof that this happened but the administration continued to press the claim and encouraged Congress to investigate the matter.

The claim ignited a firestorm. Critics were outraged that President Trump would accuse former president Obama of such serious actions without a shred of evidence to support his claims. Even Republicans in Congress wanted the administration to provide evidence that these events really happened.

It was ultimately revealed that the FBI did get a FISA warrant to monitor Carter Page, a former foreign policy advisor to the Trump campaign, for his connections to Russian interests. The warrant was also renewed on more than one occasion. The Trump administration distanced itself from Page, claiming that his role in the campaign was only a minor one.[139]

It is important to emphasize that warrants of this type would emanate from the Justice Department, not the White House. There is no evidence to suggest that President Obama was in any way involved in the warrant or surveillance process. President Trump also accused Obama's National Security Advisor, Susan Rice, of illegally seeking information on surveillance targets (in this instance Page).[140] Rice did inquire about the investigation but such inquiries do happen on occasion and are not illegal. There was no evidence to suggest that this FISA warrant was issued for political purposes.

This turned out to be the extent of any wiretapping related to the Trump campaign. Representative Devin Nunes, Republican Chair of the House Intelligence Committee and Trump supporter, declared a few weeks later that there was no evidence that Trump's phone was tapped.[141] FBI director James Comey also affirmed, in testimony before Congress, that Trump's charges against Obama were false and that there was "no information to support them."[142]

A second electronic surveillance story also involved FBI director James Comey. The early months of the Trump administration were dominated by an investigation into whether Trump or his campaign had any illegal communications with Russian contacts during the 2016 presidential election. This stemmed from U.S. intelligence community's conclusion that the Russians had purposely attempted to influence the outcome of the presidential election via a variety of electronic means. National Security Advisor Michael Flynn was forced to resign in the midst of the probe and Trump was alleged to have inappropriately pressured Comey to drop any FBI investigation into Flynn's activities with Russia.

Trump ultimately fired Comey, leading many critics to speculate that the reason was Comey's refusal to drop the investigation as allegedly requested by the president. While conflicting stories about the reason for Comey's firing circulated, Trump cryptically tweeted that "James Comey better hope that there are no 'tapes' of our conversations before he starts leaking to the press."[143] This immediately raised the specter of another presidential administration—Richard Nixon's—that actually did keep secret recordings of Oval Office conversations with the president, including conversations designed to cover up criminal activity associated with the Watergate break-in.

For weeks President Trump refused to confirm whether any such tapes or taping system existed in the White House. For his part, Comey asserted that he had nothing to hide. He told Congress, "I've seen that tweet about tapes. Lordy, I hope there are tapes."[144] Finally, in a series of tweets, President Trump announced: "With all of the recently reported electronic surveillance intercepts, unmasking and illegal leaking of information, I have no idea whether there are 'tapes' of recordings of my conversations with James Comey, but I did not make, and do not have, any such recordings."[145] It is worth noting that the president did not say that there were no tapes, just that he did not make or have any.

Electronic Surveillance: Remaining Issues

Government's ability to conduct electronic surveillance will continue and grow as technology continues to advance. This particular policy area is one marked by a history of secretive executive branch surveillance programs punctuated by periodic congressional oversight and occasional judicial attention. This pattern continued after 9/11 when secret surveillance programs in both the Bush and Obama administrations were publicized. Congressional oversight has been late in coming, haphazard, and generally ineffective.

Congressional Republicans, particularly those in the leadership, were the first ones to come to the defense of the Bush administration's TSP. They were also the ones who pushed for retroactive immunity for the telecommunications companies as part of the 2008 bill that revised the Patriot Act. Too often partisans on both sides of the aisle acted more out of defense for "their" president rather than as advocates for institutional prerogatives.[146] The impact of this partisan approach to surveillance policy is that it was very difficult to pass any legislation that did not receive the blessing of the White House since it would be difficult, if not impossible, to override a presidential veto. This was evident in the passage of the 2007 and 2008 Acts as well as the USA Freedom Act. This partisan dynamic ultimately led the 9/11 Commission to conclude in 2004 that "congressional oversight for intelligence—and counterterrorism—is now dysfunctional."[147]

Perhaps the most important lesson that can be gleaned from examining the post-9/11 executive and congressional responses in the area of electronic surveillance is that FISA needs to be replaced. Many of scholars and legal experts who have followed the development of FISA over its decades of existence agree.[148] It was a law built for another time when technology was considerably simpler. This was one of the key reasons offered by the Bush administration when it circumvented FISA with the TSP. FISA was not "quick" or "agile" enough to meet the challenges of a decentralized terrorist threat in a technologically changing world.[149]

While Congress deserves credit for continually updating the law, there eventually comes a time when no amount of tinkering is going to get things right. It is just best to start over again. This does not mean abandoning the guiding principle of FISA, the idea that there needs to be checks on executive branch electronic surveillance. If anything, presidential activities since 9/11 have reinforced the belief that Congress needs to retain some type of legislatively mandated oversight control over the executive branch regardless of whether Democrats or Republicans are in the White House.

While Congress managed to pass the USA Freedom Act, it was not designed to take the place of FISA. It was an important piece of legislation that increased accountability and transparency in executive branch surveillance programs. As the Trump administration's first year winds down, there is no significant movement afoot in Congress to seriously tackle FISA reform so any legislative efforts in this area are likely to be minor.

Oversight

If post-9/11 events have proven anything in the area of electronic surveillance, it is that strong congressional oversight is needed more than ever.

It also shows that existing oversight arrangements are in serious need of revision. The same pre-9/11 pattern has continued. The executive branch conducts secret electronic surveillance programs, the media reveals the nature of these programs, Congress is outraged and passes some type of legislation, and then it returns to slumber while the executive branch goes back to its electronic surveillance activities, promising to be more accountable and transparent. Then the whole cycle repeats itself. While there are some initial signs that the USA Freedom Act has increased transparency, it is too early to make a definitive judgment.[150]

Meaningful oversight can only be done when members of Congress have access to the information they need to make informed judgements about the efficacy and legality of executive branch surveillance programs. All reports coming out of the government since 9/11 paint a picture where the executive branch controls the flow of classified information about surveillance programs and sets the rules when this information is shared with Congress. Congress can and should demand a more robust sharing of information.

This can take a variety of forms. First, Congress can insist that the circle of members who are "read in" on surveillance matters be extended beyond the Gang of 8 or even beyond the intelligence committees. Second, members of Congress should have the opportunity to bring appropriately cleared staffers and counsel to these briefings. This would increase their ability to ask thoughtful questions about the efficacy and legality of surveillance programs. This policy area is highly technical and it is unreasonable to expect members to have the capacity to parse these highly complex programs.[151] The executive branch has frequently opposed expanding briefings by raising the fear that Congress will leak sensitive classified security information. However, many observers argue that this fear is overblown and that the congressional track record when it comes to keeping secrets is, in some respects, better than that of the executive branch.[152]

The Snowden leaks illustrate the problems associated with weak congressional oversight. If people who work in executive branch and have issues with surveillance programs feel that that reporting potential issues through conventional channels will not be productive then they may be more inclined to either not report abuses at all or leak them to the media. Neither solution is optimal. Congress can help address this issue by strengthening whistleblower protections for employees engaged in national security operations.

Judicial Reforms—FISA Courts and Article III Courts

The judiciary is often viewed as a potential check on executive branch behavior but when it comes to reviewing surveillance programs the structural limitations of the judiciary have become all too clear. The judiciary's role is not altogether disconnected from that of Congress. As a result, Congress can also help strengthen judicial oversight of the executive.

When Congress passed FISA in 1978, it created a new set of legislative courts in the FISC and the FISCR. These courts were ostensibly designed to handle the unique pressures associated with classified national defense surveillance programs. The aftermath of the 9/11 attacks significantly altered both the scope and nature of what these courts do and how they do it. The FISC now hears a staggering number of warrant applications for government surveillance. Revisions in FISA since 9/11 have also expanded the scope of these courts, while also requiring the FISC and the FISCR to interpret these revisions and determine how they can be legally and constitutionally applied.

FISA courts have been criticized on several grounds. First, FISC judges have been accused of being rubber stamps for government warrant proposals. The judges themselves bristle at this suggestion, but as noted earlier in the chapter, the sheer number of applications and the lack of institutional resources to verify the government's application information preclude any rigorous review of the government's information. Congress could pass legislation that provides FISC judges with more resources to assist them in providing a meaningful check at the warrant application stage.

Second, the numerous amendments to FISA that have been passed at various times since 9/11 have created situations where it is difficult for the executive branch to determine what the rules exactly are. The resulting confusion resulted in mistakes and over-collection of data by both Republican and Democrat administrations.[153] Replacing FISA, as opposed to adding to the existing patchwork of rules and regulations, may make it easier for the executive branch to produce more accurate warrant applications.

Third, FISA courts have been asked to decide weighty issues of constitutional origin that were perhaps unintended when FISA was written. While judicial review by Article III courts (e.g., the U.S. Supreme Court) is possible, it has yet to occur and is not likely to in the near future. The fact that these decisions have been issued after hearing only one side (the government's) and in opinions on classified matters that are secret from virtually the entire government has done little to bolster the faith of those seeking transparency and accountability in government.

Making this process more adversarial and more transparent will help restore faith that the United States is not being governed by "secret law." The USA Freedom Act's provisions for third-party amici in FISA court hearings is a step in the right direction as is its provision for the release of (redacted) FISA court opinions where practicable. There are those who have called for an entire revamping of the FISA court structure but there does not appear to be any widespread support for such a dramatic overhaul of the system as President Trump is completing his first year in office.

The experience of litigants in surveillance cases in Article III courts since 9/11 has illustrated the difficulties in relying on the judiciary as a primary check on executive branch surveillance programs. Judicial deference to the executive in national security matters has routinely been on display as has the use of threshold issues such as standing to preclude a judicial ruling on the underlying constitutional issues. Finally, the extensive use of the State Secrets Privilege, and the judiciary's general acceptance of it, has also proved a formidable barrier to those seeking judicial review of their legal and constitutional claims.[154]

Unfortunately, for those seeking a larger role for the judiciary in electronic surveillance law, many of the restraints that hinder broader judicial review are largely self-imposed and done out of a culture of judicial deference that is unlikely to change any time soon. Congress may be able to make some changes around the edges by more clearly articulating how surveillance law provisions may be challenged and who may do so.

Conclusion

The policy area of electronic surveillance is a good example of the give and take that can occur between political institutions in an attempt to design and refine policy that is sensitive to ever-changing technological advances. The USA Freedom Act is a step in the right direction. Initial returns seem to indicate that it has indeed increased executive branch transparency. The public and members of Congress now have greater access to FISA court opinions. Reporting requirements can also let members of Congress know how many warrants the FISC is granting, how many have been modified, and how many have been rejected. The provision appointing third-parties to represent the public interest before the FISCR also shines some light on the FISA courts.

There are certainly limits to transparency in this area. Often forgotten in the various oversight reports that have been filed are the lines that cryptically remind the public that there are still other government surveillance programs about which the public (and perhaps even members of Congress) know nothing. Much of the information and the means by which it is gathered are—and should be—classified.

The ability to use electronic surveillance to track terrorist enemies of the United States is one of the great advantages the United States has in the WOT. The NSA and other government agencies have capabilities that no terrorist group can match. The ever-growing extent of the NSA's abilities has given many civil libertarians pause. The question is not whether the government can do something. More and more often the answer is "yes" it can do that. The better question to ask is what *should* the government do? Focus on the latter question is key, otherwise technology trumps policy rather having an openly debated policy that defines the parameters of government surveillance action.

CHAPTER THREE

Interrogation and Torture

Among all of the controversies surrounding government policies in the War on Terror (WOT), the ones most passionately debated are those regarding the treatment of detainees. In the days following 9/11, the "gloves came off."[1] President Bush left no doubt about this. "Any barriers in your way," he said to his national security team, "are gone." When Secretary of Defense Donald Rumsfeld pointed out international law imposed some legal constraints on U.S. action, the president responded, "I don't care what the international lawyers say, we are going to kick some ass."[2]

It was this mind-set—articulated at the top—which set the tone for polices that have resulted in hundreds of allegations of detainee abuse and the death of dozens of detainees under U.S. government control. The media feeding frenzy grew as news of the Bush administration's interrogation tactics became public and revealed a host of controversial actions. Stories about detainee treatment at Guantanamo Bay and pictures of abuse at the Abu Ghraib prison in Iraq stunned members of the public. Congress and the American people wanted to know whether these actions were just the product of a few rogue interrogators or part of a more systematic attempt by executive branch officials to implement interrogation policies that threatened to cross the line into torture.

Policies governing interrogation can be particularly difficult to discuss because they often lie at the intersection of public policy and morality. The U.S. experience in the WOT epitomizes this. On the policy side of the coin, it is imperative to ascertain which interrogation policies are effective and which are not. Which model—criminal justice or military (or both?)—should guide decision making? How can rules regarding interrogation best be developed and enforced, and what role does Congress have in this process? Policy questions cannot be asked in isolation because there are important moral issues as well. Are there certain interrogation tactics that should never be used? Can torture be justified in certain circumstances (e.g., the "ticking time bomb scenario")?

While repeatedly asserting that it did not sanction torture, the Bush administration defended many of its harsh interrogation techniques. As Vice President Dick Cheney explained:

> We also have to work, though, sort of the dark side.... A lot of what needs to be done here will have to be done quietly, without any discussion, using sources and methods that are available to our intelligence agencies, if we're going to be successful. That's the world these folks operate in, and so it's going to be vital for us to use any means at our disposal, basically, to achieve our objective.[3]

"I was and remain," Cheney added in a 2009 speech to the conservative American Enterprise Institute, "a strong proponent of our enhanced interrogation program" as it was "legal, essential, justified, successful, and the right thing to do" in preventing the deaths of thousands, if not hundreds of thousands of U.S. citizens.[4] Former National Intelligence Director Mike McConnell was equally enthusiastic: "Have we gotten meaningful information? You betcha. Tons! Does it save lives? Tons! We've gotten incredible information.... We have people walking around in this country that are alive today because this process happened."[5]

Critics continue to be infuriated by what they feel is a lack of remorse for legally sanctioned torture and an unwillingness of Bush administration officials to acknowledge all of the negatives associated with the administration's interrogation programs. They have pushed for investigations into Bush administration interrogation programs and argued those responsible for propagating these policies be held accountable.

The incoming Obama administration made a pointed effort to reject the rhetoric and policies of the previous administration. Some changes were made to U.S. interrogation policy, and President Obama vowed to close the detention facility at Guantanamo Bay. However, these changes were done almost exclusively via executive order.[6] In other words, they lack an important degree of permanence. Any future president could change these policies with the stroke of a pen (in either direction—making them tougher or more lenient). As a presidential candidate in 2016, Donald Trump's harsh rhetoric brought these issues back into the spotlight. Trump's stated desire to bring back waterboarding as an interrogation tool alarmed many, and questions remain as to whether his administration can and will revive many of the harsh, Bush-era interrogation policies.

This chapter will explore U.S. interrogation policies in the WOT by reviewing the history of U.S. interrogation policy followed by a review the of Bush and Obama administration's interrogation policies after 9/11. This review will attempt to assess patterns, similarities, and differences while focusing particularly on the role that Congress has played in the design, implementation, and oversight of interrogation policy.

The Criminal Justice Model versus the Military Model

Before examining the history of interrogation in the United States and its subsequent iterations after 9/11, it is important to note the two different models for dealing with terrorists in the United States. The first model is the criminal justice model. This model treats terrorism as a crime and prosecutes terrorists as criminals. The second model views terrorism as an act of war and treats terrorists as combatants in a military conflict. Congress has roles to play in each model though it arguably plays a larger role in the criminal justice model because it is usually limited to domestic politics. This is an arena where Congress traditionally has had more clout vis-à-vis the president than it has in foreign military affairs.

The United States has tended to use the criminal justice model most frequently throughout history because terrorist acts are almost invariably crimes. However, the Bush administration frequently invoked the military model in the wake of 9/11, referring to the attacks as an act of war. As a result, the United States has used both models in the WOT, and this mixture is partially responsible for some of the disagreement and confusion about interrogation policies.

While there are similarities between the two models, there are also some important differences and assumptions that underpin them. These similarities and differences help determine what the ground rules are when it comes to interrogation—why terror suspects are being interrogated and how it is done. Torture is prohibited by law in either model so it is not as if adopting one particular model as opposed to the other will allow torture to be used. However, the lines for what are considered acceptable interrogation techniques can vary.

In the criminal justice model, suspects are detained and interrogated to solve crimes. It is generally a more backward-looking model. Authorities use interrogations to gather evidence. In America, this is done in accordance with the legal and constitutional norms of the criminal justice system, which contains a wide variety of protections designed to prevent government abuse when solving crimes and punishing criminals.

The military model is based on the assumption the country is at war with another country or group of people (e.g., Al Qaeda). The enemy is detained and interrogated for two primary reasons. First, the enemy is detained to prevent them from returning to the battlefield to fight again. Second, enemy captives are interrogated to obtain information that can be used to help defeat the opponent (e.g., troop movements and strength). Interrogation rules are different than those found in the criminal justice system. International law becomes more relevant and constitutional protections (to the degree they even apply) are applied differently and usually to a lesser extent.

This model is a more forward-looking model. The government is seeking information that can help defeat the enemy in the future. If fighting an enemy that has the capacity to do considerable damage (e.g., the 9/11 attacks), then obtaining information from detainees perhaps understandably takes on a new sense of urgency. This sense of urgency existed in the days following 9/11 and was primarily driven by a fear that there would be additional attacks, attacks the Bush administration was determined to prevent at almost any cost.

Defining Terms

It is important to determine what is meant by "torture" at the outset of a discussion about interrogation methods in the WOT; otherwise it is possible to get bogged down in arguing about whether particular actions are torture and perhaps lose sight of other important questions. This is particularly true when phrases like "coerced" interrogations or "enhanced" interrogations are frequently invoked to describe U.S. interrogation policies. It is also important to state upfront that torture is unequivocally prohibited by both international and U.S. domestic law.

International Law and Torture

The United States is a party to a number of international agreements that prohibit torture and cruel, inhuman, and demeaning punishment. This means that even if one views the WOT and the treatment of detainees through the lens of the military model, there are laws and treaties that must be observed. The impact of the international legal community on U.S. interrogation policy is difficult to measure. When the United States signs and ratifies treaties, they are considered the law of the land and government officials are obliged to abide by them. However, there are significant differences in the implementation mechanisms between domestic and treaty law, which often make international law more difficult to enforce.

Defining torture over the years has been a challenge for both the legal community and policy makers. The Convention against Torture (CAT), perhaps the most recent definitive international statement on the subject, defines torture in Article I:

> [A]ny act by which severe pain or suffering whether physical or mental, is intentionally inflicted on a person for such purposes as obtaining from

him . . . a confession . . . when such pain or suffering is inflicted by or at the instigation of or with the consent or acquiescence of a public official or other person acting in an official capacity.[7]

This definition still leaves questions as to what specific actions constitute torture. While most authorities would agree that electric shocks, mock executions, and prolonged, severe beatings constitute torture, there is less consensus on techniques such as sensory deprivation and stress positions.

The Universal Declaration of Human Rights (UDHR), passed by the United Nations General Assembly in 1948, while not a binding treaty, unequivocally denounced the propriety of torture in Article 5 stating, "[n]o one shall be subjected to torture or to cruel, inhumane or degrading treatment or punishment."[8] The United States is also a signatory to the Geneva Conventions (1949), which the Senate ratified in 1955.[9] The conventions are a comprehensive set of guidelines for the humanitarian treatment of civilians and prisoners of war. Common Article III of the conventions prohibits "violence to life and person . . . mutilation, cruel treatment and torture" for those not taking part in active hostilities (including detainees). "Outrages upon personal dignity . . . in particular humiliating and degrading treatment," while perhaps less easy to define, are also prohibited.[10] In 1966, the United Nations adopted the International Covenant of Civil and Political Rights (ICCPR).[11] The language in Article 7 of the ICCPR is comparable to that of Article 5 in the UDHR. The United States signed the ICCPR in 1977 and it was eventually ratified by the Senate in 2002.[12]

In addition to prohibiting torture, Article 16 of CAT also requires states refrain from "cruel, inhumane or degrading treatment" of detainees.[13] The United States signed CAT in 1988 and President Reagan sent it to the Senate for ratification with a number of important reservations.[14] The Reagan administration (and later other administrations as well) attempted to define the scope of U.S. obligations under CAT narrowly so that the "torture" it forbade was only the "worst of the worst" behaviors. Defined this narrowly, torture would only account for a handful of abuses, ones already prohibited by U.S. law and rarely (if ever) engaged in by U.S. officials.

The "cruel, inhumane or degrading treatment" would be limited to behavior prohibited under the Fifth, Eighth, and Fourteenth Amendments. This standard would theoretically allow abusive treatment that didn't rise to the level of constitutional violations under these amendments. The George H.W. Bush administration also insisted that torture under CAT required specific intent as opposed to general criminal intent. This means a person would have to specifically intend to commit torture in order to be prosecuted for it. Reckless or negligent behavior that resulted in torture would not violate CAT standards.[15]

It is also worth noting that countries may be bound by international law even if they are not a party to a particular treaty. Legal scholars have recognized the concept of customary international law, and even the U.S. Supreme Court has held that customary international law can be binding on U.S. officials. "Like all the laws of nations," wrote the Court in 1900, "it rests upon the common consent of civilized communities. It is of force, not because it was prescribed by any superior power but because it has been generally accepted as a rule of conduct."[16] As a result, it is possible to argue (though U.S. courts have never decided this) prohibitions against torture are enforceable norms under customary international law whether Congress has enacted legislation to implement them or not.[17]

Collectively, this body of customary and codified international law represents a growing international consensus against the use of torture. Gaps still remained in the application and enforcement of these international norms. The United States has historically been of two minds when it comes to international law. The United States has generally had an interest in the promotion of peaceful international norms and has been a key player in the development of international human rights law. On the other hand, U.S. government officials have often viewed international law skeptically and attempted to define its reach in such a way as to jealously guard against applications of it that might intrude on U.S. sovereignty. Congress has played an important role in the development of international law in this area ratifying important treaties such as the Geneva Conventions, the ICCPR, and CAT.

Domestic Law and Torture

In U.S. domestic law, there are both constitutional and statutory provisions meant to prevent the government from engaging in torture. In the criminal justice system, unlawfully obtained (i.e., coerced) confessions could violate the Fourth, Fifth, Eighth, and/or Fourteenth Amendment rights of criminal suspects if officials attempt to introduce these confessions into court. In addition to this, government conduct which "shocks the conscience" may also violate the substantive due process rights of an individual if it is "unjustifiable by any governmental interest" whether the coerced statements are introduced in court or not.[18] This supports the principle that the needs of the criminal justice system do not excuse the use of extreme tactics by the state.

A second line of cases in the U.S. court system deal with confinement conditions while one is incarcerated. These are usually Eighth Amendment challenges (which bans cruel and unusual punishment), though it is often difficult for prisoners to be successful with them as the courts have set the bar high. Prison inmates must show that incarceration conditions are so bad as to deprive an inmate of "the minimal civilized measure of life's necessities."[19] Inmates must also show that officials were "deliberately indifferent" to inmate suffering. These types of claims are usually difficult to prove and, and prior to the 9/11 attacks, no court had applied this line of cases to incarcerated terror suspects.

Federal statutes also directly address torture. The Federal Torture Statute is located in Title 18 of the U.S. Code and provides harsh prison terms (and even death in some instances) for Americans who commit or attempt to commit torture.[20] While such a statute might appear to some to be a deterrent with some teeth, no U.S. court has ever heard a case involving the federal torture statute.[21]

In 1996, Congress passed the War Crimes Act (WCA). The act originally was designed to serve as an enforcement mechanism for the Geneva Conventions and punish "grave breaches" (e.g., willful killing, torture, or inhuman treatment) of Common Article 3.[22] A year later, at the urging of the State and Defense Departments, Congress amended the WCA to cover additional war crimes. The act applies to behavior both inside and outside the United States committed by or against U.S. citizens/military personnel. Long prison terms are prescribed for violations, even the death penalty in some instances. Still, like the Federal Torture Statute, no one has ever been prosecuted under the WCA.[23]

Internal government memoranda and discussions reveal numerous figures in the Bush administration sought clarification as to whether the more coercive interrogation techniques they were being given the opportunity to use ran afoul of these domestic statutes. In short, they wanted a legal guarantee that they would not later be brought up on charges under these torture statutes for their aggressive interrogation techniques. The Bush administration accommodated, going to great lengths to characterize its interrogation activities as wholly consistent with international and domestic law.

Another issue interrogators needed to consider was whether the individual in question would ever be tried in the criminal justice system. If the government ever wanted to try a detainee, it needed to make sure that any interrogation techniques used against that individual complied with criminal justice system norms. Any techniques that did not comply with these norms potentially tainted any prospective criminal case against that individual even if those interrogation tactics were acceptable under the laws of war. These often conflicting models and goals made developing interrogation policy during the WOT difficult.

Interrogation and Torture: A History

It is a truism to say that torture, especially as an instrument of statecraft, is universally condemned in this day and age. Still, it is not difficult to find incidents of torture in many countries around the world. The United States has its own history when it comes to interrogation and torture, and while it may arguably have a better record than many countries, it is not a spotless one.

Military Interrogations/Treatment of Prisoners

In one of first large-scale military conflicts in North America, the English were pitted against the French in what is often referred to as the French & Indian War (or the Seven Years' War). Treatment of war prisoners during this conflict varied considerably. While British and French regulars who fought by the "civilized" rules of conventional European warfare generally received humane treatment, the same cannot be said for those captured by Native American forces who played by a very different and more violent set of cultural norms. As a result, many English and colonials suffered harsh treatment.[24]

At the outset of the American Revolution, the Second Continental Congress adopted the American Articles of War, which were almost exclusively based on the British Articles of War. These Articles included provisions for the humane treatment of war prisoners. Treatment of war prisoners was complicated during this conflict by the fact that the British refused to recognize the Americans as a legitimate country entitled to fight under the conventional laws of war. As such, American prisoners were often treated harshly.[25] Political scientist Louis Fisher also notes U.S. military leaders like George Washington generally attempted to make a practice of prohibiting cruelty to captives.[26]

A few years after the conclusion of the Revolutionary War, the United States entered into the Treaty of Amity and Commerce with Prussia. In what would become a model for future international agreements, both countries agreed that if they were ever involved in a conflict, they would attempt "to prevent the destruction of prisoners of war." They were to be put in "wholesome situations" and "shall not be confined in dungeons, prison-ships, nor prisons, nor be put into irons, nor bound." Prisoners were also to be given the same rations as the other side's soldiers.[27]

The norm that emerged during the 18th and 19th centuries for the United States was if an opponent fought in a "civilized" (i.e., European) manner, then civilized treatment would be returned in kind. That included the humane treatment of prisoners. The Mexican-American War was one example of this kind of reciprocity. However, troubles occurred in conflicts where the opposing forces were not recognized as legitimate combatants.[28]

During the Civil War, both sides initially exchanged prisoners. However, this task was difficult because the North refused to officially recognize the South. As the war dragged on, supply shortages—particularly in the South—hampered each side's ability to house prisoners of war. The notorious Andersonville prison in Georgia held over 45,000 Union soldiers over the course of the war. Over 13,000 died from various causes such as malnutrition, poor sanitation, and exposure to the elements.[29]

A similar issue arose during the Spanish-American War when U.S. forces fought to quell unrest during the occupation of the Philippines at the turn of the 20th century. Americans viewed enemy militants as guerillas, making prisoners ineligible for the protections and privileges granted to soldiers of civilized nations. American foreign policy was also heavily colored during this time period by the idea of Manifest Destiny, the belief that a virtuous America had a duty to spread its virtues across the globe, civilizing the uncivilized. Those opposed to this American perspective were viewed as standing in the way of America's solemn moral responsibility and also not entitled to be treated as civilized warfare combatants.[30]

The United States generally avoided international humanitarian treaties during most of the 19th century. However, this did not mean the United States had no interest in participating in the development of standards to protect prisoners of war (POWs). The "Lieber Code" was created for the Union Army in 1863 by former Prussian soldier and Columbia University professor Francis Lieber. This guide to the rules of warfare would turn out to be extraordinarily influential both in U.S. and international circles. It included recommendations on the humane treatment of prisoners.[31]

World Wars I and II each saw the abusive treatment of prisoners. In fact, the atrocities committed during both world wars on prisoners and civilians served as an impetus for the development of international treaties designed to mitigate the harshness of war such as the Geneva Conventions and the UDHR. The United States was among those who hailed these international agreements and the goals to which they aspired.

Although the United States was publicly condemning abusive behavior, it was surreptitiously developing its own coercive interrogation programs. The advent of the Cold War prompted U.S. agencies, especially the newly created Central Intelligence Agency (CIA), to explore coercive interrogation techniques. Many of these tactics were in response to perceived Soviet advances in interrogation practices (e.g., "brainwashing"). As a result, early CIA agents were made to feel that the country was "in desperate peril" and any means necessary should be used to defend it.[32]

In the 1950s, the CIA developed a wide variety of interrogation methods grounded in "human behavioral controls" including the use of drugs, hypnosis, truth serums, and sensory deprivation. Republican and Democratic administrations alike tacitly supported these programs.[33] Many of these interrogation tactics were codified in the CIA's 1963 KUBARK counterintelligence intelligence training manual.[34] Some of these harsh tactics were even practiced on American soldiers. In the early 1950s, Survival, Evasion, Resistance, and Escape (SERE) training exposed American soldiers to harsh interrogation tactics in an attempt to prepare them in case of capture by the enemy.[35] MKULTRA, approved in 1953 and funded for over a decade, provided CIA funding for over 180 researchers at dozens of universities and hospitals across the country in the development of such tactics.[36] These tactics would eventually be used in U.S. military conflicts and Cold War proxy wars around the globe during the 1960s and 1970s.

The 1980s ushered in a new approach to coercive interrogations in the United States and a general shift from the use of coercive techniques. Opposition to such tactics also grew, especially as their existence gradually became public. In 1988, the CIA's KUBARK manual and the updated version, the 1983 Human Resource Exploitation Training Manual, became public for the first time. Many were shocked and outraged that the United States would engage in such behavior.[37]

The CIA was unrepentant however. In a 1988 Senate hearing, Deputy Director Stolz testified that the new manual contained "harsh" techniques but that none of them amounted to torture. In fact, he added, it was always CIA policy "not to encourage interrogation which results . . . in torture." In many circles this claim was taken at face value.[38] Others noted there was no explicit CIA policy statement on interrogation protocol prior to 1985.

As the Cold War focus shifted to Central America during the 1980s, U.S. counterinsurgency efforts in that region of the world intensified as well. The CIA provided training to a number of countries (sometimes openly, sometimes surreptitiously) and its interrogation tactics proliferated around the globe as a result.[39] Some government agencies began to outsource detainees for coercive interrogation so that the U.S. image would not be tarnished. This "interrogation by proxy" served the dual purpose of being able to get the information wanted by the U.S. government, while allowing someone else to actually do the dirty work of extracting it from detainees.[40]

During this time period, most other U.S. government agencies began to move away from the use of coercive interrogation tactics. By the early 1990s, the U.S. Department of Defense had revised its manuals to remove many controversial interrogation practices and bring the department's policies more in line with Geneva Conventions and the UDHR. SERE training continued for many U.S. military personnel but the changing culture and controversial nature of the program itself generated numerous lawsuits (allegations of sexual assaults and physical/mental abuse) against the government arguing that military trainers had gone too far.[41]

The interrogation and treatment of prisoners in military conflicts has been an uneven one for the United States. Steeped in the "civilized" European art of war, the United States has generally accorded humane treatment to POWs in most conflicts. Congress has played an important role in codifying policies to provide protections to POWs. Troubles have occurred though when opposing belligerents were not viewed as worthy of humane treatment (e.g., guerilla fighters).

The Cold War also proved to be a training ground for some of the tactics that surfaced in the WOT. Mental stresses and sensory deprivation became key tools in the arsenal of Guantanamo interrogators. The Cold War also saw government agencies engage in rendition policies similar to those which would also occur during the early years of the Bush administration.

Criminal Justice

Behavior that is considered torture today was often part of the legal code in ancient civilizations. Prisoners and slaves in Rome, Greece, and Egypt were often subjected to public torture that frequently consisted of flogging, the rack, burning, crucifixion, or gladiatorial contests. While there were incidents of torture in colonial America (e.g., Salem witch trials in 1692), the colonists generally did not import the more common instruments of torture used by the English Privy Council or the Star Chamber.[42]

There is some evidence to suggest the framers of the Constitution included the Fifth Amendment's self-incrimination clause and the Eighth Amendment's prohibition against cruel and unusual punishment in part to prevent torture.[43] One of the key underlying principles in the U.S. criminal justice system is that the accused is innocent until proven guilty and that the burden is on the government—through fair methods—to prove a person guilty beyond a reasonable doubt.

Police violence, especially against certain segments of society (e.g., the poor, racial minorities, drunks), was widespread at various times throughout U.S. history. Sometimes referred to as the "third degree," abuses included the use of boxing gloves, beating subjects, stripping them, tying a rope around the suspect's neck, rubber hoses, and sleep deprivation. These tactics were frequently used as late as the early 20th century because police officers often justified such interrogation practices as necessary to obtain confessions and solve crimes.[44] In 1931, the Wickersham Report publicly chronicled the "arbitrary and coercive character" of these tactics and provided an impetus for cracking down on this type of police behavior.[45]

Prior to the Wickersham Report, the U.S. Supreme Court had not heard any state cases involving interrogation techniques and the admissibility of a defendant's confession.[46] This would soon change. In 1936, the U.S. Supreme Court held that confessions obtained using coercive methods violated the Due Process Clause of the Fourteenth Amendment.[47] In 1944, the Court continued this trend when it overturned a murder conviction obtained using a coerced confession. Writing for the Court, Justice Black resolved:

> The Constitution of the United States stands as a bar against the conviction of any individual in an American court by means of a coerced confession. There have been, and are now, certain foreign nations with governments which convict individuals with testimony obtained by police organizations possessed of an unrestrained power to seize persons suspected of crimes against the state, hold them in secret custody, and wring from them confessions by physical or mental torture. So long as the Constitution remains the basic law of our Republic, American will not have that kind of government.[48]

In *Rochin v. California* (1952), the Court concluded that pumping the stomach of the defendant to retrieve illegal drugs he had ingested during his arrest constituted police conduct that "shocks the conscience. . . . They are methods [pumping the stomach] too close to the rack and the screw to permit constitutional differentiation."[49] A few years later, the Court ruled that the prolonged detention and frightening of a retarded man produced a coerced confession that violated his due process rights. "Neither the body nor the mind," the Court opined, "may be twisted until it breaks."[50]

This line of cases by the courts culminated in one of the best-known Supreme Court decisions of the century: *Miranda v. Arizona* (1966). The fundamental underlying principle that drove the Warren Court's reasoning in *Miranda* was the belief that police custodial interrogations were inherently coercive. As a result of this imbalance, law enforcement officers are required to read the now-familiar *Miranda* warnings to remind suspects that they have a variety of constitutional rights they may exercise in the face of police questioning. By the 1960s, U.S. courts had established a solid track record of taking law enforcement officials to task when it came to interrogating suspected criminals. Definite limits on the amount and type of physical and mental pain police interrogators could impose while remaining within constitutional boundaries were established.

Interrogation, Torture, and the Law: Pre-9/11

This brief history begins to illustrate the differences between interrogation under the military model and the criminal justice model. Norms under each model have developed differently over time. Understanding how far they have developed and the manner in which they have done so is important in setting the stage for post-9/11 detention and interrogation.

Under the military model, Congress often set broad parameters such as passing the Articles of War and the Lieber Code, while presidents and military commanders have often had more say about how these policies were implemented in the field. International law has gradually broadened protections for detainees, but the United States has been vigilant about defining its participation in these agreements carefully, lest they be interpreted to provide detainees with more rights than they would customarily receive under U.S. law. Norms in the criminal justice system have evolved such that the interrogation of criminal suspects is more transparent now than it has historically been; numerous Supreme Court decisions have strengthened this position. All of these factors make it difficult for the state to engage in interrogation abuse on a widespread scale.

The development of parallel systems with similar, yet different, rules was bound to make detainee interrogation and treatment after 9/11 complicated. Although the United States had a long history of prosecuting terrorists in the

U.S. criminal justice system, the Bush administration largely—though not completely—adopted a military approach from the outset of the WOT. This mixing of models proved to be problematic for a host of reasons.

Interrogation and Torture: The Bush Administration

Fighting Al Qaeda and the Taliban regime in Afghanistan meant casualties, but it also meant war prisoners. The Bush administration had to make decisions about where to keep these prisoners and what legal status they would have. Both decisions were ultimately made with an eye toward maximizing legal and military flexibility. The answer was the American naval base at Guantanamo Bay, Cuba, a place Secretary of Defense Donald Rumsfeld once referred to as the "least worst" place to hold detainees.[51]

The naval base at Guantanamo Bay originally served as a coal refueling station in the 19th century. It was leased from Cuba indefinitely following the Spanish-American War, meaning the United States could maintain the base as long as it wished but if it closed the base and left, the property would ultimately revert to Cuba.[52] The base addressed many of the concerns held by the Bush administration. Officials were reluctant to house any potential terrorists captured on the battlefield in facilities in the United States for fear that they might escape or draw another terrorist attack in the United States. Guantanamo was close but not actually in the United States. A related fear was that housing detainees in the United States might implicate procedural rights under the U.S. Constitution, a legal status the Bush administration wanted to avoid at all costs. By housing detainees in Guantanamo, the administration was able to keep them out of the United States and diminish any potential legal rights they would have under the U.S. Constitution.

A related part of this strategy was determining what rights Al Qaeda and Taliban fighters would have under international law. A series of internal memoranda during the Bush administration's first term in office chronicle the decision-making process surrounding the legal status of the detainees and which interrogation techniques would be allowable. All of these memoranda were initially classified so Congress was left largely in the dark on these matters and had no formal role in the development of interrogation policy at the initial stages of the WOT.

In early 2002, there was a pitched debate within the administration regarding detainee rights under international law. On one side was the State Department, who encouraged President Bush to accord both Al Qaeda and the Taliban full protections under the Geneva Conventions. Opposing this was the Defense Department and the Justice Department, which argued that neither group should receive these protections.[53] On February 7, 2002, President Bush issued a memorandum siding with the Justice Department. He concluded that neither Al Qaeda nor Taliban fighters were eligible to receive protections under the Geneva Conventions. Al Qaeda fighters were not eligible because Al Qaeda was a group, not a state signatory of the Conventions. Neither group fought or abided by the norms of international law and therefore neither was afforded its protections.

This had the important effect of denying both Al Qaeda and Taliban prisoner of war status, stripping them of numerous protections. Despite this decision, the president's memorandum concluded, "As a matter of policy, the United States Armed Forces shall continue to treat detainees humanely and, to the extent appropriate and consistent with military necessity, in a manner consistent with the principles of Geneva."[54] By holding detainees in Guantanamo Bay, an area under U.S. military control yet not a part of the United States, and denying them combatant status under international law, the Bush administration created a group of detainees who—at least in its opinion—resided in a legal black hole with no protections under either domestic or international law.

At one point in time, almost 800 detainees were housed in the Guantanamo Bay detention facility. Government interrogators spent considerable time attempting to extract valuable intelligence from them. Eventually, interrogators requested permission to use additional methods on subjects who were not cooperating. The Bush administration debated what limits should apply for U.S. interrogators in Guantanamo. Two memoranda particularly illustrate the issues high-level officials considered.

On August 1, 2002, Assistant Attorney General Jay Bybee drafted a memorandum assessing the applicability of U.S. statutes prohibiting torture to the interrogations taking place in Guantanamo. Bybee concluded that only the most extreme tactics would be prohibited.

> Physical pain amounting to torture must be equivalent in intensity to the pain accompanying serious physical injury, such as organ failure, impairment of bodily function, or even death. For purely mental pain or suffering to amount to torture under Section 2340, it must result in significant psychological harm of significant duration e.g., lasting for months or even years.

Bybee also concluded that statutes prohibiting interrogations that involve torture might be unconstitutional if they limited the president's ability to perform his duties as commander in chief. Necessity and/or self-defense could also justify interrogation methods that potentially violated any statutes prohibiting torture.[55]

In retrospect, the memorandum is remarkable for several reasons. First, it defines torture very narrowly, leaving interrogators a considerable amount of flexibility to use harsh methods which—according to Bybee's analysis—would still not technically amount to torture. Second, Bybee advanced the proposition that the laws prohibiting torture could not bind the president if

Interrogation and Torture

he was acting in his capacity as commander in chief. This essentially set the president above the law. Finally, Bybee concluded that even if interrogator conduct did rise to the level of torture, there might still be legal protections they could invoke. This was the legal cover interrogators were seeking from the executive branch.

When some high-value detainees still refused to cooperate, interrogators sought permission to use additional techniques. The following techniques were all eventually approved for use: yelling, deceptive techniques, stress positions, use of falsified reports/documents, isolation, light/sensory deprivation, forced standing for up to 4 hours at a time, hooding, removal of all clothing, playing on a detainee's phobias, and interrogation lasting up to 20 hours. Secretary of Defense Rumsfeld signed off on these techniques adding his own handwritten note—"However, I stand for 8–10 hours a day. Why is standing limited to 4 hours?"[56]

Both the Bybee memorandum and Rumsfeld's approval of additional techniques were largely done out of the sight of Congress. This is important because it shows how the Bush administration took laws passed by Congress and secretly interpreted them in a manner that maximized executive power and justified the types of actions that the administration wanted to perform.

One of the ongoing power struggles in the Bush administration was pressed by the Judge Advocate Generals (JAGs), the military's lawyers. This group of legal experts often objected to the introduction of harsh techniques but their objections were generally discounted at the highest levels of the Bush administration. In fact, the JAGs were frequently left out of the decision-making process altogether, depriving the administration of a valuable legal perspective.

Eventually, Federal Bureau of Intelligence (FBI) agents began to complain to their supervisors about the techniques being used by military interrogators in Guantanamo.[57] Interrogators were accused of using a variety of questionable tactics including: shackling, allowing detainees to soil themselves, sleep deprivation, sensory deprivation (extreme heat/cold), forced enemas, listening to loud music/sounds. A handful were even electrocuted and burned.[58] One Justice Department memo outlined how a detainee could be "walled" (thrown into a wall) one time in order for the interrogator to "make a point . . . or twenty to thirty times consecutively when the interrogator requires a more significant response to a question."[59] Aside from the issue that these types of tactics might constitute torture or cruel and degrading treatment, their use seriously jeopardized the federal government's ability to use information extracted in any kind of criminal justice proceeding.

This type of treatment was particularly concerning to individuals and groups who questioned the dangerousness of the detainees in the first place. The Bush administration constantly repeated the refrain that the Guantanamo detainees were the worst of the worst. They were exceedingly dangerous killers and terrorists.[60] Normal measures should not apply to this abnormally dangerous group of people.

One claim Guantanamo proponents often pointed to was that numerous released detainees went back to fighting in terrorist groups against the United States. One Director of National Intelligence (DNI) estimate put the number of released detainees who returned to terrorist activities at roughly 17 percent. This specter resonated with the American people and their representatives in Congress. No one wanted these detainees in the United States where they could possibly escape and commit future terrorist acts.[61]

Critics disputed these assertions about how dangerous these detainees were. Many were turned over to the American forces for bounty money. Others, stated one official, were probably caught simply because they were the slowest ones on the battlefield.[62] Even former Guantanamo Bay commander, General Michael Dunleavy, estimated that about half of the detainees were there by mistake. Over the course of his presidency, President Bush ultimately arranged for the transfer of 533 of these individuals to other countries.[63]

The international community was almost uniformly opposed to Guantanamo Bay. Even allies complained about the treatment of detainees at the facility. Numerous human rights organizations such as Amnesty International, the American Civil Liberties Union, the Red Cross, and Human Rights Watch conducted investigations of detainee treatment and filed reports chronicling detainee abuse.[64]

The Central Intelligence Agency

About a week after the 9/11 attacks, President Bush issued a secret presidential directive giving the CIA broad authority to kill, capture, or detain Al Qaeda members anywhere in the world.[65] Congressional leaders were briefed with only "skeletal details" of what the CIA was doing on this front.[66] By 2004, the CIA established secret prisons in over half a dozen countries around the world (e.g., Syria, Jordan, Egypt, and Thailand) where terrorist suspects were detained and interrogated "off the books."[67] Sometimes the CIA interrogated these detainees themselves, but on occasion they were shipped to other countries with reputations for being far more aggressive with interrogation techniques.[68] The total number of detainees in CIA custody is unclear, but the number is estimated to be between 100 and 150.[69]

The CIA had clearance to use more aggressive interrogation techniques on high-value detainees than military interrogators did. Still, CIA agents expressed concern at times that these techniques might run afoul of WCA.[70] This is one of the reasons the Bush administration Office of Legal Counsel (OLC) prepared various memoranda providing legal cover for interrogators. By 2004, the CIA suspended a number of its "extraordinary interrogation techniques" (e.g., stress positions, sleep deprivation, feigned suffocation) even though they had been approved by the White House.[71]

Perhaps the most infamous technique used by the CIA was waterboarding. Waterboarding occurs when a cloth is placed over a person's mouth and nose and water is poured through it to create the sensation of drowning. The controversial technique was reportedly used by the CIA on three high-value detainees: Abu Zubaydah, Abd al Nashiri, and Khalid Sheikh Mohammed (KSM). Government documents subsequently revealed KSM was waterboarded 183 times over the course of his detention.[72]

The use of waterboarding, even though it was only used on a handful of detainees, became symbolic of the Bush administration's get-tough approach to detainee interrogation. There was a very public debate about whether waterboarding rose to the level of torture and, more fundamentally, whether it was an effective interrogation technique. A 2014 poll of Americans revealed that 70 percent of those surveyed thought waterboarding was torture. However, over 57 percent also believed that waterboarding and other aggressive interrogation techniques often or sometimes produced useful information from detainees.[73] Former vice president Dick Cheney continued to defend the practice even after his term in office, claiming that waterboarding produced "phenomenal" results, some of which led to the raid that resulted in the death of Osama bin Laden.[74]

The CIA rendition program and some of its more aggressive interrogation tactics did not become public knowledge until a June 2006 White House press conference. President Bush acknowledged the existence of the program while assuring the American public that the agency's actions were safe, legal, and constitutional.[75] However, increasing public scrutiny called the president's claim into question.

The case of Maher Arar, a Canadian citizen, garnered critical public attention and illustrated many of the issues associated with the CIA's rendition program. While traveling through the United States with his family, Arar was detained by the U.S. government on suspicion that he had ties with members of Al Qaeda. He was taken into custody and held incommunicado. He was finally taken to Jordan and transported to Syria where he was beaten and confined in a grave-like box for almost a year. Eventually, Arar was returned to Canada. The Syrian government later admitted that it found no evidence linking Arar to any terrorist groups.[76]

When Arar went public with his story, U.S. officials were quick to deny any wrongdoing. Attorney General Alberto Gonzalez explained:

> Well, we were not responsible for his removal to Syria, I'm not aware that he was tortured, and I haven't read the Commission report. Mr. Arar was deported under our immigration laws. He was initially detained because his name appeared on terrorist lists, and he was deported according to our

laws. Some people have characterized this as a rendition. That is not what happened here. It was a deportation.[77]

The U.S. government had received assurances that Arar would not be tortured and that was good enough for the Bush administration.

Arar later sued the Bush administration seeking punitive damages for violating his Fifth Amendment due process rights and for violating the Torture Victims Protection Act. The United States invoked the State Secrets Doctrine, arguing that being forced to defend against Arar's claims would jeopardize national security. Federal district court judge David Trager accepted this argument and dismissed Arar's case,[78] a decision affirmed by the Second Circuit Court of Appeals.[79] The U.S. Supreme Court declined to hear Arar's appeal putting an end to his judicial challenges.

An angry Congress held numerous hearings. Arar testified before two House subcommittees and the Senate Judiciary Committee. Senator Pat Leahy (D-VT) blasted Attorney General Alberto Gonzalez:

> We knew damn well if he went to Canada, he wouldn't be tortured. He'd be held; he'd be investigated. We also knew damn well if he went to Syria, he would be tortured. And it's beneath the dignity of this country, a country that has always been a beacon of human rights, to send somebody to another country to be tortured. You know and I know that has happened a number of times in the past five years by this country.[80]

Other members of Congress were equally critical of the administration's rendition policies. President Bush ultimately put an end to overseas CIA detention sites, but given most information on the issue is classified, it is difficult to tell exactly how many secret detention facilities there were, how many people were held there, or what types of interrogation techniques were used.

Information about CIA interrogation tactics continued to trickle out into the public domain. In December 2007, the public became aware the CIA destroyed 92 video tapes that portrayed the waterboarding of terrorist suspects. Many critics were outraged and claimed the CIA was attempting to destroy evidence of its harsh tactics. CIA officials argued that the destruction of the tapes was completely legal. They were destroyed because they had no investigative value and to protect the identity of CIA officers. Officials also stated congressional committees were aware of the existence of the tapes and the CIA's decision to destroy them.

Some members of Congress disputed this claim stating that while they were told of the existence of the tapes but were not consulted on the legality of their destruction. Senate Intelligence Committee member Jay Rockefeller (D-WV) said Congress did not learn about their destruction until a year after they had already been destroyed.[81] It was incidents like these that kept an interest in congressional inquiries into CIA activities alive even into the Obama administration. These calls would culminate in an exhaustive Senate Intelligence Committee report into the CIA's interrogation methods under the Bush administration.

Abu Ghraib

While most of the focus on torture and prisoner abuse by U.S. interrogators focused on Guantanamo Bay, another facility, the Abu Ghraib prison in Iraq, also became notorious for abusive behavior perpetrated by the U.S. military against detainees. In March 2003, the U.S. and allied military forces launched Operation Iraqi Freedom. The stated reason of the invasion was to prevent Iraqi president Saddam Hussein from obtaining weapons of mass destruction. While no weapons of mass destruction were ever found, the U.S. military coalition quickly defeated Iraqi forces and removed Saddam Hussein from power. Despite the fact that major military operations were complete, pockets of resistance continued for a period of time.

Abu Ghraib prison was built in the 1950s by the British and used extensively by Saddam Hussein during his time in power. Thousands of prisoners were held here and many were tortured extensively. Thousands more were executed and mass graves containing the bodies were located nearby.[82] The prison was largely deserted when the United States invaded in 2003, and it became one of the main U.S. detention facilities in Iraq, housing over 10,000 prisoners.[83]

In January 2004, it was discovered that U.S. military personnel had been routinely abusing detainees held in Abu Ghraib. Somewhat ironically, days before the scandal broke, the Bush administration's solicitor general, Paul Clement, argued the case of detainee Jose Padilla before the Supreme Court. Padilla was an American citizen who had been designated as an unlawful enemy combatant and held incommunicado. When justices inquired about the scope of presidential detention power, the treatment of military detainees, and the possibility of torture, Clement responded that it was not the purview of the Court to monitor those things. Just because executive discretion "can be abused," he argued, "is not a good and sufficient reason for judicial micromanagement of that authority."[84] Essentially, Clement's answer was other political actors just have to trust the president. That trust was about to be severely tested.

Explosive photographic evidence of the detainee abuse at Abu Ghraib was published a few days after the Supreme Court hearing. Pictures included images of Iraqi corpses and U.S. troops having sex with one another. Others showed naked detainees stacked into a pyramid, a detainee being led around on a dog collar, and a detainee being forced to masturbate in front of female U.S. soldiers.[85]

Outrage and disgust was instantaneous. Senate Majority Leader Bill Frist (R-TN) called the scenes "appalling," while House Intelligence Committee member Jane Harman (D-CA) said, "I saw cruel, sadistic torture."[86] Even members of the Bush administration were forced to acknowledge the repulsive nature of the situation. President Bush reacted to the photographs "with deep disgust."[87] In early May, he publicly apologized on Arab television for the abuses that occurred at the prison.[88]

However, even as the Bush administration was forced to recognize the seriousness of the situation at the White House, it denied that the acts in question amounted to torture. Secretary of Defense Donald Rumsfeld argued, "what has been charged thus far is abuse, which I believe technically different from torture. . . . Therefore I'm not going to address the 'torture' word."[89] The White House insisted the abuses were perpetrated by a handful of rogue individuals rather than as part of a systematic operation designed to intentionally abuse detainees. "The system is working," said Rumsfeld, by which he meant that the rogue perpetrators were uncovered and steps were being taken to punish them and ensure no future abuses would occur.[90] Congress was less certain.

Congress immediately held hearings on the matter to determine if the system really was working. Even Republicans such as Lindsey Graham (R-SC) wanted to make sure that a thorough investigation was done in order to avoid making people in the lower ranks scapegoats for actions approved at the higher ranks. Both Democrats and Republicans were unhappy with Rumsfeld for not letting them know in advance about the abuses at Abu Ghraib before the images hit the news media. While some Democrats called for Rumsfeld's resignation over the matter, he was defiant, asserting he wouldn't resign "simply because people try to make a political issue out of it."[91] Republicans rallied to Rumsfeld, arguing that while mistakes were certainly made he deserved the benefit of the doubt. Vice President Cheney growled Rumsfeld's critics should just "get off his case."[92]

The Abu Ghraib scandal ultimately produced a dozen congressional hearings and over 10 military investigations in an attempt to determine just how far up the chain of command responsibility went.[93] Two of the more prominent reports were the Schlesinger Report and the Mikolashek Report. Both concluded that individuals and a permissive command environment were largely to blame for the abuses at Abu Ghraib. Neither addressed whether these failures extended upward to top civilian officials such as Secretary of Defense Rumsfeld.[94] A few months before Barack Obama took office, the Senate Armed Services Committee released a report that laid much of the blame for detainee abuse at the feet of Rumsfeld, blaming him and other civilian leadership for poor leadership.[95]

The Red Cross also conducted an investigation that concluded U.S. practices at Abu Ghraib violated international law. "The construction of such a system," the report read, "whose stated purpose is the production of intelligence, cannot be considered other than an international system of cruel, unusual and degrading treatment and a form of torture."[96] The Bush administration was nonplussed by the report with Rumsfeld's spokesperson simply stating that's "their point of view."[97]

Congress Responds

Despite keeping a variety of detainee interrogation memoranda secret, the Bush administration claimed Congress had complete knowledge of its interrogation practices. As early as 2002, the administration regularly briefed the Gang of Four—the majority and minority leaders of the House and Senate Intelligence Committees. When detainee abuses came to light later in the Bush administration, there were conflicting accounts on just what Congress knew and when they knew it.

Democrat Nancy Pelosi (D-CA) claimed that while the CIA discussed waterboarding, they never said they were actually doing it to anyone. When it came to light that several detainees had been subjected to waterboarding, Pelosi accused the CIA of intentionally misleading her. Senator Bob Graham (D-FL) had no recollection of being briefed on specific interrogation techniques during these briefings.[98] Republican Porter Goss (R-FL) took exception to Pelosi's charges responding, "Not only was there no objection, there was actually concern about whether the agency was doing enough."[99]

Some critics speculated that Pelosi made her claims only after the CIA's interrogation tactics were revealed to avoid criticism herself. Why, they argued, did she not object when she had the chance in 2002? Her defenders responded that filing protests with the Bush administration about WOT activities was largely a waste of time because they were "minimally responsive" to those types of inquiries.[100]

Trying to figure out exactly what happened and who was informed of what was problematic because of the small number of people involved. The Bush administration generally limited its interrogation-related briefings to the Gang of Four until 2006 when it broadened those briefings to include the entire House and Senate Intelligence Committees. Sometimes these briefings were led by the vice president. "We all approved it [waterboarding]," he said. "I'm a strong believer in it. I think it was the right thing to do."[101]

As more stories and allegations about the Bush administration's interrogation practices became public, Congress clamored to know more. Congressional Democrats attempted to subpoena White House documents related to interrogation practices, but the Republican majority blocked these attempts. Partisan lines were clearly drawn. What Democrats referred to as "stonewalling" and a "cover-up," Republicans called a "fishing expedition" and a "political ploy." Senator Orrin Hatch (R-UT) argued that full transparency was not always in the nation's interest, particularly when lives were at stake.[102]

The Bush administration wholeheartedly agreed. Despite these calls, the administration doggedly clung to the position that public discussion of particular interrogation techniques was inappropriate because it would give terrorists inside information about U.S. interrogation techniques. Armed with this information, they could prepare themselves and be more difficult to interrogate.[103] Some administration officials went even further, arguing it was not good policy to publicly debate the scope of the president's powers during wartime.[104]

However, between the allegations of abuse at Guantanamo Bay and Abu Ghraib, the congressional tide had turned against the Bush administration. In December 2004, the Senate voted 96–2 to ban torture, and inhuman treatment by all intelligence agencies. The provision was dropped in conference with the House only after what was described as "intensive, closed door negotiations."[105] Supporters of the provisions made it clear they would try again.

The next opportunity to limit executive interrogation power took the form of the Detainee Treatment Act (DTA). The amendment, introduced by Senator John McCain (R-AZ), contained two parts. The first made the *Army Field Manual* the uniform standard for all Defense Department interrogations. The second stated that no individual in the custody of the U.S. government "shall be subject to cruel, inhuman, or degrading treatment or punishment."[106] The Bush administration furiously opposed the amendment stating unequivocally that the president would veto the bill if McCain's amendment was attached. Vice President Cheney also lobbied McCain hard behind the scenes including a "contentious" October 2005 meeting where the vice president failed to get McCain to back down.[107] When it became clear that McCain's amendment would pass with a veto-proof majority, the White House acquiesced and signed the bill.

However, the White House issued a signing statement that appeared to call some of the act's provisions into question. Signing statements are attached to bills by the president when he signs them into law.[108] They can signal a variety of things. At times, they may be ceremonial, congratulating lawmakers for their efforts. In other instances, they can offer clarity regarding how the presidential administration will interpret particular sections of the legislation. This may not be controversial if the sections are open to a variety of interpretations, but it can be if the president's interpretation appears to squarely contradict or undercut the meaning of a section.

This is what occurred when Bush signed the DTA. Despite the act's seemingly clear prohibition against torture and cruel and degrading punishment, Bush's signing statement said:

> The executive branch shall construe Title X in Division A of the Act, relating to detainees, in a manner consistent with the constitutional authority of the President to supervise the unitary executive branch and as Commander in Chief and consistent with the constitutional limitations on the judicial power, which will assist in achieving the shared objective of the

Congress and the President, evidenced in Title X, of protecting the American people from further terrorist attacks.[109]

Some administration critics were furious, claiming that the president's language essentially reserved the right for the Commander in Chief to use whatever interrogation methods he chose if he felt them necessary to protect Americans from terrorism, unencumbered by the limitations found in the DTA.

Closing Guantanamo Bay

Bush administration critics spent a considerable amount of time and effort attempting to convince the administration to close the detention facility in Guantanamo Bay. This was difficult for two reasons. First, there was support in the administration for using Guantanamo. It served a purpose. "If you didn't have it," Vice President Dick Cheney said, "you'd have to invent it."[110] Second, closing it would mean that the administration would either have to release detainees or find somewhere else to house them. Given the administration's continued assertions that the detainees were "killers" and the "worst of the worst," the former was unthinkable. Finding somewhere else to house them was equally challenging. Some countries did not want any detainees. Others could not guarantee to provide the security assurances sought by the United States.

During a June 14, 2006, White House news conference, President Bush surprised some observers when he publicly expressed a desire to close Guantanamo. "But," he cautioned, "I also recognize that we're holding some people that are darned dangerous, and that we'd better have a plan to deal with them in our courts."[111] President Bush continued to articulate a desire to close Guantanamo, but made little progress in doing so. Finally, toward the end of his second term in office he admitted defeat, concluding there were "too many legal and political risks to be acceptable."[112]

This was mere weeks before the 2008 presidential election, an election where both Democrat Barack Obama and Republican John McCain advocated closing Guantanamo. Rather than castigating President Bush for being insincere about his desire to close the detention facility, one official argued that people underestimated how difficult the process was. He predicted, "The new president will gnash his teeth and beat his head against the wall when he realizes how complicated it is to close Guantanamo."[113]

Interrogation and Torture: The Obama Administration

As a presidential candidate, Barack Obama promised to close the U.S. detention facility in Guantanamo Bay. "Under my administration the United States does not torture. We will abide by the Geneva Conventions," stated the incoming president.[114] Some of his first actions as president were intended to address just these issues.

President Obama issued a series of executive orders during the first week of his presidency related to terrorism and interrogation. The first called for a new review of Guantanamo detainees and the closure of the base "as soon as practicable," but not later than one year from the order.[115] The second order revoked all previous orders related to detention and interrogation practices by the CIA and declared the *Army Field Manual* to be the sole guide as to allowable interrogation techniques. The CIA was also instructed to close any existing overseas detention facilities it might still have.[116] A third executive order established a task force to determine what detention policy options the administration had, particularly for those individuals in Guantanamo.[117]

Bush administration critics cheered this new direction, but not everyone was supportive. Former vice president Dick Cheney argued that the CIA programs "were programs that have been absolutely essential to . . . defeat further attacks against the United States."[118] Some former CIA officials concurred, arguing waterboarding and other harsh techniques helped prevent "a wave" of terror attacks in the wake of 9/11.[119] There was also some concern in the agency that the incoming administration would criminally prosecute agents for their past use of these harsh tactics.

The Obama administration seemed intent on making a clean break with the Bush administration's interrogation policies. Obama's new attorney general, Eric Holder, flatly testified before the Senate Judiciary Committee that he unequivocally viewed waterboarding as torture and the United States should follow the interrogation procedures outlined in the *Army Field Manual*.[120] Incoming DNI Dennis Blair seconded Holder's views. There would be no waterboarding and no torture in the Obama administration.[121]

Having charted a new course that broke with many of the Bush administration's past practices, one of the key questions for the new president was whether to investigate the prior administration's actions to determine if they were unlawful. Many Democrats, now in control of both Congress and the White House, were eager to punish Bush administration officials for what they deemed abusive and unlawful policies. Senior Senate Democrat Pat Leahy (D-VT) floated the idea of a "truth commission" to look into the Bush administration's detention policies, an idea which received only lukewarm support even among congressional Democrats.

The political pressure to conduct investigations ratcheted up as some of the Bush-era internal memoranda began to trickle out into public view. Democrats in particular were highly critical of the legal reasoning employed by Bush administration legal advisors such as Jay Bybee and John Yoo. Congressional Democrats pressed ahead with committee investigations.[122] The Senate Armed Services Committee jumped quickly into the fray, publicly concluding the Bush administration did engage in torture and it "damaged our ability to collect accurate intelligence that could save lives . . . and compromised our moral integrity."[123] The Senate Judiciary Committee also began what would ultimately be a six-year investigation into the CIA's interrogation practices in the Bush administration.

President Obama expressed a deeper reluctance than congressional Democrats to revisit the previous administration's interrogation policies, fearing the appearance that a Democratic administration was seeking "victor's justice" on the previous Republican one. He wanted to look forward rather than backward.[124] In particular, Obama wanted to avoid any prosecution of rank-and-file CIA and Defense Department interrogators wherever possible. In his mind, they were largely subordinates who were just following policies established by higher-ranking civilian officials. He did, however, leave open the possibility of prosecuting the officials who designed and advocated those policies.

Both President Bush and President Obama were able to exercise a considerable amount of discretion when it came to determining the scope of executive branch and military interrogation policies. Internal memoranda and executive orders allowed interrogators considerable latitude under the Bush administration. This scope was somewhat limited by Congress when it passed the DTA and limited the actions of military interrogators. President Obama further narrowed this flexibility with new executive orders that also limited the CIA and other intelligence agency interrogators.

In an effort to make interrogation policies less susceptible to the whims of future presidential administrations, Senators John McCain (R-AZ) and Dianne Feinstein (D-CA) added a provision to the 2016 National Defense Authorization Act which would—by law—limit *every* U.S. government agency to interrogation techniques found in the *Army Field Manual*. The amendment passed the Senate with overwhelming support, 78–21.[125]

Civil Suits

A number of lawsuits were filed contesting the legality of the Bush administration's detention and interrogation policies. Ultimately, these suits—like those in other WOT policy areas—were largely unsuccessful, demonstrating once again how difficult it is to use the judiciary to challenge executive branch policy making. Two suits in particular illustrate these challenges and the associated difficulties.

Shortly after the 9/11 attacks, a Pakistani cable television installer from Long Island named Javaid Iqbal was arrested and detained for alleged ties to terrorists. He was held in a maximum security administrative detention wing where he claims he was subjected to beatings, strip searches, and religious persecution. Iqbal's terrorist ties proved unfounded, but he was convicted of document fraud (using another person's social security card) and deported to Pakistan.[126]

Iqbal sued prison officials for his ill treatment. Attorney General John Ashcroft and FBI director Robert Muller were also named in the suit. Iqbal alleged that policies created and propagated by Ashcroft and Muller led to his detention and that those policies singled him out for detention solely based on his nationality and religion in violation of the First and Fifth Amendments to the U.S. Constitution. Ashcroft and Muller both contended that they were entitled to qualified immunity from civil suits related to their official duties.[127]

On May 18, 2009, a five justice majority on the U.S. Supreme Court ruled against Iqbal, concluding that he failed to state sufficient facts to justify his assertion that Ashcroft and Muller engaged in purposeful and unlawful discrimination.[128] There was not enough of a direct connection to show that the government designed these detention policies to purposefully discriminate against Muslim individuals as opposed to some other purpose, like national security or fighting terrorism. The Court's decision had the effect of making it very difficult to civilly sue Bush administration officials for their detention and interrogation policies even if it was established that some abuses occurred in the implementation of those policies.

Jose Padilla, an American citizen, was arrested in 2002 and held as an unlawful enemy combatant and accused of plotting terrorist activities with Al Qaeda. The conditions of Padilla's detention soon became the focus of a legal challenge. Padilla was being held at a naval brig in South Carolina without access to an attorney. Padilla argued that the U.S. Constitution afforded him a variety of due process rights such as access to an attorney and a right to be charged or released. Padilla's case eventually reached the U.S. Supreme Court where the Court sidestepped the constitutional issues instead holding that Padilla had filed his case in the wrong federal court.

While Padilla attempted to refile his case in the correct court, the government suddenly opted to remove Padilla from military detention and filed criminal charges against him. Padilla was eventually tried and convicted in federal court of Conspiracy to Defraud the United States, Conspiracy to Aid Terrorists, and Conspiracy to Commit Murder. He was sentenced to 21 years in prison.[129]

Padilla's treatment during his time in custody was a key issue during his criminal trial. Although he was found competent to stand trial, he had clearly endured treatment that was out of the ordinary. On January 4, 2008, Padilla filed a civil suit against former Bush administration Justice Department official John Yoo.[130] Padilla argued that while in government custody he had been subjected to:

> prolonged isolation; deprivation of light; exposure to prolonged periods of light and darkness . . . extreme variations in temperature; sleep adjustment; threats of severe physical abuse; death threats; administration of

psychotropic drugs; shackling and manacling for hours at a time; use of "stress" positions; noxious fumes . . . loud noises . . . forced grooming; suspensions of showers; removal of religious items . . . incommunicado detention.[131]

Yoo was named in the suit because, Padilla argued, Yoo's memoranda had told administration officials that this type of treatment was legally and constitutionally permissible. Padilla's suit was dismissed in May 2012 by the Ninth Circuit Court of Appeals. The court held that even if the actions alleged by Padilla did amount to torture, they were not clearly defined as such at the time. As a result, Yoo could not be held liable.[132] Once again, the difficulty of seeking relief through the judiciary was illustrated.

Closing Guantanamo Bay

At its peak, the detention facility at Guantanamo housed just under 800 detainees. The Bush administration made considerable efforts during the president's second term to reduce those numbers. As a result of these efforts, Guantanamo housed roughly 240 detainees when Barack Obama took office in 2009. President Obama issued an executive order instructing his administration to close Guantanamo within one year. This was consistent with his campaign promise, but critics doubted his administration's ability to accomplish this.

Any closure of Guantanamo meant that the detainees would have to be transferred somewhere else (or released). This created a variety of complicated scenarios. One option was to transfer detainees to other countries and have those countries detain them. Both the Bush and Obama administrations made concerted efforts to transfer detainees to other countries. This process was complicated by the fact that security assurances needed to be obtained and some countries did not want any detainees (even their own nationals). Congress made this process even more difficult by requiring the executive branch to notify it of pending transfers.

A second option was to transfer any remaining detainees to maximum-security federal prisons in the United States. This option was also met with howls of protest from members of Congress, particularly if the detention facility in question was in that particular member's state or district. These members were responding to public opinion that indicated Americans were afraid that housing Guantanamo detainees in the United States would either provide targets for additional terrorist attacks or create the potential that terrorists could escape from these facilities and kill Americans. President Obama made some overtures to blunt this criticism. He pointed out, "We're already holding a bunch of really dangerous terrorists here in the United States . . . and there have been no incidents. We've managed it just fine."[133] However, Congress and the public remained unconvinced.

From almost the outset of the Obama administration, Congress erected roadblock after roadblock that prevented the closure of Guantanamo. In May 2009, the Senate voted against the appropriation of money to close the facility. The following month, Congress banned the transfer of Guantanamo detainees to the United States for any reason other than prosecution. By December, Congress banned any detainee transfer to the United States.[134]

During his last year in office, President Obama made one final push in an effort to convince Congress to close Guantanamo. Even though there were less than 100 detainees housed in the facility in 2016, the president said, the cost to American taxpayers was over 450 million. He also reminded members that keeping Guantanamo open would cost over 200 million per year going forward.[135] This effort was also ultimately unsuccessful.

Some observers argued the Obama administration never really put forth a concerted effort to close the base. It was never a priority (like health care) that the administration was willing to spend political capital on to achieve. Guantanamo remained open as President Donald Trump took office in 2017.

Senate Torture Report

Continuing demands for inquiries into CIA interrogation tactics after 9/11 eventually culminated in a multiyear investigation by the Senate Intelligence Committee. The product of this investigation was a report that stretched over 6,700 pages in length. The report was approved for release in December 2012 over the objection of almost all committee Republicans who argued that it was substantially flawed and incomplete. The executive summary was declassified and made available to the public. The report was highly critical of the CIA, and its findings included the following:

- The CIA's use of its enhanced interrogation techniques was not an effective means of acquiring intelligence or gaining cooperation from detainees.
- The CIA's justification for the use of its enhanced interrogation techniques rested on inaccurate claims of their effectiveness.
- The interrogations of the CIA detainees were brutal and far worse than the CIA had represented to policy makers and others.
- The CIA actively avoided or impeded congressional oversight of the program.
- The CIA impeded effective White House oversight and decision making.
- The CIA rarely reprimanded or held personnel accountable for serious or significant violations, inappropriate activities, and systematic and individual management failures.[136]

The CIA was unhappy with the content of the report and disputed many of its conclusions. As it was reviewing the full Senate version report to determine what information could be declassified, CIA officials determined that Senate investigators had obtained—in the eyes of the CIA unlawfully so—an internal CIA memorandum examining CIA interrogation practices. But it was not the memorandum, but rather the manner in which the CIA discovered it, that eventually became a point of focus.

On March 11, 2014, Senate Intelligence Committee Chair Dianne Feinstein (D-CA) took to the floor of the Senate to make an extraordinary accusation. She claimed that the CIA had illegally broken into Senate computers and read investigators' e-mails. She described the actions as an attempt to "intimidate" congressional staffers. CIA director John Brennan publicly and emphatically denied the charges saying, "When the facts come out on this, I think a lot of people who are claiming that there has been this tremendous sort of spying and monitoring and hacking will be proved wrong."[137]

A few months later the facts did come out in the form of an internal CIA investigation. The CIA's own inspector general confirmed Feinstein's claims. The investigation determined several CIA officials did surreptitiously break into Senate computers and monitor investigators' e-mails. These CIA officials also recommended (using false information) Senate staffers be brought up on criminal charges for obtaining the internal memorandum.

When this news became public, Director Brennan offered an apology to Senator Feinstein. A number of senators expressed concern that CIA officials would so brazenly interfere with a Senate investigation into their activities, but some Republicans demurred. Senate Intelligence Committee member Richard Burr (R-NC) asserted, "I personally don't believe anything that goes on in the Intelligence Committee should be discussed publicly."[138]

The full version of the Senate report remains classified, despite continued efforts on the part of numerous senators and public interest groups to declassify and release the entire report. When the full report was initially completed, the Senate Intelligence Committee sent eight copies to executive branch agencies asking them to incorporate it into their agency records. This would potentially have made the report available to the public via a Freedom of Information Act (FOIA) request. However, none of the executive branch agencies performed this action. Public interest groups filed lawsuits in hopes of forcing agencies to publish the entire report, but the judiciary held the report was a congressional record and therefore not subject to the FOIA.[139]

A month before exiting office, President Obama designated a copy of the full report as a "presidential record." This has the effect of preserving a copy, but it would not be available for public inspection—by law—for a period of at least 12 years. Even then, the report would have to go through a declassification process so there is no guarantee that the public will ever have access to the full report.[140]

While interest groups were continuing their attempts to gain public access to the entire report, Senate Intelligence Committee Chair Richard Burr (R-NC) sent requests to the executive branch that they return their copies of the entire report to the Senate Committee. Burr had been critical of the report since its release calling it nothing more than a "footnote in history."[141] The Trump administration acquiesced and returned the copies.

Democrats were furious. They viewed Burr's act as an attempt to bury all existing copies of the report. Senator Feinstein openly rebuked her colleague: "No senator—chairman or not—has the authority to erase history. I believe that is the intent of the chairman in this case."[142]

One additional full copy of the Senate torture report exists outside the executive branch. As a part of his ongoing trial before a military tribunal, legal counsel for Abd al Nashiri, a Guantanamo detainee accused of bombing the USS Cole in 2000, attempted to have the full Senate report preserved for his military tribunal hearings. The full report contains an entire chapter dedicated to the CIA's interrogation and treatment of al Nashiri that is not covered in the already-released executive summary. While the tribunal judge denied this request, Federal District Court Judge Royce Lamberth ordered a copy of the full Senate report to be maintained at a secure judicial facility in the event that it may be needed in a civil proceeding in the future.[143]

Summary

While President Obama continued some Bush administration WOT policies, his administration clearly differed when it came to interrogation policies. Obama immediately and publicly rejected CIA rendition sites and coercive interrogation tactics. He also attempted (unsuccessfully) to shutter the detention facility at Guantanamo.

The biggest challenge during Obama's administration was the struggle between groups that wanted a full inquiry into the Bush administration's interrogation policies and those who just wanted to leave the matter in the past and move forward. President Obama generally opted for restraint even though the Democrats controlled both the White House and Congress. There were investigations and some of these were critical of Bush administration officials, but there was no widespread criminal probe designed to target high-ranking officials for their conduct while in office.

Trump Administration

During the 2016 presidential campaign, Republican nominee Donald Trump was quite outspoken about his belief in harsh interrogation methods. He vowed to bring back waterboarding "and worse." "Torture works," he said, "only a stupid person would say it doesn't work." And, he added doubling

Interrogation and Torture

down, even if it does not work "they deserve it anyway for what they're doing."[144] These statements alarmed a considerable number of people who thought the United States stopped these types of tactics for good with the end of the Bush administration.

This alarm was magnified when the media published a draft executive order during the Trump administration transition period that contemplated reopening CIA prisons abroad. The order called for keeping the detention facility at Guantanamo Bay open, suspending the transfer of any detainees housed there, and making increased use of military tribunals.[145] The order also called for a review of existing interrogation policies to determine if the *Army Field Manual* tactics should be revised and whether to "recommend to the President whether to reinstate a program of interrogation of high-value alien terrorists to be operated outside the United States and whether such a program should include the use of facilities operated by the Central Intelligence Agency."[146] When pressed about the document, White House officials disavowed any knowledge of it, claiming it was not an official administration document.

In testimony before Congress during his confirmation hearing, CIA director nominee Mike Pompeo confidently asserted that the United States would absolutely not torture. However, he hedged somewhat in his written remarks when he noted that he would be open to changes in existing interrogation policy if experts believed that existing policy was an impediment to gathering information and protecting national security.[147]

Critics of these harsh techniques were quick to point out they were prohibited by President Obama's executive order and also by law, given the National Defense Authorization Act of 2016 banned the use of any interrogation techniques not found in the *Army Field Manual*.[148] Senator John McCain, the man at the forefront of this battle during the Bush administration years, was quite clear about his feelings on the matter. "The president can sign whatever executive order he wants," stated McCain, "But the law is the law. We are not bringing back torture in the United States of America."[149]

Remaining Issues

Torture is universally condemned as a tool of statecraft and is prohibited by domestic and international law. Regulating the interrogation of military prisoners has always been a difficult business. On one hand, it is important that there are clear regulations against the use of torture so detainees will not suffer abuse. On the other hand, it is also important to give interrogators the tools and the flexibility they need to be successful because interrogation can get information and information can save lives.

The issue of torture has been particularly difficult in the WOT for several reasons. First, the scope of the 9/11 attacks make preventing another attack of that magnitude of primary importance. Second, it is clear that many Al Qaeda operatives have been trained to resist many conventional interrogation tactics making information more difficult to obtain. The combination of these two factors contributed to the excesses that occurred under the Bush administration and prompted Congress to play a more active role in monitoring executive branch and military interrogation practices.

Congress has placed bans on torture and cruel and degrading treatment in multiple pieces of legislation so, at least on paper, these types of behavior clearly appear to be prohibited. The legislation that restricts interrogators to techniques found in the *Army Field Manual* also allows that manual to be periodically reviewed. This allows for some flexibility. Congress also has the capacity to call for regular, periodic reviews of the *Manual* if it wishes.

One scenario that is inevitably raised during discussions of interrogation tactics is the "ticking time bomb" scenario. If a detainee has been captured and has knowledge of an impending, imminent attack, are more extreme measures—even torture—justified? Some say yes, particularly if we are talking about saving hundreds or thousands of lives. Others argue that extreme measures are never justified even in situations such as this.

The current legislative scheme admits no exceptions for situations such as this, leaving interrogators at risk of prosecution if they use extreme measures even in seemingly dire situations. There are some scholars who have called on Congress to pass legislation that allows for a more nuanced approach should this type of situation ever arise. Congress could write legislation allowing for the CIA to use extreme measures in these types of rare circumstances, but only at the written direction of the president, who then must immediately inform the congressional intelligence committees of his decision.[150]

Allowing for some ambiguity, particularly in extreme circumstances, might also prove useful since many Al Qaeda members have clearly been trained to resist "standard" interrogation techniques. There is something to the Bush administration's claim that the United States should not give them a road map to tell them everything U.S. interrogators will potentially do. The difficulty lies in achieving clear limits while retaining some ambiguity, a difficult needle to thread.

Congress also has the capacity to impose some limits on the rendition of detainees to other countries. While the Bush administration was highly criticized for its "extraordinary renditions," the U.S. government has been using renditions for decades now, finding it a useful tool on occasion. While Congress might not want to tie the hands of the executive by banning rendition altogether, it might pass legislation that limits how long the government can hold someone before either charging or releasing them.

Interrogation and Torture

Congress might also require that the U.S. government receive more rigorous assurances before an individual is transferred to a country where he fears he might be tortured.[151]

The current Republican-controlled Congress has given no indication that it wants to close the detention facility at Guantanamo Bay. In fact, the majority seems perfectly content to let the handful of individuals detained there simply remain there indefinitely. If anything, Congress appears open to sending additional detainees to Guantanamo rather than closing it. President Trump has also expressed a desire to continue its operation so it appears that the status quo on Guantanamo will likely last at least as long as President Trump is in office.

Perhaps the most important thing that Congress can do going forward in this area is to engage in vigilant oversight of the CIA. The hacking incidents surrounding the CIA's activities in the Senate torture report clearly indicate that there are elements in the agency that require close oversight. This appears to be true regardless of which political party occupies the White House. After all, it was the Obama administration CIA that hacked a report prepared by Senate Democrats.

Conclusion

Increasing gridlock in the American political system has also led to an increase in unilateral executive policy making. In one sense, this serves as an outlet so that timely decisions can be made even if there is not a consensus in Congress. Presidents issue executive orders and other executive branch policy directives. Where law is not specific, presidents "fill in the cracks." This is what happened with interrogation policy.

The Bush administration framed the U.S. government's response to the 9/11 attacks under the military model rather than the criminal justice model. The primary purpose of interrogating detainees was not to bring criminal charges against them but rather to obtain valuable information that could be used in the WOT. The Bush administration held detainees outside the United States to minimize any rights they might have under domestic U.S. law. It then defined the nature of Al Qaeda and Taliban combatants in such a manner as to virtually strip them of any protections under international law. The administration then designed policies consistent with this legal status. The extraction of information, Americans were told, was essential to national security.

There was a serious lack of transparency with the Bush administration's interrogation policies. One of the themes repeated time and again was the assertion that it was unwise to even have a public discussion about U.S. interrogation methods because discussion would inform the enemy about what tactics interrogators used and allow the enemy to prepare for them. It is difficult to have transparency when an entire subject is deemed inappropriate for public discussion.

CIA actions, particularly its secret rendition program, were even more problematic. Detainees were just swept up and "disappeared" to facilities that no one admitted even existed in countries around the world. In some instances, the CIA used harsh, coercive techniques though documentation of this is difficult to obtain (recall the CIA destruction of interrogation tapes).

None of these actions seems consistent with a U.S. system of justice that prides itself on openness and transparency. Detainees are treated humanely and interrogations are limited. Policies are clearly articulated by Congress and courts have the opportunity to review instances where the executive branch is accused of abuses. All these ideals have been lacking in the WOT. Even attempting to determine what happened after the fact has been problematic. The Senate torture report's executive summary publicly took the CIA to task for its actions, but the bulk of the report remains classified and there is considerable doubt as to whether it will ever be made public.

A review of interrogation policy also provides a good opportunity to explore the issue of accountability. Detainee abuse undoubtedly occurred. Partisans can debate the scope of the abuse and whether particular tactics, or combinations of tactics, rose to the level of torture, but it is clear that improper and periodically unlawful behavior occurred at Guantanamo and Abu Ghraib. When these abuses came to light the natural question was who to blame for these actions?

Interrogators who realized they were going right up to the lawful limits of what they could do sought assurances from the White House that they would not be retroactively prosecuted if, or when, their actions ever became public. The White House legal team drafted a series of memoranda that gave these assurances. It defined torture narrowly, approved "enhanced techniques," and made it clear that interrogators had permission to push boundaries. Perhaps predictably, this approach produced abuses.

Subsequent investigations into Abu Ghraib and Guantanamo did result in some prosecutions for lower level officials and some of these investigations laid blame at the feet of rogue interrogators, a few "bad apples." Others argued that individuals further up the chain of command—people such as Secretary of Defense Donald Rumsfeld, Attorney General John Ashcroft, John Yoo, and others—should also be held accountable for drafting and approving aggressive tactics and promoting an atmosphere where abuses would be more likely. Civil lawsuits against Bush administration officials for their actions have been unsuccessful. Neither President Obama nor President Trump showed any genuine interest in pursuing any type of investigation against Bush administration officials.

The American people were told that harsh interrogation policies were sometimes needed to protect national security and prevent another terrorist attack. These policies sometimes lead to abuses. This is undeniable. However, the scope and severity of the abuses has been hotly contested among partisans on both sides of the political aisle making transparency and accountability difficult to achieve. To its credit, Congress did take steps to legislatively ban torture, hopefully preventing future recurrences of the worst abuses.

CHAPTER FOUR

Military Tribunals

While military tribunals are unlikely to be the first image that comes to mind when one thinks about the American justice system, these courts have a long history in the United States. Military tribunals gained renewed attention shortly after the 9/11 attacks when President George W. Bush announced that his administration would use them to try suspected terrorists.

Presidential legal advisor John Yoo lamented that the Bush military tribunal system was the "most practical, yet least successful antiterrorism initiative."[1] Others offered a less charitable assessment of the policy. Some contended suspected terrorists should be tried in federal civilian courts. Others complained the tribunals proffered by the Bush administration lacked important procedural safeguards and violated international law. Finally, some claimed the president lacked the authority to create military tribunals without legislative approval in the first place.[2]

This chapter examines the history of military tribunals in the United States and their use after 9/11. As the history makes clear, no single branch can lay exclusive claim to these courts. Presidents (and their military subordinates in the executive branch) have convened them, Congress has authorized their use, and courts have issued numerous decisions regarding their appropriate scope. The chapter will then review how military tribunals have been used during the War on Terror (WOT), first under the Bush administration, and then under President Barack Obama. It will conclude by examining the challenges Congress faces as it attempts to create a military tribunal system that identifies and punishes terrorists and does so in a fair manner.

Military Tribunals: A Primer

The terms "military tribunals" and "military commissions" are considered "virtually interchangeable" by many scholars.[3] Military tribunals emanate from the common law of war and find their basis in the U.S. Constitution, statutes, and military precedent. Unlike courts-martial, which are the primary military court for the U.S. system, military tribunals are more transitory in nature. They are convened and dissolved as needed, usually by presidents or their military subordinates. Military tribunals can have jurisdiction over two general types of offenses: civil crimes that lie outside the jurisdiction of civilian courts and violations of the laws of war.[4] They have been used at various times throughout U.S. history to try American soldiers, civilians, enemy belligerents, and citizens in countries under U.S. occupation.

Many scholars differ about whether the ability to constitute military tribunals is an executive or legislative power, leading one to conclude that it "lies at a constitutional crossroads."[5] While Richard Pious notes that the prerogative to unilaterally establish military tribunals has always been claimed by the executive,[6] other scholars have concluded that the United States adopted the fundamental principle that military tribunals flowed from congressional legislation.[7]

Both sides point to the U.S. Constitution for support. Executive advocates argue that the president's Article II commander in chief power includes the right to capture, detain, and process enemy soldiers. As a result, the president may establish military tribunals to carry out this constitutionally enumerated power. Some also argue the power to establish military tribunals is inherently executive in nature and is reserved to the president via this particular avenue.[8]

Legislative advocates point out that Congress is given the express power in Article I, Section 8 to "make rules for the Government and Regulation of the land and naval forces," "provide for organizing, arming, and disciplining, the Militia," "define and punish . . . Offenses against the Law of Nations," and "make Rules concerning Captures on Land and Water."[9] Collectively, they argue, these powers point to congressional dominance in the creation and regulation of military law.[10]

All agree military tribunals are not considered Article III courts. This means the judiciary plays no role in the creation of military tribunals and, as a general matter, military tribunal decisions are not reviewable by Article III courts.[11] There is one notable procedural exception. Anyone tried before military tribunals may file a writ of habeas corpus to an Article III court challenging the legality of his or her detention. It is in this capacity the judiciary has historically played an extensive role in shaping the nature and scope of military tribunal power.[12]

If the constitutional foundations of military tribunals are somewhat murky and contested, historical practice has provided patterns of behavior that sometimes flows from these foundations. Presidents, adopting broad visions of executive power, have convened them. Congress has shaped and limited them on occasion, and the courts have, at times, circumscribed their excesses.

The History of Military Tribunals in the United States

Early Military Tribunals

The Continental Congress enacted the Articles of War during the Revolutionary War to govern military matters including the use of military tribunals. The most noteworthy individual tried by a military tribunal during the Revolutionary War was Major Andre, the British officer who conspired with Benedict Arnold. Andre was tried before a military tribunal, found guilty, and hung.[13] After ratification of the Constitution in 1789, the U.S. Congress passed a statute codifying the Articles of War. These early efforts by legislative bodies buttress the arguments of those who believe the power to govern military tribunals lies with the legislature.

A more ignominious chapter occurred during the War of 1812 when General Andrew Jackson used military tribunals while in command of U.S. forces defending New Orleans. Jackson, having already defeated the British, kept the city under martial law. When a newspaper reporter printed an opinion critical of this, Jackson had him jailed and ordered him before a military tribunal. The reporter requested a writ of habeas corpus before the local district court judge who granted it. The judge agreed martial law and trial by military tribunal was no longer justified for civilians in light of the military victory.

Jackson ordered the judge jailed and removed from the city. The military tribunal failed to convict the newspaper editor and the judge returned to the city, holding Jackson in contempt and fining him $1,000.[14] Virtually all parties—President Madison's Secretary of War, the House, the Senate, and even Jackson's own subordinates—agreed Jackson's actions were unwarranted.[15]

Jackson also apprehended two British subjects accused of inciting the Creek Indians against the United States during the Seminole Wars. Jackson convened a military tribunal, and when the tribunal acquitted the two, he overrode the tribunal's decision, ordering one of the captives shot and the other hung. A House committee issued a report highly critical of Jackson's actions, but a resolution to censure Jackson failed on the House floor. The Senate issued a similarly critical report, but ultimately took no action on the matter.[16]

During the Mexican War, General Winfield Scott instituted a system of martial law in his campaign in Mexico. This included the use of military tribunals. He did this because he was concerned about the potentially disruptive behavior of his volunteer soldiers.[17] These military tribunals eventually tried 409 individuals in Mexico/California, convicting 234 (mostly American soldiers). The procedures they employed were very much like military courts-martial and punishments were limited to those comparable of what one would find in U.S. states.[18]

Sensitive of the potential ramifications of his plans for martial law and military tribunals, General Scott sent a copy of his order to Secretary of War William Marcy and the Polk administration's attorney general. There was no opposition. The order was then forwarded to Congress who declined the opportunity to pass legislation to authorize a tribunal system. Marcy returned the order to Scott "silently . . . as too explosive for safe handling."[19] Scott instituted his order and it appeared to have the desired effect. Looting and disruptive behavior by U.S. troops was kept at a minimum.

The Civil War

Military tribunals were also widely used during the Civil War. Thousands of cases were decided over the course of the conflict. These tribunals usually had procedures which closely resembled ones found in courts-martial. Their findings were only periodically reviewed by the judiciary, and then only via habeas challenges.[20]

When it came to military tribunals, President Lincoln was a watchful commander in chief. He often overturned tribunal verdicts when they failed to provide the procedural safeguards found in courts-martial.[21] Two examples illustrate this point. When Union General John Fremont issued a sweeping declaration of martial law and announced the use of military tribunals to try a wide variety of offenses, Lincoln limited the scope of the proclamation and subsequently overturned a number of guilty verdicts emerging from Freemont's military tribunals. A second example concerns the use of military tribunals in the wake of fighting against the Sioux in 1862. Military tribunals convicted 323 Sioux and recommended that 303 be hanged. Lincoln again intervened, concerned about the summary nature of the tribunals. He reduced the number of executions to 39 and commuted the sentences of the remainder.[22]

One of the more noteworthy military tribunals convened during this time period was the one used to try and convict those who conspired to assassinate President Lincoln. Although there was some legal question of whether it was appropriate to try civilians via military tribunal after the war was over, the tribunal was convened. All eight conspirators were convicted. Four were sentenced to prison and the remainder (including Mary Surratt) to death by hanging. In 1865, Captain Henry Wirz, the former commander of the infamous Andersonville prison, was also tried by a military tribunal, convicted, and ordered to hang.[23] Some scholars argue these two high-profile tribunals served to stain the reputation of all Civil War military tribunals by rushing to judgment and engaging in "summary justice."[24]

Military tribunals continued to be widely used after the war. Over 1,435 were convened between 1865 and 1869.[25] During this period, courts heard numerous cases on the nature and scope of military tribunals, occasionally

Military Tribunals

limiting their use. In *Ex Parte Milligan* (1866), the Supreme Court concluded that military tribunals cannot be used to try civilians when civilian courts are open and functioning.

Congress responded to *Milligan* and other judicial inquires by passing the Military Reconstruction Act of 1867. This act gave military commanders in southern states the right to use military tribunals.[26] Congress also passed legislation to limit the Court's jurisdiction in cases involving military law.[27] It also gave indemnity to all government and military officials who implemented presidential proclamations from 1861 to 1866 with respect to martial law and military tribunals stating "no civil court of the United States, or of any state, or of the District of Columbia, or any district or territory of the United States, shall have or take jurisdiction of, or in any manner reverse any of the proceedings had or acts done as aforesaid."[28]

World War II

Military tribunals were once again used extensively during and after World War II, both domestically and abroad. In the wake of the December 7, 1941, attack on Pearl Harbor, the governor of Hawaii transferred considerable power to the military. Martial law was imposed and military tribunals replaced civilian justice. These tribunals generated a number of cases where federal courts were asked whether military tribunals could appropriately try civilians for civilian offenses. In several instances, lower courts viewed the rulings of these tribunals skeptically.[29] In 1945—after the war was over—the Supreme Court rejected the use of military tribunals in Hawaii to try civilians for civilian offenses, especially once the threat of Japanese invasion was past. While Congress authorized the ability to declare martial law, the Court held, civilian courts were open and capable of hearing cases.[30]

The most notable use of a military tribunal during World War II occurred in the case of the Nazi saboteurs. In 1942, eight German agents arrived on the U.S. coast via submarine in two teams with instructions to commit acts of sabotage. They were quickly captured and President Roosevelt issued an order convening a military tribunal to try them for violating of the laws of war.[31]

FDR insisted on a military tribunal to avoid the embarrassment that might be associated with a civilian trial (the saboteurs were caught only because one turned himself in to the Federal Bureau of Investigation [FBI]), and ensure a "proper" penalty (i.e., the death penalty). FDR considered having the death penalty as an available punishment "almost obligatory." The tribunal was convened and the defendants tried. They filed habeas petitions with the Supreme Court, claiming their trial by military tribunal was unlawful and they should be tried in civilian courts.

In *Ex Parte Quirin* (1942), the Supreme Court upheld FDR's right to convene the military tribunal. In a hastily convened special session, the Supreme Court concluded the defendants were unlawful combatants and subject to military justice.[32] Having lost their appeal in the Supreme Court, the defendants were summarily tried and convicted. Six of the eight were executed. Only months after the executions did the Supreme Court issue a full written opinion explaining its decision, an experience Justice Robert Jackson later described as "not a happy precedent" for future behavior.[33] *Quirin* has since been the subject of much study and the recipient of "sharp criticism" from a number of legal scholars both for the manner in which the Supreme Court handled the case and the legal reasoning found in its opinion.[34]

A second important military tribunal case involved prisoners captured in China and charged before U.S.-convened military tribunals with violating the laws of war. In *Johnson v. Eisentrager* (1950), the Supreme Court held since the defendants were being held outside the territorial United States, they had no right to file habeas writs in U.S. courts. This effectively precluded any judicial review of the tribunal proceedings.[35]

Postwar military tribunals convened in Japan and Germany heard thousands of cases. In Japan over 3,000 individuals were sentenced to prison and over 920 to death. Top Japanese commanders Tomoyuki Yamashita and Masaharu Homma were tried before tribunals and charged with failing to prevent war crimes by those who were under their command. Each was sentenced to death and filed a writ of habeas corpus with the U.S. Supreme Court.[36] Rejecting the appeals by a count of 6–2, the Supreme Court determined it was not the purview of the Court to review the evidence presented to the tribunals.

Justice Wiley Rutledge dissented, objecting to military tribunals that authorized "forced confessions to be received as evidence."[37] Homma's lawyer concurred, concluding Homma "was not hanged because he was in command of troops who committed atrocities. He was hanged because he was in command of troops who committed atrocities on the losing side."[38] These tribunals illustrate one of the dangers of convening military tribunals, the danger they will be perceived as "victor's justice."

Military tribunals were also used to try over 1,700 Germans shortly after the war.[39] The Nuremberg Trials were the most notable of these. Over two dozen German political, military, and economic leaders were tried for the Holocaust and other war crimes. Several were sentenced to death and hanged for their actions during the war.

Postwar Developments

The Uniform Code of Military Justice (UCMJ) was passed by Congress and signed into law by President Truman in 1950. The UCMJ was an attempt by Congress to make military justice among the various service branches more streamlined and uniform. The UCMJ provides for military tribunals and gives presidents considerable leeway in prescribing trial procedures. Article 36 states military tribunal procedures should reflect "principles of law and rules of evidence generally recognized in the trial of criminal cases in the United States district courts" to the extent practicable. Presidents have generally been given great deference in determining what is "practicable." Similarly, all military tribunal rules should be uniform and as alike courts-martial as possible.[40]

The post–World War II period also saw the growth of a considerable body of international law regarding the rights of detainees and the legal procedures governing them. A number of human rights treaties such as the International Covenant on Civil and Political Rights also addressed these issues.[41] In particular, the Geneva Conventions state prisoners of war are entitled to be tried in "the same courts according to the same procedure" used to try the captor's own troops. These treaties, and the general trend toward providing detainees more civil, legal, and political protections, impacted the scope and procedures of future military tribunal systems in the United States.[42]

Summary

One thing that this short history makes clear is all three branches of government have played a role in shaping the usage and limits of military tribunals. Presidents and their military commanders have clearly been the main figures, convening military tribunals during times of war to try enemy spies, their own troops, and even occasionally civilians who violated the laws of war. Numerous presidents have claimed the commander in chief power provides them with the unilateral ability to convene military tribunals, determine their procedures, and establish their penalties. Some have argued they can do this without (or even contrary to) statutory authorization. However, the Supreme Court has never squarely ruled on this claim.[43]

Military tribunals prior to 9/11 generally hewed closely to the procedures found in courts-martial. The overwhelming number of military tribunals used during the Mexican War, the Civil War, and post–World War II followed this trend. Executives and their surrogates have often been quite cognizant of the importance of providing procedural safeguards in these tribunals as illustrated by the care in crafting and oversight exhibited by President Lincoln and General Scott during the 19th century.

There are some glaring and high-profile exceptions and abuses. While the general historical trend has have been to offer strong procedural protections in military tribunals, there are also examples of presidents and generals overruling tribunal acquittals and designing tribunals with the seeming express purpose of providing a swift proceeding, certain conviction, and a harsh penalty (often death). FDR's Nazi saboteur tribunal, the tribunals used to try Henry Wirz and the Lincoln conspirators during the Civil War, and those used to try Japanese military officials following World War II are striking examples of this. It is perhaps these abuses that make the best argument for close congressional and judicial oversight in this area.

Congress has played an important role in the historical development of military tribunals since the founding by codifying their existence, first in the Articles of War, and numerous additional times in subsequent legislation such as the UCMJ. One can argue this role is important because it sets boundaries, however broad and skeletal they may be. Congress has also often been passive, leaving the formation and the execution of these tribunals to the executive branch so long as their procedures were generally comparable to those found in courts-martial.[44] The use of tribunals in the Mexican War illustrates this. Even when General Scott sent his tribunal proposals to Congress for review and/or ratification, Congress demurred, leaving the whole affair to the discretion of the military.

Another factor to consider is the role of congressional oversight. In the high-profile instances noted earlier where military tribunal proceedings gave the appearance of "victor's" or summary justice, Congress often either supported the executive's actions or, as illustrated in the case of General Jackson, offered a muted response, expressing some disapproval but rarely taking any consequential actions.

Despite the fact that the path from military tribunal to Article III court is a narrow one, the historical record shows that the judiciary has had numerous opportunities to provide oversight and shape the use and scope of military tribunals. Here again, the record is mixed. While the Supreme Court has repeatedly expressed reservations about claims that the president alone has the power to create military tribunals, it is also true that its strongest objections have come in the wake of wartime conflict.

Quirin and *Eisentrager* were important precedents for the Bush administration legal team in the days following 9/11. They were used to support the contention that President Bush had the authority to convene military tribunals for detainees in Guantanamo Bay. The administration also argued that, per *Eisentrager*, these detainees were not being held in the United States so they could be denied access to U.S. courts.

This brief history provides a general sense of how military tribunals have been used throughout American history and how each branch has had a role to play in their design, use, and scope. The following section will examine how the Bush military tribunal system, designed and implemented after the 9/11 attacks, comported with these general patterns. It will review why the administration chose to revive the use of military tribunals, how it

Military Tribunals

went about devising its tribunal system, and how Congress and the courts ultimately responded to these policy initiatives.

The Bush Administration and Military Tribunals

The Bush administration moved quickly to place the United States in a position to use military force against Al Qaeda and its allies in Afghanistan following the 9/11 attacks. This involved action on several fronts. President Bush put White House counsel Alberto Gonzales in charge of a small group of officials who were tasked with developing detention plans for suspected terrorists captured by U.S. forces.

On November 13, 2001, President Bush publicly issued a military order that instructed the Defense Department to create a system of military tribunals for captured Al Qaeda fighters and other suspected (non-American) terrorists.[45] The administration argued that these tribunals were the best forum to bring terrorists and killers to justice. As international outlaws, they deserved no better.

This announcement took many by surprise, particularly members of Congress. In subsequent congressional testimony, administration officials admitted that they had considered including military tribunals in the Patriot Act, but ultimately decided they had the power to create tribunals without the need of legislation.[46] They had remained coy about their intentions regarding the creation of tribunals. Senate Judiciary Chair Patrick Leahy (D-VT) inquired about a military tribunal system after the 9/11 attacks. In an October 18, 2001, letter, Attorney General John Ashcroft responded to Leahy's request for information by informing him that "it would be inappropriate for the Department to make premature pronouncements concerning the feasibility of this or other particular methods of trying hostile terrorist forces."[47]

President Bush ultimately concluded the executive branch had the power it needed to create a military tribunal system without any congressional input. This conclusion was consistent with the advice the president was getting from his Office of Legal Counsel (OLC). In a November 2001 memorandum to the president, Deputy Assistant Attorney General Patrick Philbin articulated a powerful vision of the president's ability to convene military tribunals. Reading the president's commander in chief powers broadly, Philbin argued that the president enjoyed the "full powers necessary to prosecute successfully a military campaign." This included the power to convene a system of military tribunals. History and practice, he added, supported this conclusion.[48] The Bush administration's OLC concluded working with Congress to establish a tribunal system was certainly an option, but the president was definitely not required to do so. While most constitutional scholars rejected this muscular vision of president power, some concurred with the administration's assessment.[49]

The Bush administration was not wholly unified on the question of military tribunals. While Philbin and John Yoo were writing memoranda justifying expansive uses of presidential power, others were left out of the decision-making loop entirely. Some members of the Bush administration were caught by surprise when the military order was announced. *Washington Post* reporters Barton Gellman and Jo Becker subsequently outlined a process that described the key role played by Vice President Dick Cheney and his Chief of Staff David Addington, two individuals who were consistently in agreement with Philbin's vision of executive war powers in the WOT.

The order for the military tribunal system was drafted by Addington and shared with President Bush during a private luncheon with Vice President Cheney. Mere hours later, the president signed the order and the military tribunal system was born. The military order was reported on the news that evening. For some senior administration officials, such as Secretary of State Colin Powell and National Security Advisor Condoleezza Rice, it was the first time they had been informed of its existence. They were stunned that such an important decision had been made without their input.[50]

Why Military Tribunals?

Military tribunals were not the only option available to the Bush administration when it came to prosecuting terrorists. Having decided it had the power to create tribunals, the next question that needed to be asked was should it? Civilian trials and courts-martial were the two most readily identifiable alternatives to specially constituted military tribunals. The Bush administration rejected these alternatives and offered several justifications in support of the president's military order.

Many critics argued that suspected terrorists should simply be tried in U.S. civilian courts, particularly since there was considerable historical precedent for this approach. However, the administration argued tribunals had numerous advantages compared to civilian trials. They reduced the risk judges or civilian jurors might be the subject of intimidation by terrorist groups. They also more easily allowed for the closure of proceedings where appropriate to prevent the disclosure of classified national security information.[51] Tribunals reduced the chance that a "rogue" juror might acquit an obviously guilty terrorist.[52] A military tribunal would also lessen the risk of a trial being turned into theater by terrorists who desired a public platform to air their viewpoints.[53] The administration argued tribunals would provide swifter justice than civilian courts. Tribunals also had the virtue of being able to provide more secure physical settings to try suspected terrorists than

Military Tribunals

public courthouses across the country.[54] Finally, military tribunals could provide a sentence in proportion to the nature of the offense against the United States (i.e., one could get the death penalty in military tribunals where it might not be a sentencing option in many civilian trials).[55]

Perhaps the simplest explanation offered for the use of tribunals was articulated by Attorney General John Ashcroft when he said, "Foreign terrorists who commit war crimes against the United States . . . are not entitled to and do not deserve the protection of the American Constitution."[56] Trying these individuals before military tribunals, added Vice President Dick Cheney, shows the world that these people are international outlaws.[57]

The U.S. public supported the use of military tribunals as well. Polls taken in 2002 showed two-thirds support for Bush's military order and the tribunal system.[58] This was despite the fact that over three-quarters of those polled thought the government somewhat or highly likely to overuse them.[59]

Congress and Military Tribunals

The November 13 tribunal announcement took most in Congress by surprise. The administration had not consulted with it on the need for military tribunals nor provided advance notice that the military order was forthcoming. In fact, the failure to involve Congress in the tribunal decision from the start was roundly criticized, especially given that November 13 order had specified no exigent circumstances that would have precluded consultation with Congress.[60]

Republican senator Arlen Specter (R-PA) immediately called for hearings so the administration would be forced to explain why it failed to consult with Congress on such an important matter. Specter flatly stated that the Constitution gave Congress, not the president, the power to establish military tribunals.[61] Many cheered this, urging Congress to pass legislation codifying any military tribunal system.

Congress soon held hearings. When administration officials testified, they assured the Senate Judiciary Committee they considered Congress a "full partner" in the WOT. "How can you talk about full partnership," Specter asked doubtfully, "when nobody let us know this executive order was coming down?"[62] Democrats were equally skeptical. In a statement that would ultimately prove prophetic, senior Democrat Patrick Leahy asserted failing to consult with Congress "fundamentally jeopardizes the separation of powers that undergirds our constitutional system, and it may undercut the legality of any military tribunal proceeding."[63] Representative John Conyers (D-MI) added the tribunal system was based on the "thinnest of legal precedents" and could serve to upset American allies in the WOT.[64]

Rather than appearing chastised, administration representatives Michael Chertoff and John Ashcroft took the offensive. They admitted the White

House had been considering the use of military tribunals since shortly after 9/11 even though it never publicly addressed the issue.[65] There was no reason to have a discussion, they insisted, because legislative action on the subject was not necessary. It was the president's decision, and his alone.[66] Ashcroft famously delivered a tongue-lashing to senators who were critical of the administration's policies: "We need honest, reasoned debate, and not fear-mongering. . . . Your tactics only aid terrorists, for they erode our national unity and diminish our resolve."[67]

Most Republican senators rushed to the administration's aid. Mitch McConnell (R-KY) worried that trying terrorists in civilian courts would risk an "O.J. Simpson trial, complete with the grandstanding by the defense lawyers."[68] Orrin Hatch (R-UT) complained, "rapid-fire oversight hearings are aimed less at providing information and more at demonizing the administration and our Attorney General for partisan purposes."[69] Criticisms of the president's military order, he argued, were "unfair . . . almost hysterical."[70]

The administration's frontal assault took the steam out of any congressional desire to legislate on the matter. Several members of Congress introduced legislation, but none of the bills ever made it out of committee. Despite the occasional public bluster and the criticism of Ashcroft in particular, Senate Majority Leader Tom Daschle (D-SD) noted that "there is overwhelming support" to give Ashcroft "all the power he needs."[71] Even noted civil libertarian Senator Russ Feingold (D-WI), the only senator to vote against the Patriot Act, said he did not necessarily oppose a tribunal system in principle.[72]

Congress demurred, perhaps taking the view it was unwise to block a tribunal system that the public clearly favored. If the administration's system turned out to be problematic in the future, Congress could always criticize the administration and then pass a new law. Some, like Senator Leahy, realized that passing any tribunal legislation in 2001 without the support of the White House would be very difficult. "You're not going to be passing legislation in a situation like this," said Leahy. "I'm not unaware of the polls." However, this did not mean there was no role for Congress. "What can be done," he added, "is to have real oversight."[73]

The Bush Military Tribunal System

While the military order authorizing the tribunals was issued in November 2001, the first set of tribunal procedures was not issued until March 2002. The first charges against a detainee were not filed until February 2004.[74] This delay was largely the result of the fact that the administration started from scratch when it came to devising the tribunal procedures, a delay John Yoo lamented essentially defeated the purpose of using military tribunals in the first place (to dispense quick, sure justice).[75]

Supporters of the Bush military tribunal system argued it provided the accused "unprecedented" rights. Defendants were presumed innocent until proven guilty. They received notice of the charges against them, had the ability to retain counsel, and could call witnesses.[76] The tribunals also complied with international law norms. They were not, these proponents argued, vehicles for summary justice.[77]

Critics of the administration's tribunal system argued the president's system significantly departed from historical conventions in scope and process. Rather than particularly identifying a group of potential defendants Bush's order applied to any "noncitizens," a term of extraordinary breadth. Similarly, the order contained no requirements a defendant been captured on a battlefield, meaning the order could be applied to non-U.S. citizens anywhere in the world.[78] Bush's order also tracked FDR's Nazi saboteur order by prohibiting judicial review of the proceedings. Initially, the government also reserved the right to monitor defendants' conversations with their lawyers, a procedure later changed when it became difficult to get defense lawyers to agree to such conditions. Other critics objected to the lack of procedural safeguards and the concentration of power within the executive branch of government. Finally, some objected to the fact that the administration freely admitted on several occasions that even an acquittal before one of these tribunals might not necessarily lead to the release of a defendant.[79]

The initial criticisms following Bush's November 13 order prompted the administration to proceed cautiously as it developed the actual rules for the tribunal system. The administration consulted outside experts in the field, even officials from previous administrations. When the rules were eventually released in March 2002, members of Congress—even though they had not been consulted—quickly expressed approval.[80] Congress would eventually have more to say about the composition of military tribunals, but that would come later.

Guantanamo Detainees

Chapter 3 chronicled how the Bush administration used the naval base at Guantanamo Bay, Cuba, to detain captured terrorist suspects. The manner in which these individuals were treated and their right to challenge those conditions has already been discussed, but their legal challenges also pertain to the use of military tribunals. A number of these detainees were charged and set to be tried before the Bush administration's military tribunal system.

In the 2004 *Rasul v. Bush*, the Supreme Court held Guantanamo detainees had access to U.S. courts.[81] This decision essentially allowed the detainees to pursue two different types of challenges. They filed writs of habeas corpus to challenge their continued detention and treatment. They also attempted to prevent their cases from being heard in the military tribunal system, arguing that it was constitutionally and procedurally flawed.

The Detainee Treatment Act

While there were a handful of individuals who cheered the Supreme Court's 2004 decision in *Rasul*, a large majority in Congress was inclined to respond to the Court's decision by imposing limits on the legal rights of detainees. One of these efforts was the Detainee Treatment Act (DTA) of 2005. The act's limits on interrogation techniques were already recounted at length in Chapter 3. However, the act also contained provisions that impacted the ongoing military tribunals.

John Yoo later asserted the DTA was Congress's way of telling the Supreme Court that it went too far in *Rasul*, and the legislation served as a clear warning for the courts to avoid meddling in matters best left to the political branches of government.[82] In one sense, Yoo was correct. The legislation expressed congressionally mandated limits on detainee interrogation procedures. However, other aspects of the DTA were less clear.

One of the things the DTA did was to limit detainee access to the U.S. federal courts. The act stated: "[N]o court, justice, or judge" would have jurisdiction to consider any type of legal action brought by Guantanamo detainees. The sole exception to this was the D.C. Circuit Court of Appeals, which was given the power to review Combat Status Review Tribunal (CSRT)[83] decisions. Even then, the court only had the power to review whether the military followed the proper procedures. It could not review or overturn CSRT decisions on substantive grounds.[84] This would have the effect of halting all challenges to the Bush military tribunal system.

While the intent to limit judicial review was clear, the key question that was left specifically unanswered by the text of the act was whether the jurisdiction-stripping provision applied to *pending* cases or just *future* cases. In a signing statement that accompanied the act, President Bush articulated the view that the judiciary was denied the power to hear *any* cases, even pending ones.[85] The congressional record also reveals some confusion on the question. Clearly some congressional Democrats thought that the legislation did not apply to pending cases, while Republicans argued it did.[86] The question was one that would ultimately be decided by the U.S. Supreme Court.

Hamdan v. Rumsfeld: Military Tribunals, Round One

Once the rules were established in 2002, the Bush military tribunal system moved forward and began prosecutions. One of the first individuals charged was Salim Hamdan, a Yemeni national who was captured in 2001

Military Tribunals

along the Afghan/Pakistan border in the fighting following the U.S. occupation of Afghanistan after 9/11. While Hamdan admitted to serving as a driver for Osama bin Laden for a period of time, he denied he was a terrorist or a member of Al Qaeda.[87]

In 2003, President Bush declared Hamdan eligible for trial before a military tribunal. Hamdan was eventually charged with Terrorism, Conspiracy to Attack Civilians, and Conspiracy to Commit Murder.[88] Hamdan's counsel filed a habeas corpus petition in his case arguing the military tribunal system violated both military and international law. The petition also claimed that military tribunals did not have the power to charge someone with conspiracy since conspiracy was not a crime under the common law of war.[89] The case worked its way up through the federal court system until it reached the U.S. Supreme Court.

On June 29, 2006, the Court, in a 5–3 decision, struck down the Bush administration's military tribunal system concluding it violated both international law and the UCMJ.[90] However, before proceeding to the merits of Hamdan's case regarding the constitutionality of the military tribunals, the Court first had to address the threshold question of jurisdiction. Did the DTA's jurisdiction-stripping provision prevent the Supreme Court from even having the power to hear the case in the first place? The majority ultimately concluded that the legislation was intended to apply only to new detainee cases, not pending ones. As a result, the Court did have the power to address the merits of Hamdan's constitutional challenges to the military tribunal system.

Justice John Paul Stevens concluded the UCMJ, the Authorization to Use Military Force (AUMF), and the DTA recognized presidential authority to convene military tribunals, nothing more. Even when the president convened tribunals, he needed to do so in the context of the laws of war. He was not wholly free to devise his own rules and procedures. Five justices concluded the tribunal's procedural departures from the courts-martial found in the UCMJ were problematic. Departure from UCMJ procedures "must be tailored to the exigency that necessitates it" and in this instance, none was shown.[91] Four justices (Justice Kennedy declined to reach this issue) also found the tribunal procedures violated international law by not allowing the defendant to be present at all stages of his trial. This group of justices also concluded conspiracy was an offense not triable before a military tribunal. The Court did not decide whether the president had the power to convene tribunals without congressional authorization and this remains an open question.[92]

In his concurring opinion, Justice Kennedy emphasized the limits the Court saw on presidential power. While he refused to join the majority on all points, he did conclude "That this is not a case, then, where the Executive can assert some unilateral authority to fill a void left by congressional inaction. . . . Trial by military commission raises separation of powers concerns of the highest order."[93]

It was Justice Breyer who pointed the way forward when he noted that the Court's opinion ultimately rested on the premise that "Congress has not issued the Executive a 'blank check'" to do as he pleased in the WOT. Nothing prevented the president from seeking additional congressional authorization for a new tribunal system if that was what the Bush administration really wanted.[94] This was exactly the path the Bush administration chose to take.

The Military Commissions Act of 2006

The Supreme Court's decision in *Hamdan* threw the entire military tribunal process into chaos. Virtually everyone disagreed on how Congress and the president should respond. The one thing everyone did agree upon was a new military tribunal system should be devised. Unfortunately, no one agreed just what it should look like or what types of protections it should provide.

Even within the executive branch there was some division. Vice President Cheney and David Addington wanted a one-page bill that stripped the courts of all jurisdiction over tribunals and affirmed the president had the power to enact the tribunal system the Court had just struck down. They simply wanted Congress to give its stamp of approval to the old tribunal system.[95]

Others, including top military lawyers, favored a different approach that provided broader protections for detainees.[96] Some suggested the new system be modeled after the military courts-martial. This approach was rejected out of hand by senior members of the Bush administration as "not practicable."[97] Instead, President Bush promised to work with Congress on tribunal legislation but insisted any bill reflect the reality the nation was at war.[98]

Senate Majority Leader Bill Frist (R-TN) promised a new bill soon, and Congress immediately scheduled hearings on the tribunal issue. While both parties scrambled to draft a legislative response, Democrats took the opportunity to admonish the Bush administration for its original failed tribunal system. "Their whole unilateral approach," scolded Senator Carl Levin (D-MI), "made it more difficult for everybody here, and we're going to have to pick up these pieces. It would have been a lot easier if they had not ignored the Congress and not behaved as if they are the law unto themselves."[99] Senator Chuck Schumer (D-NY) piled on, calling the administration "the gang that couldn't shoot straight" and blaming the Court's decision on its "headstrong" behavior.[100]

Even within Congress there were disagreements about what form a new tribunal system should take. In the House, the Armed Services Committee supported a bill that gave the White House virtually all of what it wanted, while in the Senate both Republicans and Democrats on the Judiciary

Committee took a far less deferential approach. Long-time congressman Barney Frank (D-MA) colorfully described the impasse: "The House thinks the Senate is the cowardly lion and the Senate thinks the House is the scarecrow without a brain."[101]

Within a month, the White House introduced a new tribunal bill that would eventually become the Military Commissions Act (MCA) of 2006. The bill codified substantial parts of the old tribunal system. It suspended habeas corpus proceedings for detainees replacing them with alternative procedures previously outlined in the DTA of 2005. "Reliable" hearsay was admissible in the proceedings and defendants could be excluded from parts of the trial where classified information was being reviewed. In fact, any evidence with "probative value" could be admissible, even evidence obtained during interrogations where coercion was used (as distinguished from evidence obtained by torture, which was not admissible).[102] The bill also contained provisions that would make it more difficult for U.S. courts to enforce protections found in the Geneva Conventions.[103]

The MCA of 2006 easily passed Congress in late September with overwhelming Republican support. Democrats almost uniformly opposed the bill, but allowed a vote on it for fear of being labeled as obstructionists in the upcoming midterm election if they attempted to block it. Senate amendments, which would have prevented the suspension of habeas corpus and set a five-year sunset provision on the bill, were defeated.[104]

The habeas-stripping provision in the MCA was particularly controversial. Senators Leahy and Specter introduced the amendment to keep habeas protections for detainees, but it failed to receive the necessary support. Conservative Republicans had no interest in providing habeas protections for Guantanamo detainees. "The consequences of granting the habeas right would be horrendous," Senator Jon Kyl (R-AZ) concluded. "These are dangerous, dangerous killers. This is not some law school exercise that we're going through here."[105] Senator Specter eventually voted for the bill with the habeas-stripping provisions though he predicted the Supreme Court would likely find them unconstitutional. He expressed a hope that Congress could revisit the issue and "clean up" provisions he viewed as constitutionally questionable.[106]

One additional point of contention was the codification of conspiracy as a war crime. Traditionally, war crimes have historically included things such as genocide, using poison gas, or killing innocent civilians. Now, per the MCA, conspiring or planning to engage in these activities would also be considered a war crime. Critics argued that adding these as war crimes was designed to make it easier to prosecute detainee cases where the evidence was weak.

This approach was potentially problematic for two reasons. First, there is debate about whether conspiracy can properly be defined as a war crime. In

Hamdan, a plurality of justices that addressed the issue concluded that it was not. Justice Kennedy failed to offer an opinion on the issue so it was uncertain whether the Supreme Court would strike this provision.

The second problem was related to the timing of the act. Would it be possible to charge Guantanamo detainees with conspiracy before a military tribunal for actions that happened years before conspiracy was even labeled a war crime? Some observers worried that this provision might be struck down by the courts as an ex post facto law, which is forbidden by the U.S. Constitution. Senator Barack Obama was one of the opponents of this provision.

Despite these concerns, President Bush signed the bill into law on October 17, 2006. Administration supporters such as John Yoo applauded the new legislation concluding that the administration had received just about everything it wanted.[107] Others argued this was an example of Congress stepping up to the plate to offer a legislative solution through an open and deliberative process. The result, concluded two congressional scholars, was "vastly different and in most respects a more comprehensive and fair system of adjudication than the one the President had championed."[108]

After the Democrats swept the House and the Senate in the 2006 midterm elections, Senators Leahy and Specter attempted to revisit the habeas-stripping provision in the MCA but were unsuccessful.[109] Meanwhile, the Bush administration quickly informed federal courts that, per the MCA, they no longer had jurisdiction to consider Guantanamo detainee habeas corpus petitions. In January 2007, the Pentagon released a revised 238-page military tribunal rule book and the new tribunal system was up and running.[110]

Boumediene v. Bush: Military Tribunals, Round Two

Detainees with pending military tribunal cases immediately petitioned federal courts to challenge the constitutionality of the habeas-stripping provisions found in the MCA of 2006. The U.S. Supreme Court eventually agreed to hear one of these cases, *Boumediene v. Bush*. On June 12, 2008, a sharply divided Court ruled that the habeas-stripping provisions found in the MCA of 2006 were unconstitutional.[111] Writing for a five-justice majority, Justice Kennedy ruled the right of habeas corpus extended to the detainees in Guantanamo. Congress, the Court held, had the right to suspend habeas corpus—which it had effectively done for detainees with the MCA—but it needed to provide an adequate substitute that would allow government detainees to challenge the legality of their detention. The DTA of 2005, which outlined legal procedures and protections for the Guantanamo detainees, failed to provide that adequate substitute, therefore, the suspension in the MCA was unconstitutional.

Four justices dissented from the Court's ruling. Justice Scalia and Chief Justice Roberts each authored opinions that took issue with the majority's

Military Tribunals

conclusions. Both questioned whether the right of habeas should be extended to enemy detainees housed outside of the United States. The dissenters also took issue with the majority's characterization of the procedures and protections found in the DTA. The dissenting justices concluded Congress did provide a constitutionally adequate substitution for the habeas rights that the MCA had suspended.

This was another significant blow to Bush administration. It had unilaterally created its own system that the Court had struck down. So the administration went to Congress and passed the MCA of 2006. The administration then went before the Court in *Boumediene* and argued that the Court should defer to the military tribunal system put in place by Congress and the president. Solicitor General Paul Clement said, "Congress here has spoken. The political branches have spoken. They have struck a balance."[112] It was a balance, concluded Clement, the Court should respect. But the Court refused to do so. As a result, the future of military tribunals was once again in doubt as President Bush approached the end of his second term in office.

The Court's decision came in the midst of the 2008 presidential campaign. This was particularly relevant because both candidates—Democrat Barack Obama and Republican John McCain—were serving in the Senate and had voted on the MCA. While McCain stated that the *Boumediene* decision "obviously concerns me," Obama reminded voters, "I voted against the MCA because its sloppiness would inevitably lead to court, once again, rejecting the [Bush] administration's extreme legal position."[113]

Summary

It was perhaps unsurprising to see military tribunals used in the wake of the 9/11 attacks, but the unique nature of the WOT also produced some interesting wrinkles in the historical patterns exhibited by the president, Congress, and the judiciary in this area. The Bush administration pulled out all the stops after 9/11, asserting the president's war powers to their fullest with no apologies and little tolerance for opposition from Congress or the courts. The rollout of the administration's initial tribunal system in November 2001 was a harbinger of things to come. The administration, it was subsequently revealed, had planned for the use of military tribunals since shortly after the attack. But it viewed them as an executive prerogative so there was no need to consult with Congress.

Initially, Congress deferred to the administration's decision to use tribunals. Despite holding hearings, it was clear at the outset that most members of Congress were perfectly willing to give the Bush administration the tools it needed to fight the WOT. Only after the Supreme Court struck down the administration's tribunal system in *Hamdan* did Congress genuinely enter the discussions about military tribunals in a serious way. Some criticized Congress for essentially codifying much of the administration's previous tribunal system without seriously addressing its shortcomings. However, after *Hamdan*, Congress began to play a much more active role. This would particularly be on display with the transition from the Bush administration to the Obama administration.

While historically the judiciary has been mostly deferential in this policy area during military conflicts, the *Hamdan* Court insisted on a joint presidential-congressional approach on the design and implementation of a military tribunal system. The Court also noted the importance of international law and human rights law on U.S. tribunal systems, reflecting a rise in importance of these sources as protectors of civil and political rights.

The Obama Administration and Military Tribunals

As a senator and a presidential candidate, Barack Obama was highly critical of the Bush administration's approach to the creation and use of military tribunals. "By any measure," he said, "our system of trying detainees has been an enormous failure."[114] Senator Obama voted against the MCA of 2006 and constantly reminded voters of this during his presidential campaign. "I have faith in America's courts," said Senator Obama in an August 7, 2008, statement. "I'll close Guantanamo, reject the Military Commissions Act. . . . Our Constitution and our Uniform Code of Military Justice provide a framework for dealing with the terrorists."[115]

However, upon taking office, President Obama hedged on his earlier rhetoric. During the presidential transition, there was a vigorous debate between national security and Justice Department officials about the best way to prosecute Guantanamo detainees.[116] The incoming administration eventually decided to suspend rather than abolish the existing military tribunal system. This allowed the administration to review detainee cases and then determine which approach was best.

In one of his first acts as president, Obama issued Executive Order 13492. This executive order called for the closure of the detention facility at Guantanamo Bay, a review of all detainees currently being held, and a halt to all military commission proceedings.[117] In a major policy speech at the National Archives a few months later, President Obama announced the administration's plans for trying detainees. The president stated his administration still preferred to use civilian courts to try suspected terrorists whenever possible, but recognized some cases were best suited for military commissions. President Obama announced that the military tribunal system would resume prosecuting cases at some point in the future, but he pressed Congress for procedural reforms, many of which were intended to provide detainees with more due process rights than they had under the MCA of 2006.[118]

The president also indicated a preference that any future tribunal proceedings be held on military bases in the United States.[119] This would be necessary if the Obama administration was successful in the president's wish to close Guantanamo. However, Congress had other ideas. In the first of a series of votes that occurred over a several year period, the Senate voted 90–6 to block the transfer of Guantanamo detainees to the United States.[120] Several months later the House followed suit when it also voted to prohibit detainees from being transferred to the United States.[121] These congressional votes would ultimately limit the Obama administration's options when it came to the Guantanamo detainees and military commissions.

The Military Commissions Act of 2009

When he announced he was willing to keep military tribunals, President Obama also asserted that the existing MCA needed to be revised to provide more due process protections for detainees. Congress responded by passing the MCA of 2009 in October. This act offered some of the due process protections advocated by the Obama administration, but it also contained some constitutionally questionable provisions.

While the new version of the MCA allowed for evidence obtained by coercion, it banned evidence obtained via torture or any other cruel, inhuman, or degrading means. Hearsay evidence was also allowable as long as it was determined to have probative value. One of the questions facing the government was the use of classified evidence against detainees. Under the new MCA, the defendant could not be excluded from the courtroom during the introduction of evidence against him, even if that evidence was classified in nature. The government was now bound to present not only incriminating evidence but exculpatory evidence as well.[122]

The MCA of 2009 authorized tribunals to have jurisdiction over 32 offenses. Most of these offenses were commonly viewed as war crimes (e.g., targeting civilians, perfidy, pillaging) but Congress also added conspiracy and material support for terrorism (MST). Neither of these crimes has historically been widely recognized as a war crime, and some critics alleged that these offenses were included to bolster otherwise weak government cases. While President Obama had some reservations about including MST as an offense it remained in the final version of the act.[123]

Alternatives to Military Tribunals?

Even though the Obama administration received many of its desired due process enhancements in the MCA of 2009, the president continued to look for alternatives to military tribunals. On November 13, 2009, Attorney

General Eric Holder announced the five detainees in custody thought to be connected to the 9/11 attacks—including Khalid Sheikh Mohammed (KSM)—would be tried in civilian federal court in New York City. The underlying rationale behind this move was to demonstrate that the U.S. civilian justice system was capable of holding a fair trial that would deliver justice to the perpetrators of 9/11 in the very city in which the attacks occurred.

Perhaps predictably, there was considerable congressional backlash. Senator John Cornyn (R-TX) excoriated the Obama administration stating the decision to try KSM in federal courts "needlessly compromises the safety of all Americans. Putting political ideology ahead of the safety of the American people just to fulfill an ill-conceived campaign promise is irresponsible."[124] Other Republicans were equally outraged and made their displeasure with the administration known.

Another alternative floated by the Obama administration was to relocate roughly 150 Guantanamo detainees to a largely unused federal prison located in Thompson, Illinois. The plan was to make the prison a "super-max" run largely by the U.S. military. The plan was pitched as something that would facilitate the closure of Guantanamo, provide a secure place to hold the detainees, and create much-needed jobs for the local economy.

Again, Republicans voiced their extreme opposition to the idea. Referring to the Thompson facility as "Gitmo North," Senate Minority Leader Mitch McConnell said, "The American people and a bipartisan majority of the Congress have already rejected bringing terrorists to U.S. soil for long-term detention, and current law prohibits it." House Speaker John Boehner (R-OH) vowed not to spend "one dime" to move Guantanamo prisoners to the United States.[125] There appeared to be no room for compromise on this issue. Even when Attorney General Holder indicated detainees found not guilty in federal courts might still be held in custody, Republicans flatly rejected the idea. Congress eventually blocked funding for the movement of any detainees to the mainland.[126]

Given this resistance, the Obama administration was eventually forced to abandon plans to move Guantanamo detainees to the United States and/or try them in federal courts. On April 4, 2011, Attorney General Holder reversed course and announced that the Obama administration would try KSM and his fellow 9/11 conspirators in military tribunals. As he made the announcement, he blasted Congress for essentially forcing the administration's hand. "We must face a simple truth," said Holder, "those restrictions [preventing transfers from Guantanamo] are unlikely to be repealed in the immediate future . . . and we simply cannot allow a trial to be delayed any longer for the victims of the 9/11 attacks or their families who have waited nearly a decade for justice."[127] Holder argued federal courts were perfectly capable of hearing the case and could deliver sure and swift justice compared to military tribunals. He was convinced the opposition to the administration's plans was largely motivated by "settling ideological arguments or scoring political points."[128]

After Holder had left the Obama administration, he was asked if he had any regrets about his time in office. He named his failure to follow through on civilian trials for the 9/11 detainees as the foremost. Had the administration continued course, he said, "We'd be finished with that trial by now, and it could be something we could point to and show that we can be fair even to those we despise."[129] Congressional critics on both sides of the aisle approved of the administration's change of heart. Senate Majority Leader Mitch McConnell concluded, "This is the right outcome . . . Military Commissions, far from the US mainland, were always the right idea."[130] Even Democrat senator Chuck Schumer (D-NY) agreed,[131] relieved that Holder's announcement appeared to be the "final nail in the coffin of that wrong-headed idea."

Congress continued to pass legislation prohibiting the transfer of detainees from Guantanamo over the objections of President Obama. In a series of signing statements, the president expressed his opposition:

> Section 1027 renews the bar against using appropriated funds for fiscal year 2012 to transfer Guantanamo detainees into the United States for any purpose. . . . For decades Republican and Democratic administrations have successfully prosecuted hundreds of terrorists in Federal Court. Those prosecutions are a legitimate, effective, and powerful tool in our efforts to protect the Nation. Removing that tool from the executive branch does not serve our national security.[132]

In other statements, the language was more terse: "Under no circumstance will my Administration accept or adhere to rigid across-the-board requirement for military detention . . . this instruction would, under certain circumstances, violate constitutional separation of powers principle."[133] Despite these objections, the die was effectively cast and, as a practical matter, it became almost impossible to move detainees from Guantanamo for any reason during the remainder of President Obama's term in office.

Summary

Barack Obama rejected the Bush administration's military tribunal system as a senator. Absent the ability to strike it down, he fought for more due process protections for detainees. As president, he suspended the tribunals at the outset of his administration. But as has been the case in other areas in the WOT, President Obama ultimately came to endorse many of the same policies of President Bush. The key difference, his supporters argue, is he pressed for a fairer tribunal system. Congress responded with the MCA of 2009.

President Obama also made a number of overtures to find alternatives to military tribunals whether it was civilian trials in federal courts or moving Guantanamo detainees to facilities in the United States. In each instance, Congress—in no uncertain terms—rejected these alternatives. It repeatedly used the power of the purse to deny the administration the funding it needed to close Guantanamo, transfer prisoners to the mainland United States, or try Guantanamo detainees in federal court. The president voiced objections, but the opposition in Congress was vocal, consistent, and overwhelming. In the end, the Obama administration grudgingly resumed military tribunal proceedings, not with great enthusiasm, but rather because it was essentially the only remaining option to prosecute Guantanamo detainees.

Military Tribunals in Action

For all the sound and fury surrounding the use of military tribunals, remarkably few terrorist suspects have been subject to them. Tribunal proceedings have been stopped and started countless times for a variety of reasons. There have been multiple iterations of the tribunals, from the original Bush administration rules to the MCAs of 2006 and 2009. Updated rules were promulgated after each change. Charges often needed to be filed and refiled. Evidentiary standards changed continually. Questions about what information was admissible and what was not also slowed the prosecutions. Detainees and their counsel have challenged the legality of tribunal procedures and even the constitutionality of the tribunals themselves. There have also been periods of time where detainees boycotted their own trials.

According to the Office of Military Commissions web page, there are only six active tribunal cases as of fall 2017. Two plead guilty and received shorter prison terms in exchange for their cooperation with the government on future tribunal cases. Abd al Nashiri, who is accused of the *USS Cole* bombing in 2000, which killed 17 American servicemen, also has a pending case.[134]

The most noteworthy set of ongoing tribunal proceedings is that of KSM—often referred to as the mastermind behind 9/11—and four others associated with the 9/11 terrorist attacks. They face myriad charges including: conspiracy, attacking civilians, murder in violation of the laws of war, hijacking, and terrorism. These tribunal hearings have been stopped and started several times with no likely end in the near future. September 11, 2017, marked the 25th pretrial hearing for KSM, whose defense team has challenged just about everything conceivable. Prosecutors are hoping jury selection could occur by January 2019, but other observers are less sanguine about that timetable.

This includes KSM's legal counsel, who admitted: "There's every possibility that my client will die in prison before this process is complete."[135]

Over a dozen cases have had charges withdrawn or dismissed. Many of these instances are cases where detainees were charged with the offense of material support for terrorism (MST). The particulars include individuals accused of providing explosives training, fighting with Al Qaeda, providing financial assistance, and hiding explosives. Material support for terrorism is a crime under U.S. law. It prohibits anyone from providing training, service, personnel, or assistance to groups designated by the U.S. government as terrorist groups. What was not clear when the post-9/11 military tribunals were formed was whether or not this was a crime triable by military commission. Ultimately, the D.C. Circuit Court of Appeals held that it was not.[136]

Two cases are in the process of being appealed. The first is a high-profile case involving charges against Canadian national Omar Khadr. Khadr was accused of killing a U.S. soldier in a firefight in Afghanistan with a grenade. Despite the fact that he was only 15 at the time, Khadr was interrogated by U.S. forces and detained in Guantanamo Bay. He was eventually charged with Murder in Violation of the Laws of War. Khadr pleaded guilty and was sentenced to eight years in prison with the possibility of being transferred to Canada after one year of incarceration.[137] Khadr was released in 2015. He later appealed his conviction claiming he only pleaded guilty so that he could return to Canada.[138]

A second pending case involves Ali al Bahlul, another Guantanamo detainee, who was accused of being Osama bin Laden's personal secretary and Al Qaeda public relations director. Bahlul was convicted in 2008 of charges pursuant to the MCA of 2006. These charges included providing MST, Conspiracy to Commit Terrorism, and Solicitation of Others to Commit Terrorist Acts. Bahlul was found guilty of all charges and sentenced to life in prison.

A series of legal appeals in Bahlul's case illustrates the unsettled nature of law in this particular area. In 2014, the D.C. Circuit Court vacated Bahlul's convictions for MST and solicitation reasoning that neither were a part of the common law of war prior to 2006 when Congress included them as triable offenses in the MCA. The creation of these as military tribunal offenses after Bahlul had engaged in them amounted to an unconstitutional ex post facto law.[139] On June 12, 2015, a separate panel of the D.C. Circuit Court of Appeals vacated the conspiracy conviction concluding that conspiracy was not an offense triable before a military commission as it was not part of the common law of war.[140] This last decision was subsequently overturned by the full D.C. Circuit in 2016 when it reinstated Bahlul's conspiracy conviction. Unfortunately, the judges were badly splintered as to the underlying reasoning behind the court's decision.[141]

Even in the handful of instances where charges have been filed and guilty pleas obtained, the results have been less than satisfying. Ibrahim al Qosi pleaded guilty in 2010 to conspiracy and MST. His 14-year sentence was reduced to 2 years due to his cooperation with the U.S. government. He was eventually transferred to his native Sudan and subsequently released.[142] Less than two years after his release, he rejoined Al Qaeda Arabian Peninsula (AQAP) and became one of its most influential leaders in Yemen.[143]

David Hicks, an Australian national, was one of the first to plead guilty before a military tribunal. In 2007, he pleaded guilty to MST for training and fighting with Al Qaeda. He was sentenced to seven years in prison, but that sentence was reduced to nine months per his plea agreement. He was transferred to Australia to serve out the remainder of his sentence. In 2015, Hicks' conviction for MST was one of those set aside when federal courts concluded that it was an unconstitutional ex post facto charge.

Salim Hamdan's challenge to the original Bush military tribunal system made it all the way up to the U.S. Supreme Court. As noted earlier, the Court struck down that tribunal system. Hamdan was charged once again after the passage of the MCA in 2006. He was eventually convicted of MST and sentenced to five-and-a-half years in prison with credit for five years already spent in custody. Hamdan was eventually transferred to Yemen where he served out the remainder of his sentence. His conviction for MST was eventually overturned in 2012 by the D.C. Circuit Court of Appeals.

It is a disappointing record for military tribunal advocates. This is particularly true when juxtaposed against the number of terrorists prosecuted via U.S. immigration law and civilian criminal law. In the opening days of the WOT, the Bush administration aggressively used U.S. immigration law to detain and deport individuals suspected of having ties to terrorist groups. The Center on National Security at Fordham Law School reports that between 2001 and 2013 there were 368 prosecutions for jihadist terror crimes. Over 80 percent of these cases resulted in convictions with the average sentence of 15 years in prison.[144] These numbers also do not count hundreds of cases brought against suspected terrorists where the charges are more mundane like fraud, theft, or deceptive practices.

Still, there have been enough high-profile terrorism prosecution cases considered "failures" by members of Congress that support for military tribunals has remained strong and constant over time. Two cases illustrate this. The first is Zacarias Moussaoui. Although he eventually pleaded guilty to conspiring to murder civilians as part of the 9/11 plot, his trial lasted years and was anything but ordinary. Moussaoui at one point sought to represent himself and wanted the testimony of other known Al Qaeda associates. He also made frequent political statements about Al Qaeda, jihad, and the

American criminal justice system. Some described it as a circus-like atmosphere. Moussaoui is currently serving six life sentences.

The second case involved Ahmed Ghailani who was accused of being involved in U.S. embassy bombings in Kenya and Tanzania in 1998. Ghailani was charged with 285 counts, including 274 counts of murder or attempted murder. At the end of the trial, the jury saw fit to convict Ghailani of only a single crime, Conspiracy to Destroy Government Property. The prosecution was unable to introduce key evidence in this case because it came from an individual who had been detained and interrogated in a Central Intelligence Agency (CIA) black site. The jury also deadlocked 11–1 on the murder counts, denying prosecutors on that front. On the single charge, Ghailani was eventually sentenced to life in prison.[145]

Trump Administration

A considerable amount of Donald Trump's campaign rhetoric during the 2016 presidential campaign focused on fighting terrorism. He frequently shocked political pundits by taking a number of hard-line stances (some of questionable legality) on terrorism issues. This included the continued use and possible expansion of military tribunals.

Trump shared his thoughts on military tribunals while on the campaign trail. When asked whether he would be willing to try American citizens who were terrorist suspects before military tribunals at Guantanamo Bay, Trump responded, "Well, I know that they want to try them in our regular court systems, and I don't like that. I don't like that at all. I would say they could be tried there, that would be fine."[146] This would be a significant break from the Bush and Obama tribunals, both of which were for non-American terrorist suspects only. Senator Lindsey Graham (R-SC) downplayed this potential change when he noted, "There is no buy-in on the right or the left to do this."[147]

Once in office, the Trump administration indicated its desire to keep the detention facility at Guantanamo Bay open and the military tribunal system in place. Visiting the detention facility in July 2017, Attorney General Jeff Sessions called Guantanamo "a fine place" to detain and prosecute suspected terrorists. Sessions called for the military tribunals to continue and expressed frustration at the slow pace of the trials.[148]

In July 2017, the Trump administration signaled an interest in filing new charges against Riduan Isamuddin, a Guantanamo detainee also known as Hambali. Hambali has been in U.S. custody since 2003 and is alleged to have been responsible for 2002 and 2003 bombings in Indonesia.[149] The convening authority in charge of the military tribunal system will have to approve of the charges to open this new case. However, the new charges constitute another signal that President Trump will continue to use military tribunals as a tool against terrorist suspects.

Remaining Issues

There are a number of remaining issues that Congress has the capacity to address when it comes to military tribunals. Of course, the need for any additional action depends in large part on whether an individual thinks the existing situation is working well. There are a considerable number of people who advocate keeping the detention facility at Guantanamo Bay open and the existing military tribunal system in place. For these people, the system is currently working—if not at an optimum level, at least at an acceptable one. Terrorists are being detained and given military justice, the only type of justice that terrorists deserve.

However, there are also people who argue that important changes can be made and that Congress can play a key role in those changes. Congress has the ability to pass new tribunal legislation. It could take three different approaches. First, it could pass legislation that expands the scope of the existing tribunal system to include American citizens and/or increase the number and type of offenses that could be tried before military tribunals. Second, Congress could pass legislation that abolishes the military tribunal system for Guantanamo detainees altogether. Neither of these approaches is likely. Congress has shown little interest in recent years in radically transforming the status quo.

If Congress does choose to act it will likely be done in an incremental fashion. Congressional legislative action since 9/11 in this area has been largely reactive. It allowed the Bush administration to unilaterally devise the initial tribunal system and only legislated on the matter in the wake of the Supreme Court's decisions in *Rasul* and *Hamdan*. With President Trump in office, Congress has shown no interest in revisiting military tribunal legislation.

The Courts

Federal courts have been very active in the area of military tribunals despite the best efforts of both the president and Congress. The Bush administration originally argued Guantanamo detainees had no legal rights they could pursue in federal court. The Court rejected this position in *Rasul*. Congress joined the Bush administration by passing the DTA, again attempting to limit judicial access. When the Supreme Court struck down the Bush tribunal system in *Hamdan*, Congress was more than willing to legislate a new tribunal system that looked very much like the old Bush tribunal system. It has only grudgingly accorded detainees broader due process rights before military tribunals.

Congress has in recent years also seemed to content to let the federal courts sort through the constitutional and legal questions raised by the tribunal legislation. The MCA of 2006 and 2009, and the DTA were largely responses to judicial decisions. Federal courts have not been reticent about telling Congress and the president when they have overstepped constitutional boundaries when it comes to tribunals. In each instance, rather than simply accept the judicial expansion of detainee rights, Congress has pushed back, seeking ways to operate military tribunals with circumscribed rights that still meet the minimal constitutional standards insisted upon by the judiciary.

Guantanamo Bay

Congress has made quite clear that it prefers the detention facility at Guantanamo Bay to remain open. It has signaled this in two ways. First, it has denied funding for the closure of the facilities. Second, it has repeatedly passed legislation barring the transfer of detainees to the United States. While this potentially has implications in a number of areas, it also has an important impact on the continued use of military tribunals.

Keeping the remaining detainees at Guantanamo limits prosecution options. There remains the possibility that they could be tried in military courts with rules similar to those found in courts-martial but no one—neither the executive branch, nor Congress—has shown any interest in that approach. This transfer restriction also basically precludes their trial under federal civilian courts.

This essentially leaves only two options. The first is the continued use of military tribunals. The second is to simply continue to detain these individuals with charges or trials of any type. The Bush administration never promised that it would try all the detainees in Guantanamo, and the Obama administration publicly admitted that there was a group of individuals who could probably not be tried but were too dangerous to be released.[150]

Conclusion

From a national security perspective, military tribunals were presented as justified, necessary, and legal. Justified, because of the horrific actions taken by U.S. enemies on 9/11. Necessary, because civilian justice was not up to the task of safely trying and punishing suspected terrorists in a swift, sure manner. And legal, since the United States was at war. War-time measures such as military tribunals were lawful.

The number of terror suspects actually tried by military tribunals has been exceedingly small particularly when one considers the amount of time and money that has been spent on detaining these men in a specialized high-security military facility and for their trials, many of which are likely to go on for years to come. At this point, Congress and the executive branch seem content to assume that they are needed and so they will continue.

Transparency has been an issue from the very beginning. A group of senior officials in the Bush White House lobbied heavily for tribunals, and the military order was issued without significant debate within the administration. Both the Bush and Obama administrations have struggled to balance the right for defendants to have access to information pertinent to their cases without revealing classified information and sources to them. Allowing hearsay evidence, excluding defendants from portions of their trial where classified evidence is introduced, and the use of evidence obtained by questionable—but unrevealed—methods are all issues that have had to be addressed when it comes to tribunal transparency.

To its credit, the government has engaged in efforts to make the proceedings available to the public. This has allowed 9/11 victims' families, the media, and human rights groups the opportunity to view the proceedings. The Defense Department also maintains and updates a web page for the Office of Military Commissions. A considerable amount of information on the proceedings can be found here (though it is unlikely most Americans even know this page exists). What is missing are the "known unknowns." There is undoubtedly classified information that is being withheld from the public. That is known. What is not known is what that information is and how significantly it impacts tribunal proceedings.

If the consensus is that military tribunals have been a complete failure then who is to blame? Where does the accountability lie? There are a variety of explanations that are offered for the existing state of tribunals.

Some argue that the lawyers representing the detainees are the ones primarily responsible for slowing the processes to a crawl by challenging everything from the various courtroom procedures to the legality of the tribunals themselves. Government military bureaucracy has also been called to task. Regardless of where one wishes to assign responsibility, there are legitimate and complicated issues that need to be resolved (e.g., defendant access to classified information and the admissibility of evidence obtained under "enhanced interrogation").

There are critics that lay blame squarely at the feet of the Bush administration for getting everything off on the wrong foot by insisting (wrongly in this case) that it had the power to unilaterally design and implement a tribunal system. The administration's interrogation policies also complicated attempts to try a number of the detainees before tribunals. Congress has softened the tribunal rules around the edges but refuses to consider alternatives. It has

Military Tribunals

repeatedly prevented the executive from transferring detainees out of Guantanamo to other countries for any purpose.

Where does this leave everyone? The military tribunals slog onward, moving at a snail's pace. They have been eclipsed from the national security news by other stories. The president and Congress appear content to let things unfold as the detainees remain in Guantanamo. Even if the detainees are not convicted, it remains to be determined whether they will ever be deemed suitable for release.

CHAPTER FIVE

Drones and Targeted Killing

Advances in technology have repeatedly changed the face of war, and a host of ethical and moral questions often accompanies these changes. For instance, nuclear, biological, and chemical weapons have devastating destructive power, which certainly influences when, how, or even if they should be used. The War on Terror (WOT) is the latest conflict to usher in a new wave of technologically advanced weapons. In this struggle, the world has witnessed the rise of the drone.

This chapter chronicles the historical development of policy making in the area of unmanned aerial vehicles (UAVs), or as they are often more popularly referred to—drones. This is one area where President Obama considerably expanded upon precedents set in the Bush administration. In fact, it is probably the WOT issue most closely associated with President Obama. President Trump inherited a drone program widely considered an indispensable tool in the WOT and expressed every indication that he would continue to employ it.

Still, issues—and controversies—remain, ones that require concerted action by the U.S. Congress. It must answer important strategic and tactical questions. How does the United States best integrate drones into a comprehensive anti-terrorism strategy? What can drones reasonably accomplish? Do they work, and if so, how well? A host of legal questions abound as well. Is the use of drones to fight terrorists away from conventional battlefields legal under international and domestic law? Can American citizens be targeted, and if so, under what circumstances?

There are important political questions to ask too. What procedures can minimize civilian casualties and reduce targeting mistakes? How should Congress conduct oversight of drone operations? What role can the courts play to protect rights and liberties? It is clear drones are here to stay and that their continued development and use will remain a part of the fight against terrorism for the near future. As a result, it is imperative Congress play a central role in answering these questions.

Drones participate in such a variety of military conflicts it is worth differentiating them at the outset.[1] Drones have been a component in "mixed" warfare for many decades now. Drones operate in a "mixed" capacity when they supplement traditional military weapons on the field of battle; they do everything from conducting reconnaissance and surveillance to assessing battle damage. On the other hand, "pure" drone warfare occurs when drones operate in an independent capacity away from traditional active battlefields. It is this latter type of drone use—drones attacking targets in Pakistan, Somalia, and Yemen far away from any active battlefields—that has engendered such controversy in the WOT.

This chapter will open with a review of the evolution of drone technology in the United States with an emphasis on roles they have played in past military conflicts. This background will provide some insight as to where the United States stood leading up to the 9/11 attacks, after which President Bush immediately expanded drone use. Congress was largely invisible as it pertained to drones during this early period in the WOT, but interest and oversight activity increased as the level of drone activity increased under the Obama administration. This had the impact of bringing a variety of drone-related issues to the attention of Congress. The chapter will explore those issues and potential solutions. It appears that the use of drones is here to stay. The question is how our national security apparatus can best incorporate drones in a way that enhances security while protecting individual liberties.

The Historical Development of Unmanned Aerial Vehicles

The idea that balloons, drones, and airplanes could serve a variety of military purposes dates back over a hundred years. Balloons were used for military reconnaissance in the American Civil War and by Napoleon in early European wars. The birth of the airplane and manned flight eventually served to usher in a completely new mechanized era. The precursors of today's drones saw some limited action in World War I. This war saw the development and periodic use of aerial torpedoes.[2] Even at this early stage of drone development, multiple branches of the U.S. armed services began to develop and test drones. The Army and Navy each tested its own version of aerial torpedoes. During the interwar period, drones served as targets for antiaircraft weapons.[3]

After World War II, the United States relied heavily on the U2 high-altitude reconnaissance aircraft for surveillance over emerging threats such as North Korea, the Soviet Union, and Cuba. In 1960, the Soviet Union shot down U2 pilot Gary Francis Powers as the plane flew over Soviet airspace causing an international incident. One of the lessons the United States took from this incident was the potential value of pilotless reconnaissance aircraft. This would allow the United States to continue monitoring the Soviets without the danger of another pilot falling into enemy hands. A second assumption that drove the perceived need for pilotless aircraft at the time was a belief that the next war might be nuclear and it would not be possible to send piloted planes into radioactive areas.[4]

The United States had already been mass-producing the SD-1 Observer, and by 1960 the U.S. Army had five different drone types either working or in production (high costs ultimately led to the cancellation of most of these programs).[5] The Central Intelligence Agency (CIA) also began to develop its own drones during this period. Because of these continued technological advances, "remotely piloted vehicles" (RPVs) played an important role in the Vietnam conflict. They usually performed a surveillance or reconnaissance function where they would fly over their targets, take pictures, and then be recovered by helicopter.

The AQM-34 Lightening Bug did much of the RPV heavy lifting during this era. Over 1,000 Lightening Bugs flew roughly 3,500 combat sorties. This RPV fleet cost roughly $250 million each year to maintain (approximately 1.6 billion in 2016 dollars). The National Reconnaissance Office's "Black Budget" funded this fleet (i.e., they were funded off the books).[6] Over half were ultimately lost or destroyed, but they collectively took over 100,000 feet of film for the military.[7]

During the latter half of the 20th century, Israel was at the forefront of drone technology. The United States did not begin devoting significant resources to drones until the 1980s, during Ronald Reagan's presidency.[8] In fact, it was an Israeli-developed U.S. drone—the Pioneer—that saw extensive action in Desert Storm during the First Gulf War. The Gulf War was the first war where the United States routinely deployed drones in close battle conflict situations. Pioneers functioned as spotters for gunfire, assessed bomb damage, and provided reconnaissance for navy commando teams.[9] The Pioneer drones were largely successful and their legacy includes one incident where Iraqi troops actually attempted to surrender to one of the unmanned drones.[10]

The 1990s also marked a change in drone terminology, as RPVs became "unmanned aerial vehicles" (UAVs). While UAVs vary considerably in size, shape, and purpose, they share many common characteristics. The U.S. Department of Defense defines a UAV as "A powered, aerial vehicle that does not carry a human operator, uses aerodynamic forces to provide vehicle lift, can fly autonomously or be piloted remotely, can be expendable or recoverable, and can carry a lethal or nonlethal payload."[11]

The 1990s Bosnian conflict was really the key to the development of drone use on the battlefield. This was the first U.S. conflict where the tactical battlefield chain of command included drones. New Predator drones conducted reconnaissance and surveillance for ground troops and piloted aircraft. This was real-time information instantaneously transmitted to units via satellite. Bosnia also served another reminder about the dangers associated with manned aircraft when Air Force pilot Scott O'Grady was shot down and forced to evade capture behind enemy lines. By the end of 1996, Predator drones had flown over 1,500 missions. They monitored troop movement, engaged in surveillance, and conducted battle damage assessments.[12]

Predators eventually became the most widely known drones used after 9/11. Predator drones are 27 feet in length with a wingspan of 55 feet and a weight of 2,250 pounds. They have the capacity to stay airborne for over 24 hours and can achieve a maximum altitude of 25,000 feet. Predators have a range of 500 nautical miles and have the capacity to carry over 450 pounds of surveillance payload. While Congress supported arming the Predators as early as 1996, the Department of Defense initially opposed the move. It was not until after 9/11 that Predators were armed with two Hellfire anti-tank missiles.[13]

The successful use of drones in Bosnia led to a significant increase in congressional expenditures on drone technology. Congressional funding for drones more than doubled during the latter half of the 1990s.[14] The National Defense Authorization Act of 2001 doubled down on this spending trend. The accompanying conference report articulated congressional intent that "within ten years, one third of the U.S. military operational deep strike aircraft will be unmanned." This was an extraordinary goal given that the Defense Department had *zero* unmanned deep strike aircraft at the time.[15]

On the eve of 9/11, the drone industry was beginning to grow in significance, as was the military demand for them. This resulted in a hodgepodge of different drones and often overlapping programs in different branches of the U.S. military. Battlefields often served as the testing grounds for these new drones. Congress both encouraged the development of UAVs during this time and attempted—with varying degrees of success—to rein in interbranch competition related to drone development and use.

There were approximately 2,400 UAVs in the world on 9/11, two-thirds of which were small radio-controlled helicopters used for farming in places such as Japan. The United States had approximately 160 UAVs, while Europe (primarily Britain, France, Germany, and Italy) had roughly 480. These drones almost exclusively conducted military reconnaissance.[16] This was all about to change.

The George W. Bush Administration

For all of the controversial policies associated with the Bush administration and the WOT, its public record on the use of drones is remarkably scarce. The Bush administration laid the foundation for President Obama's expansion of drone operations particularly in Pakistan and Yemen, but the Bush administration's own drone activities received very little public scrutiny at the time.

As early as September 15, 2001, President Bush received a briefing on the use of drones in the Afghan theater. The CIA had been flying Predator drones out of bases in Uzbekistan in an effort to monitor Osama bin Laden. The president's advisors explained that the United States was able to keep one Predator in the air at all times, though it was aiming for two. President Bush, impressed with the potential of these drones, reportedly remarked, "We ought to have 50 of these things."[17] At the same Camp David meeting, CIA director George Tenet also told the president the United States had the capacity to arm Predators. He received the green light to do so in a memorandum signed a few days later.

The September 17 memorandum was one of several documents created in the wake of the 9/11 attacks designed to articulate and defend a muscular view of presidential power. Like others, it granted wide powers to executive branch actors. Drafted by CIA Director Tenet, the memorandum allowed the president to create a secret "high-value" drone target list of about two dozen Al Qaeda and Taliban commanders. While the president approved the initial list, the CIA had the power to add additional names to the list and conduct attacks on these individuals without prior presidential approval.[18] The memorandum also added that the evidence needed to place someone on the list needed to be "clear and convincing." Per statute, the president was required to issue a presidential finding authorizing the CIA to engage in these activities and report the finding to Congress. President Bush did both, notifying congressional leaders shortly thereafter.[19]

Expanding Drone Use

The use of drones on the battlefield engendered little controversy at the outset of the Afghan war. They were, in large part, just another tool at the U.S. military's disposal. It was when their use expanded beyond Afghan borders that they became much more controversial. Critics opposed the use of military weapons beyond an active battlefield, arguing it violated international law and military norms.

It is important to note the expanded use of drones was completely consistent with the Bush administration's concept of what the "battlefield" was in the WOT. The administration argued terrorists did not observe borders or fight on traditional battlefields. They could be found anywhere around the world. Therefore, military tools and tactics were justified around the world, even on U.S. soil.

It was not long before the CIA made use of its new powers under the September 17 memorandum. On November 11, 2001, Mohammed Atef, the third-ranking Al Qaeda official, was killed by a drone strike in Afghanistan. Still, it was a year later before the Bush administration authorized drone strikes outside the Afghan combat theater. On November 4, 2002, one of the architects of the *USS Cole* bombing, Abdul al-Fatahani, was killed by a drone strike in Yemen.[20]

The strikes in Yemen presaged what would be a complicated relationship between the Yemeni and U.S. governments with respect to terrorism and drone strikes. As early as 2001, Yemen had given the U.S. government secret permission to track Al Qaeda terrorists in Yemen subject to a host of restrictions. Domestic political considerations made it difficult for Yemen's government to work with the United States, but it too had no love for Al Qaeda. The United States killed al-Fatahani with a drone strike, but the Yemeni government took credit for his death at the time.[21]

The United States also developed a similar covert agreement with Pakistan. The U.S. military had been pressing Pakistan for permission to hunt suspected Taliban and Al Qaeda terrorists fleeing to Pakistan with Predator drones, but they did not receive it until 2004. The United States received secret permission to fly drones over limited areas of Pakistani airspace and in return, the United States used a drone strike to kill Nek Muhammad, a Taliban sympathizer also wanted by the Pakistani government. Publicly, the Pakistani government received full credit, but behind the scenes, the United States was now able to fly drone missions over Pakistan.[22] While it was the Bush administration that secretly negotiated permissions to fly (armed) U.S. drones outside the theater of hostilities in Afghanistan in both Pakistan and Yemen, the Obama administration greatly expanded U.S. activities under these agreements.

Signature Strikes

Once Predator drones were armed, it became a question of whom they should target. The administration quickly drew up a "kill list" of senior Al Qaeda and Taliban officials and ultimately had a substantial amount of success in killing a considerable number of Al Qaeda leaders. One of the more attractive aspects of drones was their ability to neutralize key terrorist suspects when they were located in areas where capture was all but impossible.

Drone strikes worked so well that soon "high-value" targets became scarce. Drones were a useful and effective tool, so the administration looked for additional ways to use them. Strikes had been reserved for Al Qaeda and Taliban leadership but the universe of potential targets was about to expand.

One controversial practice that emerged in this expanded targeting effort was the "signature strike." Of all the legal issues surrounding drone strikes, the use of signature strikes was perhaps the most problematic due to the level of uncertainty about the identity of the targets. As a result, the margin for error was high. In 2008, CIA director Michael Hayden proposed signature strikes and President Bush approved their use.[23]

Signature strikes do not target known terrorists but rather individuals who meet a certain profile "based on a 'pattern of life' analysis—intelligence on their behavior suggesting that an individual is a militant."[24] In other words, if you looked like terrorists often look like and do things terrorists often do, then you are a potential target even if the military has no idea who you really are. While the exact combination of activities that might make one subject to this type of attack remains unclear, factors such as age, actions, and locations buttressed by intelligence indicators are all considered. Sometimes the United States even conducted "double-tap" strikes. After striking the initial targets, the government waited to see who came to their assistance and then targeted them as well.

Human rights groups and other critics have almost universally criticized this type of strike due to the exceptionally inexact ability to know if the persons killed are indeed terrorists. Despite these issues, President Obama continued to authorize the use of signature strikes to varying degrees throughout his presidency, and his national security officials continued to defend the practice as a necessary tool for fighting terrorists.

The Obama Administration

As a U.S. senator and presidential candidate, Barack Obama was highly critical of most Bush administration terrorism policies. Obama often accused the Bush administration of not pursuing Al Qaeda leadership aggressively enough, a pattern he vowed to change when elected president. While President Obama may have rejected the idea that the United States is involved in a "global war on terror," he certainly embraced the idea that the United States was in a continuing military conflict with Al Qaeda and its associated forces. It was not, he stated, ". . . a boundless 'global war on terror' but rather . . . a series of persistent, targeted efforts to dismantle specific networks of violent extremists."[25] This belief colored the president's thinking on U.S. drone use policy.

The Obama administration took existing Bush administration drone policies and expanded on them considerably. "Let's kill the people who are trying to kill us," Obama said upon taking office.[26] The administration proceeded to do just that. Rather than offering criticism (at least initially), many in Congress cheered the administration's expansion of the U.S. drone effort. Even congressional Democrats, who had been so critical of the Bush administration's terrorism policies, were largely silent on the drone issue, perhaps fearful of criticizing a new Democratic president.

When critics did eventually emerge, they assailed the administration from all sides. Some criticized the Obama administration for being too timid. The *New York Times* reported that during classified CIA briefings on the subject, members of Congress periodically expressed outrage that the administration *failed* to kill suspected terrorists (even on occasions where the individuals in question were American citizens).[27] In other words, many members of Congress wanted the administration to employ *more* drone strikes and kill *more* terrorists.

More critics emerged as the number of strikes expanded and the number of civilian casualties grew. Conservative critics such as John Bellinger, the architect of the Bush administration's drone policy, accused the Obama administration of expanding the drone program because it was easier to kill suspected terrorists than deal with the entire myriad of issues associated with their capture, interrogation, and detention.[28] Even some of the administration's own (former) officials ultimately became outspoken critics. Numerous nongovernmental organizations such as the American Civil Liberties Association, Human Rights Watch, and Human Rights First also publicly called on the Obama administration to display more transparency about the U.S. drone program.

One of the real ironies of the U.S. drone program under the Obama administration was the very refusal to officially acknowledge its existence until April 2012, almost three years after Obama had assumed the presidency.[29] This was despite the fact that U.S. drones were clearly engaged in dozens of strikes each year around the world. The timing and occasion for the public disclosure was also somewhat odd. President Obama was conducting an online technology discussion and broached the subject in response to a question about drones and civilian casualties. He replied, "Drones have not caused a huge number of civilian casualties" and assured his audience his administration was not conducting drone strikes "willy-nilly."[30]

A host of significant questions remained unanswered. It was ultimately revealed that both the CIA and the Department of Defense conducted drone strikes, though it was unclear who was being targeted, what criteria were being used to determine who should be targeted, and where the United States was conducting drone strikes.

Drone Strikes: Who and Where?

While the Bush administration was the first to use drone strikes in the WOT, it was the Obama administration that took their use to a higher level

Drones and Targeted Killing

in countries outside the theater of the Afghan conflict. Given the secrecy surrounding the U.S. drone program, even attempts to determine something as seemingly simple as the number of drone strikes conducted has proven highly complicated. Various nongovernmental organizations (NGO) and U.S. government estimates differ considerably.

One estimate puts the number of drone strikes in Pakistan since 9/11 at 408. President Bush authorized 48 drone strikes, while President Obama authorized 353 drone strikes. The number of strikes peaked at 122 in 2010 and has since steadily decreased to just three in 2016. Similarly, the Bush administration authorized only a single drone strike in Yemen, while President Obama authorized 183 strikes in that country. The number of strikes peaked at 57 in 2012.[31] In 2012, President Obama asserted the United States was not engaging in any armed drone operations in Iraq. The only use of drones in that country was in a surveillance capacity.[32]

Even though the number of drone strikes decreased significantly after 2012, the Obama administration continued to target suspected terrorists. This continued into his final year in office. In March 2016, a massive strike in Yemen killed over 200 people. The Pentagon asserted the target in question was an Al Qaeda Arabian Peninsula (AQAP) training camp. That same month a strike aimed at the al-Shabab network killed over 150 people in Somalia.[33]

As noted earlier, President Bush approved the creation of a CIA kill list to target people with drone strikes. This practice continued into the Obama administration, though President Obama was far more involved than his predecessor was. One source reported President Obama and Chief of Staff Rahm Emanuel followed the daily CIA briefings on drone activities "avidly" bordering on "obsessively."[34] The kill list continued into the Obama administration but President Obama personally approved every name on the list and over one-third of the actual strikes on those targets.[35]

When drones eliminated an individual on the kill list, another individual replaced him. As a result, the kill list continually replenished itself. To some, this was a dangerous expansion of the war. It was almost as if the list needed restocking in order to justify the drone program itself.[36]

The Obama administration always asserted drone attacks targeted senior, or high-level, terrorists. Some critics contend this is misleading because, while the United States has certainly eliminated a number of high-level terrorists with drone strikes, it has killed far more low-level "foot soldiers" and other militants as well.[37] What began during the Bush administration as a tool to pursue high-level terrorists gradually morphed into a tool used against an increasingly wide variety of suspected terrorists across the globe. When it became widely known U.S. citizens were also on the target list, congressional interest in drone strikes quickly spiked.

Drone Casualties

It is generally accepted in policy-making circles that the United States is on some type of war footing (against "terrorism," Al Qaeda, and/or the Islamic State of Iraq and the Levant [ISIL], etc.) so it is important to remember that accurately and transparently reporting casualties is a part of war. Only in this way can Congress and the American people legitimately assess the value of drone strikes as a part of U.S. terrorism policy. Unfortunately, the government has been less than transparent in this area, though this began to change during the last year of the Obama administration.

The number and identity of drone casualties in strikes outside the Afghan theater have been the source of a considerable amount of speculation and controversy. Much like the refusal of the Obama administration to publicly and officially admit that a U.S. drone program even existed, the administration also refused to acknowledge any civilian casualties as a result of strikes even as late as 2011. A number of nongovernmental organizations took it upon themselves to track casualties, but the fact that strikes often occur in remote locations and that identifying victims is difficult made the entire enterprise an inexact one.

Testifying before a Senate subcommittee, Peter Bergen, director of the National Security Studies Program of the New America Foundation, spoke to the issue in April 2013. His organization estimated that the total number of militants killed because of U.S. drone strikes ranged from 1,600 to 2,700, while the number of civilian deaths was 260–305. The combatant status of several hundred others was unknown. Bergen put the total U.S. drone strike casualty figure (through 2013) at somewhere between 2,000 and 3,300.[38] Bureau of Investigative Journalism author Chris Woods claimed that Congress never really wanted to delve too deeply into the discussion on drone strike casualties. In his book *Sudden Justice: America's Secret Drone Wars*, he asserts that since 2010 no congressional intelligence committee member or staffer had reached out to any academic body, NGO, or news organization for more detailed information on civilian casualties.[39]

At one point, Congress inserted language into legislation that would have mandated the Obama administration publish a yearly tally of civilian deaths but this was removed at the request of Director of National Intelligence (DNI) James Clapper who successfully argued revealing those numbers might divulge classified information.[40] On July 1, 2016, the Obama administration finally released the official government casualty counts from U.S. drone strikes from the outset of the Obama administration through December 2015. The government reported 473 total strikes, with the number of combatant death ranging between 2,372 and 2,581 and the number of total civilian casualties at 64–116. The White House also issued an Executive Order instructing the DNI to publicly issue a report (with unclassified data only) on

Drones and Targeted Killing

the number of strikes outside areas with active hostilities, the number of combat deaths, and the number of civilian deaths on a yearly basis going forward. The report is also supposed to address any differences in casualty figures between the government's estimates and those of interested NGOs or news media outlets.[41]

The civilian casualty estimates from the U.S. government's initial public accounting are significantly lower than those from numerous NGOs. Why the discrepancy? Many of the differences probably lie in the fact that different entities count casualties differently. At one point in time, critics accused the Obama administration of defining any military-age male killed as a combatant even without corroborating evidence.[42] The administration later denied it calculated combatant and civilians casualties in this way.

In the same memorandum that reported its casualty totals, the government opined that casualty counts could be different for several reasons. First, the government submitted it had information other agencies did not so it was possible that they were classifying individuals as innocent civilians when the government knew in truth that they were combatants. Second, the government argued the fact it did both pre and post-strike analyses to make their figures more accurate. Finally, it suggested many agencies have a stake in overreporting the number of civilian casualties in order to make the United States look bad.[43]

The memorandum also emphasized that the Obama administration went to considerable lengths in order to minimize civilian casualties. It said American forces received training to prevent targeting civilians. They also gathered exhaustive intelligence information to help ensure proper targeting and took all feasible precautions. When civilian deaths did occur, there were policies in place designed to review the incidents. The U.S. government acknowledged its responsibility when appropriate and offered apologies and/or financial compensation when necessary.[44] The United States maintains civilian casualties are a part of war—unavoidable collateral damage—while critics claim a sufficient lack of U.S. care in this area amounts to war crimes.

Congressional Oversight

In a May 23, 2013, speech, President Obama asserted, "I've insisted on strong [congressional] oversight" of the administration's drone initiatives. The administration, he added, briefs the appropriate congressional committees and members on every drone strike that occurs outside of Iraq and Afghanistan. In that same speech the president indicated he would be willing to review new oversight proposals even though he expressed some reservations about two of the more commonly mentioned ones: a special review court and an independent oversight board.[45]

It is not difficult to find critics of both Congress and the judiciary when it comes to policy making in the WOT, and this is true for drone policy as well. These critics often claim that Congress's role in the development, implementation, and oversight of U.S. drone policy has been "politically defensive in nature" and that it should be more active.[46] Others also question the quality of congressional oversight with some going so far as to suggest many members of Congress prefer to remain ignorant of the subject for reasons of self-interest. Broader scrutiny on the issue of drones is unlikely to come because there is no real widespread congressional demand for it.[47]

Consistent oversight of the Obama administration's drone program did not occur until 2010, though the administration was adamant it kept congressional leaders (e.g., the Senate Intelligence Committee chair and ranking member) informed of its drone operations from the first day of Obama's term in office. The CIA and the Defense Department gave select members monthly briefings outlining the number of strikes and the outcomes. Members even saw videos of drone strikes. All the information, of course, was classified (e.g., the number of strikes and casualties) so members were forbidden from taking and removing any notes or materials and unable to share what they had seen with anyone else.[48]

It eventually became public knowledge that both the Defense Department and the CIA conducted drone strikes during the Obama administration. This meant two different sets of congressional committees were responsible for congressional oversight. The Senate Select Committee on Intelligence and the House Permanent Select Committee on Intelligence monitor CIA activities. The creation of these committees was part of the reforms implemented in the wake of the Church Committee hearings in the 1970s. The purpose of these committees was to provide more robust congressional oversight over executive branch intelligence agencies. Defense Department activities—including any drone strike activities—were subject to congressional oversight from both the Senate and House Armed Services Committees. The fact that both the Defense Department and the CIA engaged in drone activities resulted in divided oversight as well, creating a number of problems. While numerous congressional committees and members were able to see some part of the government's drone program, very few saw the whole thing.

Toward the end of Obama's second term in office, there was an interest in moving the drone program that existed in the CIA to the Defense Department, giving it exclusive control over all drone activities. While this move received some support from the House and Senate Armed Services Committees, the CIA vigorously resisted it and aggressively courted its allies in Congress to help it retain its drone program. It did this in part by making its case to lawmakers that it did a better, more effective, job in this area than Defense.[49]

Drones and Targeted Killing

The move to transfer all drone programs to the Defense Department ultimately failed when wording appeared in the budget making that transfer all but impossible. The conclusion appeared to be that both Congress and the White House were largely satisfied with a status quo, allowing both the Defense Department and the CIA to operate drone programs. Some critics argued it did not matter which committee was doing the oversight since both were significantly lacking.[50]

Congress Takes an Interest in Drone Strikes

While members of Congress often showed ambivalence about the use of drones abroad against suspected terrorists, their use against Americans—and particularly against Americans within the United States—received a considerable amount of attention. This occurred even though strikes against suspected terrorists who are U.S. citizens constitute an extraordinarily tiny fraction of the number of overall drone strikes. In the spring of 2013, congressional interest came to a head during the nomination of John Brennan—one of the administration's architects of the drone program—as CIA director. Senators on the Senate Judiciary Committee asked Brennan a variety of tough questions about the Obama administration's drone program and Congress was ultimately able to force the administration to address a variety of drone-related issues.

Even senior congressional Democrats such as Senator Pat Leahy (D-VT) expressed reservations about the underlying (and at that time, unknown) legal justifications for the administration's drone operations.[51] During testimony at his confirmation hearing, Brennan argued the administration was as transparent at it could be when acknowledging information about civilian death totals. "In the rare instances in which civilians have been killed," he stated, the administration conducts reviews and families receive "condolence payments."[52]

Drones and Filibusters

Various congressional efforts to obtain more information on the administration's drone program finally boiled over on the Senate floor on March 6, 2013, as the full Senate was considering the nomination of John Brennan to the post of CIA director. Rand Paul, a Republican senator from Kentucky, launched a largely impromptu "talking" filibuster on the Senate floor. Senator Paul had repeatedly attempted without success to get the Obama administration to clarify its position on whether the administration could use drones to kill Americans on American soil.

He opened his filibuster at 11:47 A.M. on Wednesday afternoon with these remarks:

> I rise today to begin the filibuster of John Brennan's nomination for the CIA . . . I will speak until I can no longer speak. I will speak as long as it takes, until the alarm is sounded from coast to coast that our constitution is important, that your rights to trial by jury are precious, that no American should be killed by drone on American soil without first being charged with a crime, without first being found to be guilty by a court.[53]

Paul's filibuster would eventually last almost 13 hours. A small, yet interesting mix of senators supported his efforts. Future presidential candidates Ted Cruz (R-TX) and Marco Rubio (R-FL) and conservative Tea Party supporter Mike Lee (R-UT) were among those taking to the Senate floor in support of Paul. Some members in Republican leadership circles such as John Cornyn (R-TX) and Senate Minority Leader Mitch McConnell (R-KY) supported Paul as well. Only one Democrat, Ron Wyden (D-OR), openly supported Paul's effort.[54]

Not all senators were enamored with Paul's tactics. Republican Lindsey Graham (R-SC), both a harsh critic of the Obama administration and a supporter of the drone program, indicated Paul's filibuster had the opposite of its intended effect on him. He initially opposed Brennan's nomination but indicated, "I am going to vote for Brennan now because it's become a referendum on the drone program."[55] Senator John McCain (R-AZ), a powerful voice in the Senate on national security, was also sharply critical of Paul. On the House side, Intelligence Committee Chair Mike Rogers (R-MI) also criticized Paul's actions, calling them "irresponsible."[56]

When Senate Majority Leader Harry Reid (D-NV) arrived at the end of the workday on Wednesday in an attempt to move ahead with the Brennan nomination, Senator Paul responded he would only relinquish the Senate floor when President Obama (or his attorney general) issued a written statement that he would not kill Americans with drones in the United States. Ultimately, Paul did receive a written assurance from Attorney General Eric Holder that the "president did not have the authority to use a weaponized drone to kill an American not engaged in combat on American soil."[57] Senator Paul eventually yielded the Senate floor at 12:39 A.M. early Thursday morning. The Senate ultimately confirmed John Brennan by a 63–34 vote.

Shortly after Senator Paul's filibuster, President Obama stated: "I do not believe that it would be constitutional for the government to target and kill any U.S. citizen—with a drone or with a shotgun—without due process, nor should any president deploy armed drones over U.S. soil."[58] Left unsaid in these carefully chosen words were two important points. First, if due process is required to target Americans in the context of their being suspected terrorists what must that due process look like? Is the bar higher, lower, or similar to the type of due process that one would receive in the criminal justice system? It is possible, given the administration's position is that we are at war, military rather than criminal justice standards might apply. Second, just because a president *should* not deploy armed drones over U.S. soil does that mean he cannot?

The Obama administration ultimately released the requested memoranda on drone policy to Congress, but only to select members of Congress who could only look at the memos in private (initially without even staffers present) and could not make copies or take notes on the information they contained. Additionally, the memos only contained information on the administration's legal opinions regarding the targeting of Americans. Still unrevealed at this point were the administration's guidelines for targeting non-Americans.

Legal Defense

The Obama administration doggedly clung to the position all drone strikes have occurred in a manner wholly consistent with international and domestic law. In his May 13, 2013, address, President Obama asserted that the administration's drone program was both effective and legal. Unfortunately, it took years for the administration's legal justifications to become public so that the American people could assess them. Meanwhile, Congress and allies around the world were forced to piece together various bits of information that explained the administration's legal rationales leading many critics to conclude the legal justifications were either "unclear or heroically strained."[59]

Like most other anti-terror programs, the broad justifications offered for the U.S. drone program were simple ones. First, both the Bush and Obama administrations claimed the Authorization to Use Military Force (AUMF) granted the president the authority to prosecute the WOT without restrictions on the particular foes or the choice of weapon used to defeat them. Both administrations also claimed the president's Article II power as commander in chief also provided him with the power to use force (including drone strikes) to protect the United States. The target and choice of weapon were decisions for the president alone and not suitable for judicial review or congressional regulation.

One sticking point has been how the Obama administration justifies hitting targets in Pakistan and Yemen that are not clearly members of Al Qaeda. The AUMF limits the president's use of force to Al Qaeda, those who participated in (or facilitated) the 9/11 attacks, and "associated forces." The administration argued that even if these terrorist targets in other countries away from the battlefield were not members of Al Qaeda, they counted as "associated forces." One problem with this approach is that the Obama administration has never publicly released a list of groups considered "associated forces." Critics worry this term could become so malleable as to include any enemy the administration wanted to target.[60]

Another legal question that lacks clarity is whether U.S. drone strikes are legal under international law. In the international arena, the foundation for most U.S. military action since 9/11 rests on the argument that the United States is in an ongoing war with Al Qaeda and associated forces that are located at places all around the world. In this view, the United States is only using military force in self-defense. It is a position viewed skeptically in many corners of the world as the line between self-defense and offense has become blurry in some instances.[61]

An additional issue related to the U.S. self-defense argument is the question of whether the particular threats posed by those targeted in drone strikes are "imminent." For states to exercise force in self-defense there must be an imminent threat. Traditionally, this has come in the form of military forces arrayed on a border or something similar. However, terrorists can strike without warning at any time.

As a result, the U.S. government has conceptualized the concept of "imminence" more liberally in the context of terrorism. A Justice Department White Paper defended the legality of the drone program. It explained that an official could conclude that the concept of imminence is met and that a strike in self-defense is appropriate "where he [the individual being targeted] is an operational leader of al-Qa'ida or an associated force and is personally and continually involved in planning terrorist attacks against the United States."[62] It is important to note the Justice Department concluded that there does not need to be knowledge of a specific attack in the immediate future. Such a requirement, the opinion argued, was an unreasonably narrow way of thinking about self-defense against a threat like terrorism.[63]

Former State Department legal advisor Harold Koh addressed many of the Obama administration's drone critics on this matter in a March 2010 speech (somewhat ironically as it was years before the administration officially acknowledged that it was even using drones). Koh argued that because the United States was in an ongoing war with Al Qaeda and associated forces, these terrorist were legitimate military targets regardless of their location around the world. The fact that the United States chooses to use a drone to attack these terrorists is also largely irrelevant. The use of force in war needs to be proportional and limited to the nature of the threat. Drone strikes are both. In fact, Koh emphasized U.S. targeting procedures were "extremely robust."[64] The problem was that very few outside the administration knew what these procedures were. At best, only a handful of Congress members did.

Drone strikes also raise sovereignty issues. Sovereignty, the idea that a state has a territory and the right to control who enters—and even who flies over it—is a fundamental, and dearly held principle in international law. If the United States does not receive permission from a country, is it lawful to conduct a drone strike within that state? As noted earlier, the United States eventually secured tacit agreements with governments in Pakistan and Yemen to conduct drone strikes, even if these agreements were not public. The United States also continues to argue that drone strikes target individuals in remote areas that are often effectively beyond the state's military or governmental control and that this mitigates any infringements on a state's sovereignty.

Rumors circulated that Obama sought to "tighten up" the drone strike targeting protocol in anticipation of the 2012 presidential election. He wanted any potential successor to have a clear set of guidelines and boundaries.[65] Publicly, he stated that the "preference is always to detain, interrogate, and prosecute" suspected terrorists rather than kill them. Before any strike, there needed to be a "near-certainty" that no civilians would be killed or injured. Respect for the sovereignty of other nations, stated the president, was paramount, though he did not specifically indicate just how.[66]

The Joint Chiefs of Staff issued a January 2013 memorandum that gave some insight into how the targeting process works and what stages it entails. First, there is a vetting of any proposed target by an interagency group. Second, there is a process to determine whether the potential target meets military and legal requirements. Third, there needs to be a positive identification of the target by the military. Fourth, the government collects collateral damage estimates. Fifth, the individual is placed on a further targeting list and forwarded to the military component commander. Sixth, Joint Forces commanders must approve the target. If the individual in question is a "sensitive target," then the secretary of defense or the president himself must approve his inclusion.[67]

It is an exhaustive process, but it is worth noting that it takes place entirely within the executive branch and the military. There is no congressional or judicial review at any stage. This arrangement has caused critics to question whether—exhaustive as the process is—it contains sufficient checks to prevent targeting mistakes and civilian casualties even when carried out in good faith by the executive branch.

As noted earlier, the possibility that the U.S. government might target Americans with drones is an issue that has received considerable attention from Congress. As far as Congress (and public opinion) is concerned, it is apparently one thing to target foreign terrorist suspects in other countries with drone strikes and quite another to target Americans who might also be suspected terrorists. The former is fine. The latter questionable. This distinction is important despite the fact that the number of strikes directed against Americans is miniscule. The targeting of Americans introduces some additional constitutional and legal concerns that the Obama administration was finally forced to address publicly.

American citizens enjoy constitutional protections even if they are located abroad. They have the right to know the nature of any criminal charges against them and they receive a variety of procedural protections found in the Bill of Rights. Both the Bush and Obama administrations returned to "laws of war" justifications for arguing any constitutional protections U.S. citizens might enjoy in this context were either diminished or nonexistent in the face of the countervailing U.S. government interest in national security. If one commits an act of war or joins enemy forces (e.g., Al Qaeda), then one is an enemy regardless of one's citizenship. Any constitutional due process a citizen might be entitled to in this type of scenario was satisfied by executive branch determinations. Judicial and/or congressional review of targeting decisions in these instances was inappropriate.[68]

The Obama administration's legal team also noted the AUMF placed no citizenship restrictions on the enemy or against whom the president could use force. One additional concern the administration needed to address was the Executive Order banning assassination as a tool of statecraft. In short, America does not assassinate people. Is a drone strike on an American citizen abroad without any charges, trial, or formal judicial determination of guilt whatsoever tantamount to assassination? The administration concluded it was not. Assassinations refer to unlawful killings and the legal team concluded American citizens who were engaging in terrorist activities are enemies under the laws of war and therefore subject to reprisal, even the use of deadly force.[69]

The Justice Department White Paper did attempt to emphasize the precautions taken when targeting American citizens. Drone use against American citizens was an acceptable option when an "informed high-level official" determines that an individual poses an imminent threat to the United States, that capture is not feasible, and that the operation occurs in a manner consistent with both U.S. law and the laws of war.[70]

Returning to the basic principles of accountability and transparency, the important thing to note about the legal defense of the Obama administration's drone program is that it remained classified/secret, even from most members of Congress, for a considerable portion of Obama's presidency, even while U.S. drone strikes away from the battlefield numbered in the hundreds. As these legal justifications for the drone program have slowly emerged and become public, members of Congress, scholars, and human rights groups have roundly criticized them.

Taking It to Court

Federal courts have had an opportunity to consider a handful of cases with respect to U.S. drone policy and forced the Obama administration to

Drones and Targeted Killing

provide some information about its drone program. Despite this, transparency advocates have been largely disappointed, as the courts have generally sided with the Obama administration's desire to withhold drone-related information for national security reasons. These claims have been especially frustrating when the administration describes drone killings in public, yet in judicial proceedings makes claims all information related to the existence of a drone program is classified information the government cannot reveal.

In October 2011, the American Civil Liberties Union (ACLU) filed a Freedom of Information Act (FOIA) request asking the Obama administration for documents related to the targeted killing of an American citizen living abroad, Anwar al-Aulaqi. District court judge Rosemary Collyer initially held that the CIA was entitled to decline the request for national security reasons. In fact, the CIA's response was that it would neither affirm nor deny the existence of any records pertaining to drones and targeted killing. The ACLU argued unsuccessfully that CIA director Leon Panetta had made substantial public comments about the drone program and that this, in effect, constituted an admission such a program existed thus negating the CIA's ability to deny records might exist.[71]

On appeal, the Second Circuit partially overturned Judge Collyer's decision. It held that given the Obama administration's public disclosures, it "strains credulity" to imagine that the CIA has no interest in a drone program. It returned the case to the district court to determine if the *content* rather than the *existence* of drone-related materials merited exemption under FOIA.[72] When the district court had an opportunity to review the government's drone-related documents, it eventually determined that the CIA could properly withhold them from public scrutiny in the interest of national security, a decision later affirmed by the Second Circuit.[73]

In a similar case, the *New York Times* filed a FOIA request with the Obama administration requesting documents related to the legal justifications behind the government's decision that it was acceptable to target American citizens with drone strikes. Despite public disclosures about the existence of such a program, the district court found in favor of the government and allowed it to withhold those legal documents. However, Judge Colleen McMahon's frustration was palpable. She referred to her decision as "Alice-in-Wonderland" in nature. "I can find," she wrote, "no way around the thicket of laws and precedents that effectively allow the Executive Branch of our Government to proclaim as perfectly lawful certain actions that seem on their face incompatible with our Constitution and laws, while keeping the reasons for its conclusions secret."[74]

The *Times* won a partial victory on appeal to the Second Circuit. The Court held that the redacted Defense Department memorandum outlining the legal justifications for targeting Americans must be released as it was neither "logical" nor "plausible" to think that its disclosure would reveal any sensitive military or intelligence matters.[75] However, the Second Circuit did uphold the remainder of the government's requests to limit the disclosure of other drone-related documents.

Anwar Al-Aulaqi

Anwar al-Aulaqi was the first American citizen to be targeted and killed by an American drone strike. The U.S. government accused al-Aulaqi, who was living in Yemen, of being a senior-level member of Al Qaeda. He was a "specially designated global terrorist" and placed on the Obama administration's "kill list." Knowing his son was a target, al-Aulaqi's father filed suit in U.S. courts in an attempt to obtain an injunction that would prohibit the government from targeting his son in any future drone strikes. He argued that as an American citizen his son had the right to due process before the government used deadly force against him.

On December 7, 2010, district court judge John Bates ruled against al-Aulaqi's father on several initial points. First, he ruled, the father did not have standing in court to file such a suit. Anwar al-Aulaqi himself was perfectly able to come before the court and file such a suit himself if he desired. Second, the decision about whom to target with drone strikes is a political question—one best decided by the elected branches of government rather than the courts. It was therefore inappropriate for the court to rule on it.[76] The U.S. government did eventually kill Anwar al-Aulaqi will a Hellfire missile strike on September 30, 2011.

After his son's death, al-Aulaqi's father once again sought redress in U.S. courts, this time with a civil suit seeking damages for the death of his son. Once again, the district court dismissed Al-Aulaqi's case concluding there were no sufficient legal grounds on which to continue the suit. Judge Collyer noted the Obama administration made the case needlessly more difficult by its "truculent opposition" to allowing the court to review any documents related to the drone program. In fact, the government went as far at one point as to suggest that she try deciding the case first without viewing those documents.[77]

For those hoping to challenge the legality of the U.S. drone program or even discover more about the nature of it, the pattern is clear. The government has been vigilant about not divulging any information about the program, going to great lengths to deny its existence in the face of overwhelming evidence to the contrary. While these public disclosures have led some appellate courts to force the Obama administration to release some redacted materials, the administration has been largely successful in keeping the drone program's details from public view.

Issues and Reforms: Work to Be Done

Slowly, but surely, the nature and scope of the U.S. drone program is receiving public scrutiny. The Obama administration eventually took steps that have certainly increased the transparency of a program it refused to admit even existed only a few short years. Now that the issue is in the public sector, it is possible for the American people and their representatives in Congress to address some of the outstanding issues and questions that remain.

Targeted Killing—Does It Work?

In 2014, the Obama administration commissioned the Stimson Center, a nonpartisan policy research center, to review the U.S. drone program. The Stimson group examined a variety of questions about the use of drones, targeting policies, and the efficacy of drones more generally. Many of these questions are unresolved and could benefit from a public debate in Congress and by the American people. The Stimson study concluded that UAV use has never (to its knowledge) "been subjected to any rigorous strategic cost-benefit analysis as a counterterrorism tool."[78]

Asking whether targeted killing works seems like a deceptively simple question when it is possible to count the number of Taliban, Al Qaeda, and other terrorists killed with drone strikes. Surely dead terrorists equal success. A true assessment likely involves contemplating and balancing a more complicated set of criteria.

It is worth remembering government officials, both those in the White House and Congress who have supported the use of drone strikes for years, have a stake in touting their usefulness. They have reason to assume that strikes are effective rather than conduct an empirical analysis or have a lengthy public discussion over the matter that might result in a different conclusion.[79] However, if the U.S. government is going to use armed drones as a tool to fight terrorism, it is imperative to know if they are effective, both strategically and tactically.

Academic research offers a far more nuanced answer when it comes to analyzing the success of drones.[80] While there is no consensus on whether targeted killing (via either drones or other means) actually works, most studies seem to suggest either it has no net impact, or its effects are more negative than positive.[81]

Aside from the actual body count of terrorist leaders, perhaps the best way to measure the success of the U.S. drone campaign in the WOT is to listen to members of the targeted groups themselves. Letters seized from Osama bin Laden's compound during the U.S. raid that resulted in his death indicate how effective the U.S. drone campaign had been in disrupting his network's efforts.[82] Commanders were reluctant to meet in large groups. Many moved from house to house each night, never sleeping in the same place twice. The Predator drones seemed omnipresent.

Other reasons often given in support of targeted killing campaigns include their capacity to remove key leaders of terrorist networks and disrupt their activities. Targeted strikes are also simpler and easier than bringing in military (or paramilitary) forces to capture individuals. They also provide another option when a trial is not possible.

Targeted strikes are usually very popular in the court of public opinion.[83] Americans have consistently indicated support for drone strikes overseas against foreign terrorists. Since 2011, two out of three Americans polled are in favor of these attacks, support that extends across partisan lines. Still, there is also some evidence to suggest this support is slowly waning over time. Public opinion can be a double-edged sword. While public opinion often favors targeted killing, it can turn if the government makes targeting mistakes and innocent civilian lives are lost. Polls have also indicated Americans are concerned drone strikes may be killing innocent civilians.[84]

The Stimson Center's analysis of U.S. drone use concluded that an extensive use of drones runs the risk of encouraging the United States to engage militarily where it might not have before, given the relative ease and low cost drone strikes offer. Some critics argue that drone use has also "fueled a whack-a-mole approach to counterterrorism" where targeting is reactionary rather than strategic.[85] Opponents of targeted killing also argue it is simply a euphemism for assassination. It is an extrajudicial killing, something illegal under international law. They also argue it runs the risk of spawning revenge killing as groups retaliate for the loss of their leaders.

Targeted killing also has the potential to backfire if the leaders who replace those killed turn out to be worse than the original ones.[86] One of the advantages noted earlier also runs the risk of being a disadvantage too. Since targeted killing is often far simpler than capturing and detaining individuals, it provides a perverse incentive to kill rather than capture, depriving the targeting power of the intelligence that captured prisoners might provide.[87]

Any review of the U.S. drone program needs to occur at two levels. First, it should determine where a drone program fits (if indeed it does) into an overall strategic plan in fighting terrorism. If drone strikes create more terrorists than they kill, is it a strategically sound policy?

The second part of the review needs to be at a tactical level. Do drones accomplish what their advocates advertise? Are they useful—or necessary—tools to help us accomplish smaller, tactical goals such as killing suspected terrorists and disrupting their operations? It may be the United States has the capacity to launch hundreds of drone strikes but the advantages and disadvantages associated with drone strikes are optimized by striking fewer times.

Drones and Targeted Killing

Congress has the power to pass legislation requiring both a strategic and tactical analysis of targeted killing to determine if it is an effective tool in the fight against terrorism. Various elements of the executive branch would surely be a part of any review including the White House, the Defense Department, the CIA, the State Department, and others. Any review should provide Congress with information needed to make important decisions about what it can do to help in terms of legislation, budget authorizations, committee structure, and oversight.

Proliferation of Drone Technology Abroad

Another issue the U.S. government, and particularly Congress, must deal with is the proliferation of drone technology. The proliferation of drone technology makes it more difficult for the United States to control who has the ability to use drones and how other countries choose to employ them. The United States now has roughly 7,500 drones (of various types) and flies drone missions out of dozens of countries around the world.[88] At the outset of the WOT, the United States had fewer than 50 drones and it was the only country who had the capability to arm them.[89] That is no longer the case. Over 20 countries now have the capacity to deploy armed drones (and the number is growing).[90]

Policy makers need to be cognizant of this because for better or for worse the manner in which the United States has employed drones in the fight against terrorism has set an example for other countries. The lessons they may currently be taking from that fight may not necessarily be the ones that the United States wants.[91] The Stimson group report warned:

> From the perspective of many around the world, the United States currently appears to claim, in effect, the legal right to kill any person it determines is a member of al-Qaida or its associated forces, in any state on Earth, at any time, based on secret criteria and secret evidence, evaluated in a secret process by unknown and largely anonymous individuals—with no public disclosure of which organizations are considered "associated forces" (or how combat status is determined or how the United States defines "participation in hostilities"), no means for anyone outside that secret process to raise questions about the criteria or validity of the evidence, and no means for anyone outside that process to identify or remedy mistakes or abuses.[92]

Ignoring world public opinion on U.S. drone policy is no longer a viable option. Policy makers need to ask themselves how others around the world perceive U.S. policies.

The versatility of drones makes their proliferation particularly troubling. Drones have the capacity for military surveillance and internal surveillance of domestic insurgent groups. They may now be armed, and many have ranges of hundreds of miles. Even terrorist organizations might be able to use drones to deliver WMDs to targets in other countries.

Over 78 countries now have developed, or are now deploying, surveillance drones. Russia, China, Iran, Israel, Taiwan, and South Korea are already building their own drones.[93] Not only are an increasing number of countries beginning to build their own drones, the global export market for them is booming as well with Israel as the largest exporter of drone technology.[94] In 2010, General Atomics, the American company that manufactures the Reaper and Predator drones, received permission to sell unarmed Predators to Egypt, Morocco, the United Arab Emirates, Turkey, and Saudi Arabia. It can also sell armed ones to Italy.[95]

The Missile Technology Control Regime (MTCR) is a voluntary group of 34 countries that seeks to control the proliferation of ballistic missile technology and drones. The Wassenaar Arrangement is another international agreement (41 nation signatories) that seeks to limit the spread of munitions and technology that has both civilian and military uses. The United States is a member of the MTCR, but other countries that are not (e.g., China, Israel, and Russia) benefit economically over countries with self-imposed limits on drone technology.[96]

Another area that should require congressional attention is strengthening drone technology nonproliferation regimes, particularly for armed technology. Drone technology is spreading rapidly across the globe. This includes technology that enables countries to arm their drones. Much in the same way Congress and the executive branch have worked together in the past to prevent the spread of nuclear, chemical, and biological weapons, they should also find ways to curtail the spread of drone technologies, particularly those conducive to the development of armed drones.

In its last few months in office, the Obama administration took an initial step to expand nonproliferation efforts with the issuance of the Joint Declaration for the Export and Subsequent Use of Armed or Strike-Enabled Unmanned Aerial Vehicles, an agreement with more than 40 signatories. While supporters were encouraged by the deal, critics pointed out the limited nature of the agreement and noted that drone exporters such as Russia, China, and Israel were not signatories.[97] Congress should support these types of efforts going forward.

Congressional regulation may prove challenging because drone technology production is now a multibillion dollar business. It is producing jobs in someone's state or congressional district, and these companies are eager to expand their global market share. General Atomics (the creator of the Predator and the Reaper) has made sizable monetary contributions and aggressively lobbies members of Congress. Nevertheless, Congress will likely need to address the issue of controlling the export of drone technology in the coming years.

Domestic Drones

While the focus of this chapter is primarily how drones can fight terrorism, it is worth noting that drones are proliferating on the domestic front as well and that the federal government is facing a variety of challenges associated with this rapidly changing and expanding technology. Drones have been increasingly popular for personal use and hundreds of organizations around the country have permission to fly numerous varieties of drones. One writer estimates there may be over 30,000 drones in U.S. airspace within the next few decades.[98] Some of these regulatory areas tie in with the larger debate about drone use in the WOT while others are largely unrelated.

First, there is a burgeoning market for small drones in the private business sector. While only a few short years ago it might have sounded like a fantasy to have drones delivering packages, that day is coming sooner than many expected. An increasing number of companies are now producing a staggering variety of drones for both business and private use. For only a few hundred dollars, individuals can now own their own drones. Many of these drones now also come equipped with cameras, video, and Wi-Fi capabilities.

This proliferation of drones has raised a number of privacy concerns. Now just about anyone has the capacity to fly drones over places previously not viewable except by aircraft. This raises constitutional and legal issues if the drone operators are law enforcement agencies. While law enforcement agencies are beginning to experiment with a variety of uses for drones (e.g., surveillance, border patrol, search and rescue) their use by domestic government agencies remains controversial.

There have been some efforts in Congress to address these issues. In March 2013, experts told a Senate Judiciary Committee panel that current laws offer very little in the way of privacy or protection against drones.[99] While there have been some attempts to draft legislation (e.g., The Drone Aircraft Privacy and Transparency Act of 2013 or the Preserving Freedom from Unwarranted Surveillance Act of 2012), there remains a considerable amount of work needed in this area.

Most congressional efforts in this area have instead focused on safety, not privacy. Congress needs to attend to privacy issues lest states legislate on these matters in a piecemeal basis. Perhaps the most significant piece of legislation in this area has been the Federal Aviation Administration Modernization and Reform Act of 2012. Under this statute, the agency was to develop a set of guidelines designed to safely integrate drones into U.S. airspace.[100]

It remains unclear how well administrative rules keep pace with ever-changing drone technology.

In the absence of congressional legislation, it is increasingly likely that state and local governments will seek to regulate drone use in their skies. Some cities have already passed resolutions restricting drone use. In 2013, 43 states introduced almost a hundred bills designed to address drone use.[101] While only a handful of these bills passed, state action seems likely to increase unless Congress adopts comprehensive legislation in this area.

Finally, the proliferation of drones domestically raises the specter of terrorists using one within the borders of the United States as a delivery system or a weapon. Congress must keep all of these concerns and issues in consideration as it addresses the use of drones in the WOT as some of these issue are indeed interrelated.

Targeting and Transparency

The U.S. drone program has been lacking transparency since its inception, and it continues to be an issue that hampers its effective implementation. The Bush administration released virtually no information on this subject. During its final year, the Obama administration finally began to provide some details about the U.S. drone program including the number of strikes, the number of casualties, and targeting criteria.[102] Judicial decisions also forced the release (albeit in redacted form) of the administration's legal justifications for its targeting criteria, but large gaps remain. It is also important to note progress made in this area could change with a new president. Since most of the regulations in this area have occurred via Executive Order, a president can change them with the stroke of a pen. It is unclear how transparent the Trump administration will be when it comes to drone programs.

There are a variety of avenues open for congressional legislation on drone policy. Carefully drafted legislation can provide future administrations with the ability to use drones to respond to new challenges (and emergencies), while providing checks and safeguards for U.S. citizens who might become targets in the future. Not only will this improve national security, it will also enhance accountability and transparency.

One avenue is to revisit the AUMF. In 2013, President Obama said he looked forward to ultimately repealing the AUMF and forcefully stated he would not sign any law that would expand it.[103] Just about any revision of the AUMF would likely increase its clarity. With respect to drones, Congress could augment the AUMF to specifically allow presidents to target individuals and groups who pose terrorist threats that are separate and distinct from those posed by Al Qaeda and its associated forces. Congress could also simply amend the AUMF (or pass a separate law) prohibiting the targeted killing of American citizens.[104]

Some critics have forcefully argued that targeted killing is nothing more than government assassination by another name. It has long been the policy of the U.S. government to forbid assassination as a tool of statecraft, and while internal Office of Legal Counsel (OLC) memoranda have distinguished between assassination (which is prohibited) and targeted killing (which is allowed),[105] codifying this position with legislation has the potential to set this type of program on more solid legal standing.

A number of reporting provisions would also enhance the transparency of any future drone activities. These provisions can include the requirement that the executive branch provide Congress with a detailed report on the legal justifications for the drone program and targeting procedures. Administrations could be required to acknowledge strikes after the fact and provide Congress with information on the number of strikes, where strikes occurred, and the number of casualties. Presidents might also be required to notify Congress when they add individuals to the "kill list" and sign off on individual drone strikes personally.[106]

As the WOT continues, it is important to recognize the vital influence both international and domestic law have on terrorism policy. Congress has the power to put the U.S. drone program on stronger footing in both arenas by passing any number of statutory provisions. As noted earlier, these can range from relatively modest reporting requirements to an outright ban on targeting American citizens with drones. The public discussion surrounding the passage of such legislation would have the virtue of providing a transparent debate before the American people on this issue and provide accountability by putting legislators on record as being knowledgeable and supportive of a drone program.

There is also room for improvement in congressional oversight, but executive resistance is likely. Both the Bush and Obama administrations have regularly asserted that internal executive branch checks on terror programs are sufficient to ensure they are legal and used properly. Some scholars agree that concluding intra-agency review might provide sufficient checks.[107] Presidents are also reluctant to lose the flexibility that accompanies vague grants of power such as the AUMF. The executive branch legal establishment has also occasionally made legal arguments that congressional ability to control the executive's actions as he fights terrorism are minimal and that expanding them would be an encroachment on the president's constitutional prerogatives. As a result, any congressional efforts to pass legislation codifying a drone program and targeting criteria would need an overwhelming unity of congressional support, something that will be difficult to achieve for a variety of reasons.

A Role for the Judiciary?

Most observers agree that the judiciary has played a minor role in the debates surrounding drones and the WOT. The courts have reviewed only a handful of cases and for a variety of reasons they have yet to answer a number of important statutory and constitutional questions. It is therefore fair to ask what role the courts will have in this policy area moving forward. There are two ways to enhance the role of the judiciary in this area. The support of Congress is key in both areas. First, Congress could create some type of "drone court" to oversee policy in this area. Second, Congress could pass legislation that would provide greater support for courts to access and review classified information in national security cases involving drones.

Numerous scholars have advocated the creation of a "FISA-like" drone court although they often differ on the type of structure it might take.[108] Much in the same way the statutorily created FISA court serves as a watchdog on electronic surveillance in the fight against terrorists, a drone court could serve a similar function. Some prefer a court that would have the power to review drone strikes before they occur, adding an extra check in an attempt to make sure individuals are being properly targeted and that a drone strike is appropriate. Others favor a drone court that would have power to review strikes after the fact that, while not preventing mistakes, would at least serve as a forum when mistakes occur. It would also allow individuals to seek redress from the U.S. government.

In addition to the potential encroachment on executive foreign policy/war powers prerogatives, the creation of any type of drone court has the potential to create a number of serious problems. First, any drone court designed to engage in pre-strike review would have to be able to move quickly since opportunities to strike targets can emerge and disappear in a matter of hours. Is it feasible to expect that any type of court or judge could exercise meaningful judicial review in that short a period? Second, some argue that there is no precedent for involving courts in the decision-making process of who, when, and how to strike in military encounters. Presidents have always viewed these decisions as executive prerogatives. There is a question of whether involving the courts is sound, constitutional policy.

A related objection to involving the judiciary in drone policy and targeting decisions is the long-standing view that the judiciary is ill-suited to make foreign policy and war powers decisions, particularly ones that need to occur quickly. Finally, there is the question of whether these types of courts would review all drone strikes or just drone strikes against American citizens. These are tall hurdles, but they are not insurmountable.

Congress should explore these proposals, particularly in conjunction with other drone policy legislation. Some high-profile members such as Senators Dianne Feinstein (D-CA) and Pat Leahy have expressed interest in a drone court in the past. President Obama indicated a willingness to consider drone courts but he also expressed some worry that they would encroach on executive war powers prerogatives. As a result, many scholars conclude that neither Congress nor the executive is likely to strongly support the creation of any type of drone court.[109]

A second, more modest, approach would be for Congress to pass legislation designed to facilitate judicial access to classified national security information on a more reliable basis. While the judiciary has the power to conduct *in camera* review of classified or sensitive information, both the Bush and Obama administrations have frequently resisted releasing documents even for this limited type of review. Sometimes judges have pushed back and demanded documents, but at other times, they have not. As a result, judges occasionally face the difficulty of deciding cases without all pertinent information. Congress has the ability to supplement or amend laws such as the Classified Intelligence Procedures Act (CIPA) to give courts more reliable access to classified national security information. This will enhance transparency by allowing for litigation in national security cases to go forward while also protecting classified information.

The Trump Administration

In January 2017, Donald Trump became the third U.S. president to have armed drones at his disposal. As a presidential candidate, Donald Trump advocated an even more aggressive approach to targeting terrorists. He appalled many when, in a FOX News interview, he stated: "The other thing with the terrorists is you have to take out their families, when you get these terrorists, you have to take out their families. They care about their lives, don't kid yourself. When they say they don't care about their lives, you have to take out their families."[110] Whether the Trump administration actually adopts this type of radical expansion of the U.S. drone program remains uncertain.

The first drone strike under the new Trump administration occurred only four days after the president took office; it marked the return of a more active drone program, particularly in Afghanistan and Yemen. While the Trump administration appears to be following the Obama administration's framework for drone use, it has made some small, but significant changes.

Recall that one of the main issues regarding drones is their use away from the battlefield. The Obama administration, recognizing this, designed a process that required White House approval for drone strikes in all noncombat areas such as Yemen and Pakistan. One of the first things the Trump administration did in 2017 was to designate both Somalia and Yemen areas containing "active hostilities." This lowered the threshold for drone use in those countries and allowed military officials to engage in drone attacks without explicit prior White House authorization.[111]

The number of drone strikes conducted by the Trump administration in 2017 represents a significant increase from 2016, especially in Afghanistan and Yemen. In his final year in office, President Obama conducted 1,071 strikes in Afghanistan. The Trump administration more than doubled that figure, conducting over 2,600 strikes. A similar trend is evident in Yemen where the Trump administration more than tripled the number of drone strikes conducted by the Obama administration in 2016. The 32 drone strikes in Somalia in 2017 also represents more than the Obama administration conducted in that country during his entire term in office.[112]

The evidence clearly supports the conclusion that the Trump administration is increasing the drone use in the WOT. Like President Bush, President Trump has delegated most of the drone strike decision making to military commanders rather than centralize it at the White House, as was the case with President Obama. This reinvigorated approach to drone use in the WOT makes it even more imperative that Congress play an active role in monitoring and regulating U.S. drone use.

Conclusion

The development and the exponential increase in the use of drones by all U.S. administrations during the WOT is the latest reminder of the ways technology changes the ways we wage war. Drone strikes have killed hundreds of terrorists, yet their use remains controversial. Congress will play a central role in addressing many of these controversies.

From a military perspective, it is important for Congress to insist on a wide-ranging review in order to best assess the strategic and tactical value of drones. This includes developing long-term strategies to develop the weaponized drones of the future. Congress is the institution best positioned to monitor the development of these weapons. It can also provide the necessary resources while being vigilant to avoid the duplication of resources.

From a legal standpoint, Congress also has the power to supplement the existing legal regime currently governing drone usage. Like many of the other policy areas discussed in this book, the legal regime that governs drone use is the result of a hodgepodge of Executive Orders and other executive branch directives, some of which remain hidden from public view. Congressional legislation in this area—even modest legislation such as reporting strike and casualty data—can begin to provide some stability to a policy area which is currently subject to change each time a new presidential administration takes office. Even the ability to discuss and debate this type of legislation would have the virtue of allowing the American people to become more familiar with drone-related issues and provide them an opportunity to provide input on how the United States should utilize drone warfare going forward.

Slowly and grudgingly, presidents are revealing some details of government's drone programs. All administrations to date have resisted efforts to divulge drone-related material in the handful of judicial challenges in federal courts. Congressional oversight can improve so that members can ask meaningful questions about the number of strikes, casualties, and targeting procedures.

A sound legal foundation and strike/casualty reporting transparence could also result in increased accountability. Mistakes will happen and civilian casualties will occur. Rather than acknowledge them only when forced to do so by the media or NGOs, it is more useful to admit mistakes when they occur, figure out how/why they happened, and work to minimize them in the future. Drones will continue to be a part of the ongoing WOT and Congress will play a key role in maximizing their usefulness as a weapon against terrorists.

CHAPTER SIX

Making Policy for the Long War

The War on Terror (WOT) and the threat of terrorism are not going away anytime soon. The nature of the threat may shift—different groups and different countries—but the threat remains. The United States will continue to engage in electronic surveillance against suspected terrorists. Terrorists will be captured, detained, interrogated, and given military justice. Drones will be a part of the U.S. arsenal going forward. Recognizing that these will be ongoing issues is one of the first steps to addressing them effectively.

Policy making since 9/11 in many of the areas covered in this book has been primarily driven by executive unilateralism and often executive secrecy. The American people have been repeatedly told the WOT is a new kind of war. This new kind of war requires new kinds of policies, ones that provide more power and flexibility so the president can respond more quickly and agilely to the 21st-century terrorist threat. This rhetoric resonated with Americans in the wake of the 9/11 attacks. No one knew if more attacks were imminent, and the pressure to respond quickly was immense. But as the immediacy of the threat recedes, the argument that there is no time to have open policy discussions on national security issues loses some of its potency.

The 9/11 attacks were not an isolated incident but rather a single salvo in a much more extended conflict. The WOT is a Long War, and a Long War requires an approach that is best designed to address a protracted conflict, not respond to an individual incident no matter how devastating the impact. Presidential policies put in place right after 9/11 were perhaps defensible when the length and scope of the conflict was uncertain. Vulnerabilities existed and they needed immediate attention.

It is now clear the United States needs to develop policies that are designed to stand the test of a long-term conflict. To do this, Congress needs to play an active role in the design and implementation of WOT policies. Congress does not necessarily have to be the prime actor in WOT policy making, but its involvement increases both accountability and transparency, and this is a good thing.

Scholars, critics, and the public have focused on the president in the WOT and often ignored the activities of Congress. However, Congress has already been much more active in the WOT than many of its critics claim. The level of activity has varied across policy areas. In some instances, Congress did not act because the executive branch was keeping its activities almost wholly secret from Congress. It is difficult to act when one does not know what the executive branch is doing. For instance, many members of Congress expressed shock and dismay when they learned that the executive branch was interpreting parts of the Patriot Act in ways designed to facilitate the bulk collection of data. When the scope of these collection activities became public, Congress acted to restrict the National Security Agency's (NSA) ability to collect bulk data.

In other instances, Congress has acted and, to the dismay of some presidential critics, essentially ratified executive branch initiatives. The passage of the MCA of 2006 is a good example of this. After the Supreme Court struck down the Bush administration's initial military tribunal system, Congress passed another, essentially codifying what the administration was previously doing.

On other occasions, Congress has acted and opposed the president. The explicit ban on torture contained in the Detainee Treatment Act (DTA) was vigorously opposed by the Bush administration, but it was forced to back down when it became clear that Congress would override a presidential veto. President Obama's desire to close Guantanamo also ran headlong into fierce congressional resistance. Eight years after instructing his administration to close the base, it still remained open.

Historical Trends

It is often useful to examine historical trends when attempting to explain current activities and events. This can be done on two levels when looking at congressional action in the WOT. First, one can examine macro trends, how institutions such as the president, Congress, and the courts identify and articulate their war and foreign affairs powers and how they interact with each other in making WOT policies. Second, one can examine policy-specific areas (e.g., electronic surveillance) to see if the activities and interactions between political institutions in the WOT reflect historical patterns or whether new dynamics are at work.

A macro analysis of WOT policy making produces few surprises. As has been the case in war and foreign affairs matters since the Korean War, presidents have dominated the policy-making stage. Presidents have been the ones to take the initiative and develop policy, often via Executive Orders and

Making Policy for the Long War

sometimes via secretive means. Congress and the judiciary have played a largely responsive role, reining in exercises of presidential power periodically.[1] This offers an important piece of the puzzle for those critical of presidential power and supportive of a more active Congress. To the degree presidents have been at the center of the WOT and Congress at the periphery, this is just a continuation of larger trends in war and foreign affairs power that have been occurring over the past 50 years. There has been little or no shift in institutional dynamics at this macro level.

However, when it comes to policy making in specific WOT policy areas, there is some variation, areas where Congress has been more active than the macro dynamics might suggest. The preceding chapters demonstrate that the historical development of policy in these areas has not been the sole prerogative of the executive branch, regardless of what advocates of presidential power have argued. Congress has—more in some areas, less in others—always played some role in the development of terrorism policy. The institutional war powers discussion in Chapter 1 and the historical summaries in each subsequent chapter set the stage for post-9/11 policy design and implementation. While many observers threw up their hands in disbelief or confusion at certain congressional actions (or nonactions) after 9/11, history often offered insight.

In some instances, the historical patterns at this level hold true. This was particularly illustrated in the chapter on electronic surveillance. Presidents of both parties have historically engaged in secret, warrantless electronic surveillance prior to 9/11, and the track record of congressional oversight was poor. This pattern recurs not once but twice during the WOT with whistle-blowers in both the Bush and Obama administrations revealing extensive secret surveillance and data collection programs. Congress eventually responded in the form of the USA Freedom Act, but it was only prompted to do so after whistle-blowers made the programs public and the public was suitably outraged.

The chapter on interrogation and torture also revisits some historical themes. Recall that there have been military conflicts in the past where the U.S. government questioned the legitimacy of opposing forces. Whether they were called rebels or guerillas, they were viewed as combatants that did not play by the warfare rules of civilized society. As a result, they were accorded few protections under the law. The Bush administration in particular illustrated this practice in the months after 9/11 when it conducted legal inquiries into the status of Taliban and Al Qaeda fighters before ultimately concluding that they were not protected by the Geneva Conventions. This approach undoubtedly contributed to some of the harsh treatment detainees received at the hands of CIA and military interrogators.

The discussion on the use of armed drones offered a similar perspective on terrorists. Members of Congress generally applauded the use of drones to track down terrorists in foreign countries. They were terrorists who did not play by the civilized rules of war so they could be hunted anywhere and with any type of weapon at the American government's disposal. However, Congress became more attentive to the ground rules surrounding drone use when it became clear that the Obama administration reserved the right to use drone strikes against American citizens if necessary. It was one thing to use drones against terrorists in foreign countries. It was another to use them against American citizens or on American soil.

Putting government actions in historical context helps to explain numerous things that have occurred in the WOT. Looking at things in historical context also helps to identify trends and patterns at work. For example, if congressional oversight of electronic surveillance has consistently, and over a long period of time, proven inadequate to the task, perhaps it is time for Congress to insist on a new oversight system that differs in substance and scope. Looking at history can also reveal where true breaks, or novel situations, are occurring. If the problem is genuinely new or different then it might be unwise to address it with the same approaches that have been historically used.

Overcoming Challenges

Each of the substantive chapters in this book identified a variety of issues and reforms that Congress can or should tackle in the interest of making stable, transparent long-term policy in the Long War. Some are fairly simple. Others are more complex. Admittedly, some of these reforms are not likely to occur. This is sometimes due to larger institutional or partisan barriers. A number of these barriers were briefly outlined in Chapter 1. To what degree have barriers, which have been historically prevalent, been on display in the WOT?

Has Congress ceded policy-making responsibility to the president because its members believe that making war is primarily an executive function? All three presidents have made repeated used of the rhetoric that it is primarily the president's responsibility to protect the American people from another terrorist attack. Congress, the narrative goes, should simply give the president whatever tools he feels he needs and get out of the way. Some members of Congress have adopted this approach. Senate Majority Leader Trent Lott, when confronted with questions about the scope of executive branch surveillance, sided with "security first," opting to trust the president and worry about the details later.[2] On more than one occasion members of Congress realized that public opinion was behind the president and his policies. As a result, they opted not to fight him.[3]

In the days following 9/11, Congress did pass very executive-friendly legislation. This is consistent with the historical pattern where Congress gives

Making Policy for the Long War

presidents new power to deal with military threats. Unfortunately, these powers are often ill-defined in scope or duration (e.g., the Gulf of Tonkin Resolution). The Authorization for Use of Military Force (AUMF) has been routinely criticized as being a far too permissive and open-ended grant of power, yet in the wake of 9/11 Congress wanted to empower the president to do something to strike back at the terrorists. The Patriot Act is another example of legislation passed in the aftermath of 9/11 that gave the president new and expanded powers. In fact, a variety of provisions in the Patriot Act had not been enacted into law prior to 9/11 precisely because Congress objected to giving presidents that much power. Even though the act had numerous sunset provisions, it became very difficult for Congress to take these powers away once they were given to the president.

The preceding chapters also clearly demonstrate the hyper-partisanship that has enveloped Washington, D.C., has impacted policy making in the WOT. It used to be that disagreements about war and foreign policy "stopped at the water's edge." At that point, it was important to Americans to present a united front. While the Bush administration received overwhelming support following the 9/11 attacks, legislating in subsequent years often took a partisan turn. Attacks on presidential policies were often dismissed as partisan smears rather than attempts to have genuine debates on important WOT policies. Similarly, presidents and their partisans were not reluctant to paint opposing members of Congress as weak on terrorism when they opposed the president's policies.

The response to Abu Ghraib illustrates this. While there were surely genuine questions about whether higher-level officials propagated or implicitly condoned the type of atmosphere that fueled the abusive behavior, Democrats who attempted to raise these questions and assign responsibility were often accused of doing so for purely partisan reasons. By the same token, many Republicans reflexively defended their own rather than conduct any searching inquiries. Democrats were guilty of this at times as well. Many who castigated the Bush administration for any number of WOT-related activities were noticeably less vocal when it came to questioning the Obama administration's drone use and targeting policies.

Another barrier relates to the challenges associated with legislating. Both President Bush, and to a lesser extent President Obama, used the threat of a presidential veto to make sure that their war powers stayed intact. Presidential administrations jealously guarded against anything viewed as an expansion of congressional participation in the day-to-day prosecution of the WOT. This essentially meant that any legislation had to enjoy the support of a veto-proof majority, a feat difficult to achieve in this contemporary partisan environment. Even when Congress was unified enough to get legislation passed, the courts sometimes struck provisions down as unconstitutional.

Presidents have also enjoyed the "first-mover" advantage, though this might be largely attributed to the fact that a number of programs—surveillance, interrogation—were done almost completely out of sight of most members of Congress. By the time they became public, the executive branch almost invariably couched these programs as vital tools in the fight against terrorism. Any member who voted to take these tools away, Congress was told, would be significantly hampering the security of the United States and inviting another terrorist attack.

Finally, members of Congress are also accused of lacking the political will to take on the president when it comes to war powers questions. No member wants to be the one to vote against giving the president or the military an important tool in the fight against terrorism and then have the country be subject to another major terrorist attack. As a result, many members have erred on the side of caution giving both Republican and Democrat presidents funding and policy approval on a host of topics ranging from surveillance to drones.

While members of Congress have often claimed to be uninformed about executive branch policies regarding drones, interrogation, and surveillance, both the Bush and Obama administrations have emphatically asserted that they have kept congressional leaders informed of their actions. This has been an ongoing point of controversy as several congressional leaders said they were misled or under informed about the true nature of executive branch policies (e.g., interrogation techniques). However, some congressional critics argue that congressional leaders came out against these policies only when they became public and the weight of public opinion was against them.

For all the talk of things that Congress does not do, it is important to remember it still retains the power of the purse. Congress has been extraordinarily supportive of presidential requests for funding for both the military and homeland defense. As of 2014, Congress has authorized over a trillion of dollars for the conflicts in Afghanistan (686 billion) and Iraq (815 billion).[4] Billions more has been spent on everything from securing high-risk targets to increasing funding for intelligence agencies.

There are even a handful of important instances where Congress has used its power of the purse to impact policy. In early 2014, Congress significantly slashed funding in Afghanistan, expediting the withdrawal of American troops.[5] Congress also consistently and forcefully refused to authorize funding related to the detention facility at Guantanamo Bay. It refused funding for closure, prohibited the executive from taking money from elsewhere to pay for it, and refused to allow any money to be spent on bringing Guantanamo detainees to the mainland United States for any purpose. As a result, Guantanamo remains open despite attempts to close it for over a decade.

Policy-Making Principles in the War on Terror

Each chapter has demonstrated that Congress has been historically active—to some degree—in all these policy areas covered in this book. Given this, it is important to dispense with the narrative that the president alone is responsible for the security of the United States. Congress and the courts also have roles to play. This is not to deny that President Bush and President Obama have been the primary drivers of policy in the WOT, nor has this book been an attempt to deny that presidents will likely be the primary actors in the Long War going forward.

In the opening chapter, separation of powers was introduced as a hallmark of the American political system. The framers thought it particularly important to the functioning of a free and effective system of government. While war and foreign affairs powers questions may "bend" the traditional assumptions about institutional roles and responsibilities, they do not just wipe them away and replace them with a unilateral system where presidents wield all power in the name of protecting the American people. As the WOT continues through its second decade, it has become clearer that Congress should provide legislative guidelines in a variety of areas so policy is not driven by a series of ever-changing Executive Orders and other presidential directives that may vary with every new presidential administration.

The rhetoric about the WOT being new type of war definitely rings true in one important respect, several of the laws currently on the books that deal with issues such as electronic surveillance and drones are inadequate for a 21st century world. Somewhat ironically (and counter to the presidency-centered narrative just noted), this new type of war calls for Congress to update (or create) legislation in a variety of areas. Foreign Intelligence Surveillance Act (FISA) is a good example of this. FISA was created in the 1970s when physical wires were still the primary means of communication. Since then satellite communications, cellular phones, e-mail, text messages, and fiber optic cables have all increased the speed and diversity of communications. The executive branch's capacity to collect communications data has increased at a staggering rate as well. Congress has placed patch after patch on FISA, but the issues raised since 9/11 such as bulk data collection and tracking terrorist communications clearly call for new legislation in this area. Any future legislation in this area needs to consider the government's new-found ability to collect staggering amount of data and privacy concerns associated with this power.

A similar discussion needs to occur regarding drone policy. The ability to arm drones and use them to hunt down terrorists around the world is a new capability, one that the United States has used extensively, and one that other countries have also recently developed. Congress has the capacity to pass legislation outlining broad principles about drone use in the WOT, both internationally and domestically, where the number of drones in American skies has proliferated exponentially.

Again, this is not a call for Congress to micro-manage the details of fighting the WOT. Congress does, however, have both the right and the responsibility to set broad guidelines in the policy areas discussed in this book. It has shown the capacity to do that in the past and it should continue in this role going forward in the WOT.

All of the policies discussed in this book have been almost exclusively associated with the presidency, even ones where Congress has passed legislation. For the most part, presidents have accepted responsibility for these policies when they have been made public, but not always. But accountability needs to be more than just accepting responsibility when a secret program becomes public; it requires honesty about one's actions. Presidential accountability needs to extend beyond "we will protect you, but you do not need to know how we are doing that." One cannot be held accountable when no one knows what programs are in place.

Other actors also have roles to play when it comes to accountability. In the WOT, the media and whistle-blowers like Edward Snowden have invested considerable time and resources attempting to make secret government terrorism programs public. Sometimes this is accomplished by investigative reporting, which occurred when the Bush administration's TSP was ultimately made public by the *New York Times*.[6] In other instances, whistle-blowers like Edward Snowden illegally revealed classified information in hopes of informing the public about government programs and stimulating a debate about their proprietary.[7]

Members of Congress repeatedly expressed shock and surprise when the media and whistle-blowers revealed the nature and extent of executive branch WOT programs, but it is incumbent upon them to remain informed of government terrorism policies. If the executive is not sharing enough information with enough members of Congress to provide appropriate, vigorous oversight, then Congress has the power to insist that it does.[8] Only then can it make informed decisions and be responsible for U.S. government terrorism policies.

Having said this, the American people must, at some level, demand that their representatives take this approach. The threat of terrorism remains very much in peoples' minds. National security and "fighting terrorism" consistently rank near the top of issues that most concern the American people.[9] Not only do the American people think about the threat of terrorism, their views are, at times, somewhat hawkish. A 2014 Quinnipiac poll found 57 percent considered Edward Snowden a whistle-blower as opposed to a traitor, but almost half also supported bulk collection programs as necessary to fight terrorists even if they implicated privacy concerns.[10] In fact, a majority polled in 2016 feared that the government would not do *enough* to monitor the terrorist communications.[11] Similarly, a majority of Americans also believe that the detention facility at Guantanamo should remain open, a sentiment that has been consistent since 2010.[12] These types of polls, though just a sample, would seem to support the idea that the American people want their government to do more in the fight against terrorism.[13] This includes Congress, where people can openly track their government's actions on this front.

One of the most common refrains from critics of U.S. policies in the WOT revolves around the lack of transparency shown by the executive branch (both the Bush and Obama administrations). All of the challenges and problems associated with national security and transparency have been on display. There was a dogged core of Bush administration officials who rejected the idea that there should be *any* public discussion or debate on many WOT policies because even having a discussion about the subject (e.g., surveillance or interrogation) could compromise programs and provide valuable information to terrorists about how the United States is fighting the WOT.

This position was rejected by a larger group of public officials and the majority of the public at large, particularly when it was discovered that many of the programs and tactics the administration did not want to even mention were highly controversial in nature (e.g., waterboarding). Other, less extreme, but often successful tactics were routinely invoked by presidential administrations to maintain secrecy. The State Secrets Doctrine has been invoked on numerous occasions to prevent any type of judicial inquiries into controversial policies. Information is withheld and classified for national security reasons, preventing informed policy discussions. In many instances, information is shared with only a handful of members of Congress.

Congress has made some progress in the effort to encourage policy making in the WOT that is more transparent. For instance, the USA Freedom Act contains provisions that require the publication of previously secret FISA court opinions (subject to screening for classified information) that allows both Congress and the public to be informed about how these courts, their judges, and the executive branch are interpreting surveillance legislation. Public and congressional interest eventually pressured the Obama administration to issue an Executive Order requiring the executive branch to report a variety of information pertaining to drone strikes and casualties. All of this is information that helps foster informed discussions about terrorism policy going forward.

At this point in the discussion about transparency it is important to remember that just about all debates on issues discussed in this book are occurring with incomplete information. There are undoubtedly more classified programs and more classified information that could be added to the discussion about policy design and implementation in the WOT. This is unavoidable when it comes to national security matters since there is a considerable amount of information that is rightly classified.

The important thing to remember is that a balance must be struck. Classifying legitimate national security information is both vital and wholly appropriate. However, in recent years, both Republican and Democratic administrations have been routinely accused of overclassifying information in the name of national security.[14] It is one thing to classify appropriate national security information. It is another to classify information because it is embarrassing to the government or it would generate discussions the government would rather not have. Information is an indispensable part of the policy-making process, even national security policy, and it is important that Congress and the American people have as much information as is practicable so that informed decisions can be made.

Congress has the capacity to address many of these information issues. There are a variety of areas—many of which have been mentioned in earlier chapters—where Congress could insist on a more vigorous oversight process, one which provides more information, or one which provides information to a greater number of people (or both). Providing more information does not have to be an all or none proposition. Change can be thoughtful and incremental and can occur despite individual and institutional barriers members of Congress face.

Congress and the Trump Presidency

There have been both similarities and differences in the WOT policies promoted by the Bush and Obama administration. This is despite the differences in rhetoric and political party. The Obama administration expanded the Bush administration's use of armed drones and continued the bulk collection of data by the NSA. Each administration also eventually made (unsuccessful) efforts to close the detention facility at Guantanamo Bay. However, the Obama administration parted ways with the Bush administration's interrogation policies and somewhat scaled back the use of military tribunals. Where does the Trump administration fit into these patterns?

President Trump's policy preferences on WOT issues during his first year in office often appear to be primarily driven by two factors. The first is a desire to appear tough on terrorism. This perhaps explains his comments regarding bringing back waterboarding "and worse," and targeting not only suspected terrorists with drones, but their families as well. The second is to do the opposite of whatever President Obama did. This "anti-Obama" tendency has manifested itself in a variety of policy areas including the WOT. Examples include President Trump's desire to bring back harsher interrogation methods and keeping the Guantanamo detention facility open.

Making Policy for the Long War

It is somewhat difficult to tell how President Trumps WOT policies are similar to or different from his predecessors, particularly in areas such as electronic surveillance and interrogation policies. Rhetoric aside, there does not really appear to be substantial public changes in these two areas. President Trump has advocated the continued use of military tribunals but has not filed any new cases during this first year in office. He has articulated a desire to continue and perhaps even expand their use.

Finally, there is one area where the Trump administration has definitely produced some notable public changes, the use of armed drones. While the number of drone strikes greatly increased during the Obama administration, the number also significantly decreased during his last few years in office. President Trump has dramatically increased the number of drone strikes, particularly in Yemen and in Africa. This is clearly an area where President Trump sets himself apart from his predecessors.

Throughout the book, a number of possible reforms have been introduced. These are things Congress might do differently as the Long War continues. How might a Trump presidency influence the likelihood of these reforms coming to fruition? There appear to be a number of variables that cut in each direction.

For those hopeful that President Trump and Congress can work together to address many of the lingering issues in the WOT, there is the fact that Republicans control both the White House and Congress. Trump's campaign rhetoric suggests that he favors hawkish WOT policies and Republicans have, on the whole, been more sympathetic to this point of view. Both parties have historically shown an inclination to be supportive of and deferential to "their" president when he is in office, even if the policies he advocates are controversial ones.

On the other hand, there are warning signs that might indicate President Trump may have difficulty working with Congress on developing long-term WOT policies. Some presidential critics wonder if a president whose most publicized foreign affairs initiative was to build a wall between the United States and Mexico really has a strong interest in building long-term WOT policy. A year into his first term, no wall has been built. Upon taking office, President Trump also instituted a travel ban on immigrants from a handful of Muslim-majority countries, ostensibly to prevent any influx of terrorists.[15] This ban, often referred to as the "Muslim travel ban," was immediately challenged in federal court, which has greatly hampered its implementation. These setbacks are compounded by the fact that the Trump administration spent most of its political capital in its first year on domestic issues like repealing Obamacare and tax reform.

On a more personal level, President Trump showed a remarkable ability to publicly feud with just about anyone and everyone in Congress during his first year in office. This included Democrats and even influential foreign policy Republicans such as Lindsey Graham (R-SC), Bob Corker (R-TN), and John McCain (R-AZ). In fact, President Trump's ability to antagonize just about everyone has led some members to turn their focus to institutional prerogatives with an eye toward increasing congressional power vis-à-vis the president.

There has even been some discussion in Congress about revisiting the AUMF, an extraordinarily open-ended piece of legislation passed shortly after 9/11. At the time, the consensus was that something like this was needed to give the president the flexibility to get the perpetrators of 9/11 and prevent another terrorist attempt. Since then, it has been used as a justification for a host of presidential actions, many of which are not explicitly mentioned in the legislation.

On September 13, 2017, Senators Rand Paul (R-KY) and Tim Kaine (D-VA) fell short on an amendment that would have repealed the AUMF in six months (with the intent of replacing it with a more focused, limited one) by a vote of 61–36. A similar effort also failed in the House Representatives. Barbara Lee (D-CA), the only member of the House to vote against the original AUMF, teamed up with Republican Scott Taylor (R-VA) to get AUMF-rescinding language in an appropriations bill. House leadership stripped it out, with Speaker Ryan calling the effort "a mistake."[16] Still, the fact that these attempts are even taking place speaks volumes about the desire of many members to tighten control over the executive management of the WOT.

The Trump administration has also engaged in a number of controversial foreign policy initiatives during his first year in office that might impact his administration's ability to work with other nations in the international community on issues related to terrorism. This includes saber-rattling with North Korea, threats to withdraw from the Iran nuclear agreement, and the withdrawal from the Paris Climate Accords. All have put the United States at odds with many long-time Western allies.

Making Policy in the Long War

The WOT shows no signs of drawing to an end. It seems to continually morph with changing enemies, strategies, weapons, and battlefields. While many of the original players are gone, the struggle continues. The U.S. government has made some progress in defining the nature of the conflict, identifying the enemy, and articulating the ground rules of the conflict but more can be done.

This book has been an attempt to articulate both a need and a role for Congress as the Long War continues. Congress, as the people's representative body, has the capacity to provide both accountability and transparency. If the United States is going to decide it wants to engage in bulk data collection of electronic surveillance, or targeting terrorists in foreign countries with armed drone strikes then Congress has the capacity to formally indicate that this is what the American people desire. Yes, the president of the United States plays a key role in the defense of the American people, but he does not do it alone. Only by working together can our government institutions produce the best terrorism polices for America in the Long War.

Notes

Chapter 1: Introduction

1. See Griffin (2013), Wittes (2008), Carafano and Rosenzweig (2005).
2. Wittes (2008), 132.
3. Devins (2003), 1146.
4. Rudalevige (2005), 212.
5. Ibid.
6. Ibid., 15.
7. Ibid., 2.
8. Farrier (2010).
9. Wittes (2008), 132.
10. Ibid., 131–132.
11. See Rossiter (1960), Rossiter and Longaker (1976), Fisher (2004), and Adler (2006).
12. Yoo (2005).
13. The weight of the academic community disagrees with this interpretation of war powers in the U.S. system. See, e.g., Adler (2006), Fisher (2004), Pious (2007), Barron and Lederman (January 2008 and February 2008).
14. U.S. Constitution, Article II, Section 2, Clause 1.
15. Yoo (2005).
16. Fisher (2004 *Pres*).
17. Fisher (2004 *Pres*).
18. Yoo (2006).
19. U.S. Constitution, Article I, Section 8.
20. Adler (1996 *Judiciary*).
21. See Pious (2007).
22. *Talbot v. Seeman* (1801).
23. Henkin (1996), 50.
24. Rudalevige (2005).
25. Davidson, Oleszek, Lee, and Schickler (2015), 481.
26. Pious (2007).

27. Moe and Howell (1999).
28. Koh (1990).
29. Yoo (2006).
30. Fisher (2004).
31. Brandon (2005), 16.
32. Linfield (1990), Cronin and Genovese (2004), Fisher (2008), and Henkin (1990).
33. Schubert (1957), 315.
34. Henkin (1996), Koh (1990), Howell (2003), Fisher (2005), Rossiter and Longaker (1976), Scigliano (1971), Schubert (1957).
35. *Youngstown Sheet & Tube Co. v. Sawyer*, 343 U.S. 579 at 641–642 (1952), Justice Jackson concurring.
36. Moe and Howell (1999).
37. *U.S. v. Curtiss-Wright*, 299 U.S. 304 at 320 (1936).
38. Adler (1996 *Judiciary*), 16.
39. Adler and George (1996 *Constitution*), 44–45.
40. *Korematsu v. U.S.*, 323 U.S. 214 at 245 (1944), Justice Jackson concurring.
41. Fisher (2004).
42. Adler and George (1996 *Constitution*).
43. Howell (2003).
44. Koh (1990), 158.
45. Henkin (1996). Article I, Section 9 allows for the suspension of habeas corpus "when in Cases of Rebellion or Invasion the public Safety may require it."
46. See, e.g., *Hamdan v. Rumsfeld* (2006).
47. Corwin (1957), 171.
48. Whittington (2003), 2–3.
49. Wood (1969).
50. Hamilton et al. (1987), *Federalist #51*.
51. Ibid.
52. Wood (1969), 451.
53. Hamilton et al. (1987), *Federalist #37*.
54. Whittington (2003), 8.
55. Harriger (2003).
56. Yoo (2001).
57. Gordon (2014).
58. Colaresi (2014).
59. Tigar (2014), 138.
60. Gordon (2014), 37.
61. J. Baker (2007), 301.
62. Obama (2009 Trans).
63. Hood (2006), 5.
64. Gordon (2014), 46.
65. Schoenfeld (2010), 259.
66. Pallitto and Weaver (2007).
67. Kitrosser (2015).

Notes

68. Davidson et al. (2015).
69. Kitrosser (2015).
70. Colaresi (2014), 1.
71. Obama (2009 Trans).
72. Gordon (2014), 81.
73. Ely (1995), IX.

Chapter 2: Electronic Surveillance and National Security

1. Risen and Lichtblau (December 2005). It was also revealed that the *Times* had known about this program for over a year and refrained from reporting on it at the request of the Bush administration.
2. Greenwald (2014).
3. Smist (1994).
4. Hamilton et al. (1987).
5. *Olmstead v. U.S.* (1928).
6. Communications Act of 1934.
7. See *Nardone v. U.S.* (1937) and *Nardone v. U.S.* (1939).
8. Linfield (1990).
9. Goldstein (1978).
10. Pallitto and Weaver (2007).
11. Linfield (1990).
12. Ibid.
13. Schwarz and Huq (2007), 30.
14. Smist (1994), 5.
15. Ransom (1975), 38.
16. *Katz v. U.S.* (1967), fn 23.
17. *Camara v. Municipal Court* (1967).
18. *Keith* (1972), 316–318.
19. Ibid.
20. Ibid.
21. Fisher (2008).
22. L. Johnson (1985).
23. See Schwarz and Huq (2007), especially Chapters 1–3.
24. Funk (2007).
25. FISA (1978).
26. Electronic Privacy Information Center (2017).
27. Wittes (2008), 227.
28. Pallitto and Weaver (2007).
29. Setty (2015), 81.
30. L. Johnson (2012), 141.
31. Lowenthal (2015).
32. L. Johnson (2012), 128–130.
33. Ibid., 21.

34. OIG (2009). Perhaps somewhat ironically, the 9/11 Commission ultimately concluded that the intelligence failures prior to 9/11 were not a result of excessive legal constraints (Setty [2015]).
35. OIG (2009).
36. Ibid.
37. Ibid., 30.
38. Risen and Lichtblau (December 2005).
39. Gellman et al. (February 2006).
40. Hutcheson (December 2005).
41. Kuhnhenn (December 2005).
42. Hutcheson (December 2005).
43. Bush (December 2005).
44. Ibid.
45. Gonzales and Hayden (2005).
46. Bruff (2009).
47. OIG (2009).
48. Pincus (February 2006).
49. Kuhnhenn (December 2005).
50. Baker and Babington (December 2005).
51. K. Clark (2011).
52. Rockefeller (2003).
53. Lichtblau (February 2006).
54. Bruff (2009).
55. USDOJ (January 2006).
56. FISA (1978).
57. Schwarz and Huq (2007).
58. Gonzales and Hayden (2005).
59. Ibid.
60. Lichtblau (February 2006).
61. USDOJ (January 2006).
62. OIG (2009), 11 (quoting Yoo's 11/2/01 OLC memo).
63. Ibid.
64. USDOJ (January 2006).
65. AUMF (2001).
66. USDOJ (January 2006).
67. Hutcheson and Kuhnhenn (December 2005).
68. Lichtblau (February 2006).
69. Babington (February 2006).
70. Babington (March 2006).
71. Lichtblau (February 2006).
72. Sugiyama and Perry (2006).
73. Babington (May 2006).
74. Lichtblau and Shane (May 2006).
75. Nakashima (May 2007). The administration's position on this was that the very War on Terror and the threat of another terrorist attack were, in and of themselves, enough to qualify as "exigent circumstances" (see OIG 2009 Report).

Notes

76. Sugiyama and Perry (2006), 168–170.
77. Lichtblau and Johnston (January 2007).
78. Ibid.
79. Mazzetti (February 2007).
80. *Terkel v. AT&T* (2006).
81. *ACLU v. National Security Agency* (2006).
82. Ibid.
83. *ACLU v. National Security Agency* (2007).
84. *Al-Haramain Islamic Foundation, Inc. v. Bush* (2006).
85. Nakashima and Hsu (August 2007).
86. Hulse and Andrews (August 2007).
87. Warrick and Pincus (August 2007).
88. Eggen and Nakashima (February 2008) and Weisman and Eggen (February 2008).
89. Lichtblau (June 2008).
90. Lichtblau (July 2008).
91. Herman (2011).
92. Lichtblau (July 2008).
93. *In re NSA Telecommunications Records Litigation* (2009).
94. Lichtblau (June 2008).
95. Risen and Lichtblau (January 2009).
96. Lichtblau and Risen (April 2009).
97. Ibid. and Risen and Lichtblau (June 2009).
98. Solomon (March 2007).
99. Lichtblau and Risen (July 2009).
100. OIG Report (2009).
101. Johnson and Nakashima (July 2009).
102. Gellman et al. (2006).
103. Herman (2011).
104. Lichtblau and Risen (July 2009).
105. OIG Report (2009).
106. *Clapper v. Amnesty International* (2013).
107. Sorkin (2013).
108. Savage (May 2011).
109. Landau (2013), 54–55.
110. Greenwald (June 2013).
111. Szoldra (2016).
112. Ibid.
113. Verble (2014).
114. Ibid., 15.
115. Landau (2013), 54.
116. Ibid.
117. See *Smith v. Maryland* (1979).
118. Obama Administration White Paper (2013).
119. Lichtblau (July 2013).
120. Landau (2013).

121. Nakashima (June 2015).
122. Setty (2015).
123. Goldfarb (2015).
124. *Klayman v. Obama* (2013).
125. *ACLU v. Clapper* (2013).
126. *ACLU v. Clapper* (2015).
127. Amash (2013).
128. Roberts (October 2013).
129. Nakashima and O'Keefe (November 2014).
130. Jacobs and Siddiqui (May 2015).
131. Ibid.
132. Hattem (June 2015).
133. Lynch and Flint (June 2017).
134. USA Freedom Act (2015).
135. Lynch and Flint (June 2017).
136. USA Freedom Act (2015). Significantly, both of these requirements could be overridden by the DNI if carrying them out in a particular instance threatened the national security of the United States.
137. Nakashima (June 2015).
138. N. Allen (March 2017).
139. Nakashima, Barrett, and Entous (April 2017).
140. Haberman, Rosenberg, and Thrush (April 2017).
141. Buncombe (March 2017).
142. Sink (March 2017).
143. Buncombe (March 2017).
144. Buncombe (June 2017).
145. Ibid.
146. L. Johnson (2012).
147. Ibid., 129.
148. Wittes (2008).
149. Bush (December 2005).
150. Lynch and Flint (2017).
151. Divoll (2011).
152. L. Johnson (2012).
153. Lichtblau and Risen (April 2009).
154. See *Terkel v. AT&T* (2006).

Chapter 3: Interrogation and Torture

1. S. Taylor Jr. and Wittes (2009), 296. Quoting CIA chief of counterterrorism Cofer Black.
2. Clarke (2004), 24.
3. Cheney (2001).
4. Walquist (2009), 41–42.

Notes

5. Wright (2008), 52.
6. Obama EOs 13,491; 13,492; 13,493 (January 2009).
7. Convention against Torture [hereafter CAT], 1985.
8. Universal Declaration of Human Rights [hereafter UDHR] (1948).
9. Geneva Conventions (1949).
10. Ibid., Article III.
11. International Covenant on Civil and Political Rights [hereafter ICCPR] (1976).
12. Parry (2009).
13. CAT (1985).
14. Reservations to a treaty are a common part of international law and can be made by signatory countries. Often they are designed to clarify how a country will interpret particular treaty provisions.
15. Parry (2009).
16. *The Paquette Habana*, 175 U.S. 677 (1900).
17. Harbury (2005).
18. Parry (2009), 1020.
19. *Rhodes v. Chapman* (1981).
20. Federal Torture Statute, 18 U.S.C.
21. Otterman (2007).
22. USC Title 18, War Crimes Act of 1996.
23. Garcia (2009).
24. Carvin (2010).
25. Ibid.
26. Fisher (2008).
27. Carvin (2010), 43–44.
28. Ibid.
29. Ibid.
30. Ibid.
31. Ibid.
32. Otterman (2007).
33. Levi (2009).
34. CIA (1963).
35. Otterman (2007).
36. Ibid.
37. CIA (1983).
38. Otterman (2007), 94.
39. McCoy (2006).
40. Levi (2009).
41. Otterman (2007).
42. Innes (1998).
43. Parry (2009).
44. Parry and White (2002).
45. Parry (2009).
46. Parry and White (2002).

47. *Brown v. Mississippi* (1936).
48. *Ashcraft v. Tennessee* (1944), at 155.
49. *Rochin v. California* (1952), at 165–172.
50. *Culombe v. Connecticut* (1961).
51. Savage (2007), 144.
52. Sweeney (2007).
53. See Powell (2002) and Yoo (2002).
54. Bush (2002). Some administration critics viewed the phrase "consistent with military necessity" as an "escape hatch," which would allow the administration to abuse detainees if it was determined to be militarily necessary.
55. Bybee (2002).
56. Haynes (2002).
57. See, e.g., Marguilies (2006), Ratner and Ray (2004), Eggen and Smith (2004).
58. Lewis (2005) and Zernike (2005).
59. Johnson and Tate (2009).
60. Rudalevige (2005).
61. Q&A (2017).
62. Golden (2006).
63. Q&A (2017).
64. McCoy (2006).
65. Schwarz and Huq (2007).
66. Ibid.
67. McCoy (2006).
68. Lue (2005).
69. Priest (2005).
70. Otterman (2007).
71. Priest (2004).
72. "CIA Waterboarded" (2009).
73. CBS News (December 11–14, 2014).
74. "Dick Cheney" (2011). Note: The Obama administration disputed Cheney's assertion about waterboarding intelligence contributing to the bin Laden raid.
75. Fisher (2008).
76. Mayer (2005) and Leung (2004).
77. USDoJ (2006).
78. *Arar v. Ashcroft* (2006).
79. *Arar v. Ashcroft* (2008) and *Arar v. Ashcroft* (2009).
80. Democracy Now! (2007).
81. Eggen and Warrick (2007).
82. Global Security.org (n.d.).
83. McCoy (2006).
84. *Rumsfeld v. Padilla* [oral arguments], (2004).
85. Babington (2004).
86. Ibid.

87. Orin and Blomquist (2004).
88. R. Wright (2004).
89. McCoy (2006), 145 and Dionne (2004).
90. Alden and Davoudi (2004).
91. Simon and Shogren (2004).
92. R.J. Smith (2004).
93. Forsythe (2011), Appendix B.
94. Schlesinger (2005) and Mikolashek (2004).
95. U.S. Senate Committee on Armed Services (2008).
96. ICRC (2004).
97. McCoy (2006), 157.
98. Kane (2009).
99. Shane and Mazzetti (2009).
100. Kane (2009).
101. Kane and Warrick (2009).
102. Dewar and Morgan (2004) and Dewar (2004).
103. McCoy (2006).
104. N. Lewis (2004).
105. Mayer (2005).
106. McCain (2005).
107. Kane and Warrick (2009).
108. Kelley (2007).
109. Bush (2006).
110. Farley (2009).
111. Ibid.
112. S. Myers (2008).
113. Ibid.
114. Abramowitz et al. (2009).
115. Obama EO 13492 (January 2009).
116. Obama EO 13491 (January 2009).
117. Obama EO 13493 (January 2009).
118. Abramowitz et al. (2009).
119. Warrick (February 2009).
120. C. Johnson (2009).
121. Pincus (2009).
122. Crabtree (2009).
123. Serwer (2017).
124. Johnston and Savage (2009).
125. Wright (2017).
126. Barnes (2008).
127. Ibid.
128. *Ashcroft v. Iqbal* (2009).
129. Associated Press (2014).
130. *Padilla v. Yoo* (2009).

131. Rosenthal (2012).
132. *Padilla v. Yoo* (2012).
133. Mason and Rascoe (2016).
134. Finn and Kornblut (2011).
135. Obama (February 2016).
136. U.S. Senate Select Committee on Intelligence (2014).
137. Mazzetti and Weisman (2014).
138. Ibid.
139. Mazzetti et al. (2017).
140. Ackerman (December 2016).
141. Mazzetti et al. (2017).
142. Ibid.
143. Rosenberg (2016).
144. Serwer (2017).
145. Savage (2017).
146. White House (January 2017).
147. Serwer (2017).
148. NDAA (2016).
149. Serwer (2017).
150. Taylor and Wittes (2009). See also Heymann and Kayyem (2005).
151. Wittes (2008).

Chapter 4: Military Tribunals

1. Yoo (2006), 204.
2. See Ball (2007), Cole (2003), Fisher (2005), Paust (2007).
3. Fisher (2005 Military).
4. Hardaway et al. (2005).
5. Hollywood (2013), see fn 97.
6. Pious (2006).
7. Fisher (2004 "Military Tribunals").
8. Yoo (2006).
9. U.S. Constitution, Article I, Section 8.
10. Fisher (2004 *Presidential*).
11. Philbin (2001).
12. See, e.g., *Ex Parte Milligan* (1866) and *Ex Parte Quirin* (1942).
13. Fisher (2004 "Military Tribunals").
14. Ibid.
15. Glazier (2005).
16. Fisher (2004 "Military Tribunals").
17. Ibid.
18. Glazier (2005).
19. Ibid., 32–33.
20. Ibid.

Notes

21. Ibid.
22. Fisher (2004 "Military Tribunals").
23. Ibid.
24. Sweeney (2007).
25. Fisher (2004 "Military Tribunals").
26. Belknap (2002).
27. See *Ex Parte McCardle* (1868).
28. Fisher (2004 "Military Tribunals"), 24.
29. See, e.g., *Ex Parte White* (1944).
30. *Duncan v. Kahanamoku* (1945).
31. Fisher (2003).
32. *Ex Parte Quirin* (1942).
33. Fisher (2005 *Military Tribunals*).
34. Vagts (2007).
35. *Johnson v. Eisentrager* (1950).
36. Fisher (2004 "Military Tribunals").
37. *In Re Yamashita* (1946) and *Homma v. Patterson* (1946).
38. Quoted in Fisher (2004 "Military Tribunals"), 56.
39. Hardaway et al. (2005).
40. Uniform Code of Military Justice, 10 USC 836.
41. Glazier (2005).
42. Vagts (2007).
43. Fisher (2004 "Military Tribunals").
44. Hansen and Friedman (2012).
45. Bush (November 2001).
46. Lardner (November 2001).
47. Ibid.
48. Philbin (2001).
49. See Fisher (2008), Paust (2007), Katyal and Tribe (2002), Bruff (2009), and Yoo (2006), Hardaway et al. (2005).
50. Gellman and Becker (2007).
51. Pious (2006).
52. McCaul and Sievert (2011).
53. Yoo (2006).
54. Biskupic and Willing (November 2001).
55. Hardaway et al. (2005).
56. Fisher (2005 *Military Tribunals*), 170.
57. Biskupic and Willing (November 2001).
58. Yoo (2006).
59. Belknap (2002).
60. Katyal and Tribe (2002).
61. Port (December 2001).
62. Lewis (November 2001).
63. Lancaster (December 2001).

64. Biskupic and Willing (November 2001).
65. Lancaster and Schmidt (September 2001).
66. Lardner (November 2001).
67. Ashcroft (2001).
68. N. Lewis (November 2001).
69. Port (December 2001).
70. Lardner (November 2001).
71. Lancaster (December 2001).
72. Robinson (December 2001).
73. Lancaster (December 2001).
74. Fisher (2005 *Military Tribunals*).
75. Yoo (2006).
76. Ibid.
77. M. Davis (2007).
78. Pious (2006).
79. Fisher (2005 *Military Tribunals*).
80. Duncan (2004).
81. *Rasul v. Bush* (2004).
82. Yoo (2006).
83. CSRTs were devised by the Bush administration shortly after 9/11 and their purpose was to give detainees a hearing to determine whether they were "unlawful enemy combatants."
84. Detainee Treatment Act (2005).
85. Bush (DTA 2005).
86. Alexander (2006).
87. Rosenberg (October 2006).
88. U.S. Department of Defense (2007).
89. Hamdan's argument was that conspiracy was not recognized as a crime under the common law of war; therefore, it could not be tried by a military tribunal.
90. *Hamdan v. Rumsfeld* (2006). Chief Justice John Roberts recused himself as he had served on the D.C. Circuit panel whose decision the Supreme Court was reviewing.
91. Ibid., at 591.
92. Ibid.
93. Ibid., at 781.
94. Ibid.
95. Gellman and Becker (2007).
96. Zernike (July 2006).
97. Cloud and Stolberg (July 2006).
98. Bush (PC 9/6/06).
99. Zernike (July 2006).
100. Ibid.
101. J. Weisman (July 2006).

102. Cloud and Stolberg (July 2006). Many observers criticized this distinction, saying it was useless for all practical purposes since the administration defined "torture" so narrowly this would allow the vast majority of evidence to be admitted.
103. Greenberger (2007).
104. Zernike (September 2006).
105. Sherman (September 2007).
106. Greenberger (2007).
107. Gellman and Becker (2007).
108. Hansen and Friedman (2012), 22.
109. Tiron (November 2006).
110. Mazzetti (January 2007).
111. *Boumediene v. Bush* (2008).
112. Greenhouse (December 2007).
113. Zernike (June 2008).
114. Finn (May 2009).
115. Shear and Finn (May 2009).
116. Ibid.
117. Obama (January 2009).
118. Savage (May 2012).
119. Finn (May 2009).
120. Wolf and Hall (May 2009).
121. Finn (October 2009).
122. Richey (October 2009).
123. Hollywood (2013).
124. Frieden and Kokenes (November 2009).
125. Perine and Epstein (December 2009).
126. Markon (July 2010).
127. Savage (April 2011).
128. Richey (April 2011) and Phillip (April 2011).
129. Savage (May 2012).
130. Richey (April 2011).
131. Phillip (April 2011).
132. Hollywood (2013), fn 326.
133. Obama (December 2011).
134. DoD OMC (2017).
135. Walters (September 2017).
136. *Al-Bahlul v. United States* (2014).
137. DoD OMC (2017).
138. Canadian Press (December 2013).
139. *Al-Bahlul v. United States* (2014).
140. Savage (June 2015).
141. Savage (October 2016).
142. DoD OMC (2017).

143. Joscelyn (December 2015).
144. Center on National Security (2013).
145. Weiser (November 2010).
146. Savage (August 2016).
147. Ibid.
148. Savage and Goldman (July 2017).
149. Ibid.
150. Hollywood (2013).

Chapter 5: Drones and Targeted Killing

1. Gusterson (2016).
2. Maass (2015). For a good discussion on the history of drones and drone technology, see Wagner (1982) or Newcome (2004).
3. Jarnot (2012).
4. Newcome (2004).
5. Ibid.
6. Shaw (2016).
7. Newcome (2004).
8. Gertler (2016).
9. Jarnot (2012).
10. Ruane (1995).
11. Newcome (2004), 1.
12. Michel (2013).
13. Gertler (2012).
14. Michel (2013).
15. Gertler (2012), 9.
16. Newcome (2004).
17. Woodward (2002), 223.
18. Risen and Johnston (2002).
19. Ibid.
20. Kaag and Kreps (2014).
21. Woodward (2002).
22. Mazzetti (April 2013).
23. Gusterson (2016).
24. Greenwald (April 2013).
25. Obama (May 2013).
26. Shane (April 2015).
27. Mazzetti and Apuzzo (April 2015).
28. Roberts (May 2013).
29. Flaherty (2015).
30. Jackson (January 2012).
31. The New America Foundation (2016). These totals reflect the numbers as of December 19, 2017.

32. Jackson (January 2012).
33. Ackerman (March 2016).
34. Klaidman (2012).
35. Lightle (2014).
36. Maass (2015).
37. Greenwald (April 2013).
38. Bergen (2013).
39. Woods (2015), 204.
40. Ibid.
41. ODNI (July 2016).
42. Becker and Shane (May 2012).
43. ODNI (July 2016).
44. Ibid.
45. Obama (May 2013).
46. Anderson (2009), 349.
47. Kaag and Kreps (2014).
48. Mazzetti and Apuzzo (April 2015).
49. Ibid.
50. Woods (2015).
51. Judicial Committee (April 2013).
52. Zakaria (February 2013).
53. Wolf (March 2013).
54. O'Keefe and Blake (March 2013).
55. Finn and Blake (March 2013).
56. Ewing (March 2013).
57. Finn and Blake (March 2013).
58. Obama (May 2013).
59. Flaherty (2015).
60. See Vladeck (2014).
61. Anderson (2009).
62. DoJ White Paper (2011), 8.
63. Ibid.
64. Koh (2010).
65. Savage (2015).
66. Obama (May 2013).
67. Joint Chiefs (2013).
68. DoJ White Paper (2011). Courts have yet to rule on this specific question.
69. Ibid.
70. Ibid.
71. *ACLU v. DoJ* (2011).
72. *ACLU v. DoJ* (2013).
73. *ACLU v. DoJ* (2015) and *ACLU v. DoJ* (2016).
74. *NYT v. DoJ* (2014; 758 F.3d), at 515–16.
75. Ibid., at 141.

76. *Al-Aulaqi v. Obama* (2010).
77. *Al-Aulaqi v. Panetta* (2014).
78. The Stimson Group (2014), 11.
79. Carvin (2012).
80. Anderson (2009) notes that the academic community is almost "entirely hostile" to the idea of targeted killing.
81. Carvin (2012)—Cronin (2009) and Hafez and Hattfield (2006) conclude that targeted killing has neither a net positive or negative effect, while Jordan (2009) and Mannes (2008) note that its net effects are negative.
82. Hayden (February 16).
83. Carvin (2012).
84. Plaw et al. (2016).
85. The Stimson Group (2014).
86. Carvin (2012).
87. Anderson (2009).
88. Bergen (2013) and Maass (2015).
89. Bergen (2013).
90. *Toronto Star* (March 2016).
91. Zenko and Kreps (2015).
92. The Stimson Group (2014), 13.
93. Zenko and Kreps (2015).
94. Bergen (2013) and *Toronto Star* (March 2016).
95. Bergen (2013).
96. Kaag and Kreps (2014).
97. Mehta (2016).
98. Black (2013).
99. Wald (March 2013).
100. Black (2013).
101. Black (2013) and Brumfield (2014).
102. Obama EO (2016).
103. Obama (May 2013).
104. McKelvey (2011).
105. U.S. DoJ (November 2011).
106. The Stimson Group (2014) and Gonzales (2013).
107. Radsan and Murphy (2012).
108. Flaherty (2015) and Vladeck (2014).
109. Kaag and Kreps (2014).
110. LoBianco (2015).
111. The Bureau of Investigative Journalism (2017).
112. Ibid.

Chapter 6: Making Policy for the Long War

1. See, e.g., *Hamdan v. Rumsfeld* (2006) and the USA Freedom Act (2015).
2. Hutcheson (December 2005).

Notes

3. Lancaster (December 2001).
4. Belasco (2014).
5. Londono and DeYoung (January 2014).
6. Risen and Lichtblau (December 2005).
7. Greenwald (2014).
8. Divoll (2011).
9. CNN Poll (October 12–15, 2017).
10. Quinnipiac (January 4–7, 2014).
11. NBC News/*Wall Street Journal* Poll (June 19–23, 2016).
12. CNN/ORC Poll (February 24–27, 2016).
13. Monmouth University Poll (September 22–25, 2016).
14. Lowenthal (2015).
15. *State of Washington v. Trump* (2017).
16. Stolberg (September 2017).

Bibliography

Abramowitz, Michael, Joby Warrick, and Walter Pincus. 2009. "Obama under Pressure on Interrogation Policy." *The Washington Post* (January 10), A1.

Ackerman, Spencer. 2016. "Massive U.S. Airstrike in Yemen Kills 'Dozens' of People, Pentagon Says." *The Guardian* (March 22). Available at: https://www.theguardian.com/world/2016/mar/22/us-airstrike-yemen-dozens-dead-al-qaida-terrorism-training-camp. Last accessed May 11, 2018.

Ackerman, Spencer. 2016. "Senate Torture Report to Be Kept from Public for 12 Years after Obama Decision." *The Guardian* (December 12). Available at: https://www.theguardian.com/us-news/2016/dec/12/obama-senate-cia-torture-report-september-11-classified. Last accessed May 11, 2018.

Adler, David G. and Larry N. George. 1996. *The Constitution and the Conduct of American Foreign Policy.* Lawrence: University of Kansas Press.

Adler, David Gray. 2006. "George Bush as Commander in Chief: Toward the Nether World of Constitutionalism." *Presidential Studies Quarterly* 36:3 (September), 525–540.

Adler, David Gray. 1996. "The Judiciary and Presidential Power in Foreign Affairs: A Critique." *Richmond Journal of Law and Public Interest* 1:1 (Fall), 1–38.

Alden, Edward and Salamander Davoudi. 2004. "Rumsfeld Broadens Inquiry into Abuse of Prisoners." *The Financial Times* (May 5), the Americas 8.

Alexander, Janet. 2006. "Jurisdiction-Stripping in the War on Terrorism." *Stanford Journal of Civil Rights & Civil Liberties* 2 (August), 259–294.

Allen, Nick. 2017. " 'This Is McCarthyism!' Donald Trump Claims Barack Obama Had His 'Wires Tapped' at Trump Tower before He Was Elected." *The Telegraph* (March 4). Available at: https://www.telegraph.co.uk/news/2017/03/04/donald-trump-accuses-barack-obama-tapping-phones-trump-tower/. Last accessed May 11, 2018.

Amash, Justin. 2013. "Amash NSA Amendment Fact Sheet—Congressman Justin Amash." (July 24). Available at: Amash.house.gov. Last accessed August 9, 2017.

Anderson, Kenneth. 2009. "Targeted Killing in U.S. Counterterrorism Strategy and Law." In *Legislating the War on Terror*, Benjamin Wittes (ed.), 346–400. Washington, DC: Brookings Institute Press.

Ashcroft, John. 2001. "Department of Justice Oversight: Preserving Our Freedoms While Defending against Terrorism." Testimony before the United States Senate, Committee on the Judiciary. 107th Congress, 1st sess. 21.

Associated Press. 2014. "Terrorism Plotter Jose Padilla Has Prison Sentence Extended." (September 9).

Authorization for Use of Military Force. 2001. Public Law 107–40. 107th Congress (September 18).

Babington, Charles. 2006. "Activists on Right, GOP Lawmakers Divided on Spying." *The Washington Post* (February 7), A4.

Babington, Charles. 2006. "Feingold Pushes to Censure President." *The Washington Post* (March 14), A8.

Babington, Charles. 2006. "Lawmakers Call for Hearings; Report May Complicate Hayden Confirmation at CIA." *The Washington Post* (May 12), A4.

Babington, Charles. 2004. "Lawmakers Are Stunned by New Images of Abuse." *The Washington Post* (May 13), A1.

Baker, James E. 2007. *In the Common Defense: National Security Law for Perilous Times*. Cambridge: Cambridge University Press.

Baker, Peter and Charles Babington. 2005. "Bush Addresses Uproar over Spying." *The Washington Post* (December 20), A1.

Ball, Howard. 2007. *Bush, the Detainees, and the Constitution: The Battle over Presidential Power in the War on Terror*. Lawrence: University of Kansas Press.

Barnes, Robert. 2008. "Supreme Court Weighs U.S. Officials' Liability in Post-9/11 Detentions." *The Washington Post* (December 11). Available at: http://www.washingtonpost.com/wp-dyn/content/article/2008/12/10/AR2008121003221.html. Last accessed January 9, 2018.

Barron, David and Martin S. Lederman. 2008. "The Commander in Chief at the Lowest Ebb—A Constitutional History." *Harvard Law Review* 121:4 (February), 944–1011.

Barron, David and Martin S. Lederman. 2008. "The Commander in Chief at the Lowest Ebb—Framing the Problem, Doctrine, and Original Understanding." *Harvard Law Review* 121:3 (January), 692–804.

Becker, Jo and Scott Shane. 2012. "Secret 'Kill List' Proves a Test of Obama's Principles and Will." *The New York Times* (May 29), A1.

Belasco, Amy. 2014. "The Cost of Iraq, Afghanistan, and Other Global War on Terror Operations since 9/11." A Congressional Research Service Report for Congress (December 8).

Belknap, Michal R. 2002. "A Putrid Pedigree: The Bush Administration's Military Tribunals in Historical Perspective." *California Western Law Review* 38 (Spring), 433–480.

Bibliography

Bergen, Peter. 2013. *Drone Wars: The Constitutional and Counterterrorism Implications of Targeted Killing.* Testimony before the United States Senate Committee on the Judiciary, Subcommittee on the Constitution, Civil Rights, and Human Rights (April 23).

Biskupic, Joan and Richard Willing. 2001. "Military Tribunals: Swift Judgments in Dire Times." *The USA Today* (November 15), A1.

Black, J. Tyler. 2013. "Over Your Head, Under the Radar: An Examination of Changing Legislation, Aging Case Law, and Possible Solutions to the Domestic Police Drone Puzzle." *Washington & Lee Law Review* 19 (Summer), 1829–1885.

Brandon, Mark E. 2005. "War and the American Constitutional Order." In *The Constitution in Wartime*, Mark Tushnet (ed.), 11–38. Durham, NC: Duke University Press.

Bruff, Harold H. 2009. *Bad Advice: Bush's Lawyers in the War on Terror.* Lawrence: University of Kansas Press.

Brumfield, Eric. 2014. "Armed Drones for Law Enforcement: Why It Might Be Time to Re-Examine the Current Use of Force Standard." *McGeorge Law Review* 46, 543–572.

Buncombe, Andrew. 2017. "Donald Trump Admits He Has No Tapes of Conversations with James Comey." *The Independent* (June 22).

Buncombe, Andrew. 2017. "Donald Trump Wiretapping Claims: House Intelligence Committee Says It Does Not Have 'Any Evidence.'" *The Independent* (March 15).

The Bureau of Investigative Journalism. 2017. "U.S. Counter Terror Air Strikes Double in Trump's First Year." Available at: https://www.thebureauinvestigates.com/. Last accessed January 4, 2018.

Bush, George W. 2001. "Detention, Treatment, and Trial of Certain Non-Citizens in the War against Terrorism." *Federal Register* 66:222 (November 13), 57833–57836.

Bush, George W. 2002. "Humane Treatment of al Qaeda and Taliban Detainees." Memo 11 in *The Torture Papers* (February 7), Karen Greenberg and Joshua Dratel (eds.), 134–135. Cambridge: Cambridge University Press.

Bush, George W. 2005. President's Statement on the Signing of H.R. 2863, the Department of Defense, Emergency Supplemental Appropriations to Address Hurricanes in the Gulf of Mexico, and Pandemic Influence Act, 2006 (December 30).

Bush, George W. 2006. "President Discusses Creation of Military Commissions to Try Suspected Terrorists." *Presidential Press Conference* (September 6).

"Bush: U.S. Must Think, Act Differently." 2005. Transcript of Presidential Press Conference (December 19). Available at: http://cnn.com/2005/POLITICS/12/19/bush.transcript/index.html. Accessed January 4, 2018.

Bybee, Jay. 2002. "Standards of Conduct for Interrogation under 18 U.S.C. Setion 2340-2340A." Memo 14 in *The Torture Papers* (August 1), Karen

Greenberg and Joshua Dratel (eds.), 172–217. Cambridge: Cambridge University Press.
Canadian Press. 2013. "Omar Khadr Explains War-Crimes Guilty Pleas in Court Filing" (December 13). Available at: http://www.cbc.ca/news/canada/omar-khadr-explains-war-crimes-guilty-pleas-in-court-filing-1.2463558. Last accessed January 4, 2018.
Carafano, James Jay and Paul Rosenzweig. 2005. *Winning the Long War: Lessons from the Cold War for Defeating Terrorism and Preserving Freedom.* Washington, DC: Heritage Books.
Carvin, Stephanie. 2010. *Prisoners of America's Wars.* New York: Columbia University Press.
Carvin, Stephanie. 2012. "The Trouble with Targeted Killing." *Security Studies* 21, 529–555.
CBS News. 2014. Survey on Torture Attitudes (December 11–14).
Center on National Security. 2013. "U.S. Prosecutions of Jihadist Terror Crimes, 2001–2013." Available at: https://static1.squarespace.com/static/55dc76f7e4b013c872183fea/t/56b88ef1356fb0ff251aa15a/1454935794120/JihadistFactSheet2001-13.pdf. Last accessed January 4, 2018.
Central Intelligence Agency. 1963. *KUBARK, Counterintelligence Interrogation* (July). Available at: https://nsarchive2.gwu.edu//NSAEBB/NSAEBB27/docs/doc01.pdf. Last accessed January 4, 2018.
Central Intelligence Agency. 1983. Human Resource Exploitation Training Manual. Available at: http://americanempireproject.com/empiresworkshop/chapter3/DODHumanResourceExploitationTrainingManual1983.pdf. Last accessed January 4, 2018.
Cheney, Richard. 2001. *NBC News: Meet the Press* (September 16).
"CIA Waterboarded al-Qaida Suspects 266 Times." 2009. *Guardian* (April 20). Available at: https://www.theguardian.com/world/2009/apr/20/waterboarding-alqaida-khalid-sheikh-mohammed. Last accessed January 4, 2018.
Clark, Kathleen. 2011. "Congress's Right to Counsel in Intelligence Oversight." *University of Illinois Law Review* 11, 915–960.
Clarke, Richard. 2004. *Against All Enemies: Inside America's War on Terror.* New York: Free Press.
Cloud, David S. and Sheryl Gay Stolberg. 2006. "White House Proposes System to Try Detainees." *The New York Times* (July 26), A1.
CNN Poll. 2017. Problems and Priorities (October 12–15). Available at: http://pollingreport.com/prioriti.htm. Last accessed January 11, 2018.
CNN/ORC Poll. 2016. Attitudes on Terrorism (February 24–27). Available at: http://pollingreport.com/terror.htm. Last accessed January 11, 2018.
Colaresi, Michael P. 2014. *Democracy Declassified: The Secrecy Dilemma in National Security.* Oxford: Oxford University Press.
Cole, David. 2003. *Enemy Aliens: Double Standards and Constitutional Freedoms in the War on Terrorism.* New York: The New Press.
Communications Act of 1934. Public Law 73–416, 73rd Congress. (June 19).

Bibliography

Convention against Torture and Other Cruel, Inhuman, or Degrading Treatment or Punishment. 1985. Available at: http://www.hrweb.org/legal/cat.html. Accessed January 4, 2018.

Corwin, Edward S. 1957. *The President: Office and Powers, 1787–1957* (4th ed.). New York: New York University Press.

Crabtree, Susan. 2009. "Sens. in Both Parties Question Leahy Idea of 'Truth Commission.'" *The Hill* (March 4), 3.

Cronin, Audrey K. 2009. *How Terrorism Ends: Understanding the Decline and Demise of Terrorist Campaigns.* Princeton, NJ: Princeton University Press.

Cronin, Thomas and Michael A. Genovese. 2004. *The Paradoxes of the American Presidency* (2nd ed.). New York: Oxford University Press.

Davidson, Roger H., Walter Oleszek, Frances E. Lee, and Eric Schickler. 2015. *Congress and Its Members* (15th ed.). New York: CQ Press.

Davis, Morris D. 2007. "In Defense of Guantanamo Bay." *The Yale Law Journal—Pocket Part.* Available at: https://www.yalelawjournal.org/forum/in-defense-of-guantanamo-bay. Last accessed January 4, 2018.

Democracy Now! 2007. "We Knew Damn Well He'd Be Tortured." Transcript of United States Senate Hearing. Available at: https://www.democracynow.org/2007/1/19/we_knew_damn_well_hed_be (January 19). Last accessed January 4, 2018.

The Detainee Treatment Act. 2005. Title X of Division A of the Defense Appropriations Act of Fiscal Year 2006. Public Law 109–148 (December 30).

Devins, Neal. 2003. "Congress, Civil Liberties, and the War on Terrorism." *William & Mary Bill of Rights Journal* 11 (April), 1139–1149.

Dewar, Helen. 2004. "GOP Senators Block Subpoena on Memos but Prod White House." *The Washington Post* (June 18), A23.

Dewar, Helen and Dan Morgan. 2004. "Senate Rejects Request or Abuse Documents." *The Washington Post* (June 24), A7.

"Dick Cheney Defends Use of Torture on al-Qaida Leaders." 2011. *The Guardian* (September 9). Available at: https://www.theguardian.com/world/2011/sep/09/dick-cheney-defends-torture-al-qaida. Last accessed January 4, 2018.

Dionne, E. J., Jr. 2004. "The System Was Working." *The Washington Post* (May 7), A33.

Divoll, Vicki. 2011. "President Obama's First Two Years: A Legal Reflection: The 'Full Access Doctrine': Congress's Constitutional Entitlement to National Security Information from the Executive." *Harvard Journal of Law & Public Policy* 34 (Spring), 494–542.

Ducat, Craig and Robert Dudley. 1989. "Federal District Judges and Presidential Power during the Postwar Era." *The Journal of Politics* 51:1 (February), 98–118.

Duncan, Stephen M. 2004. *A War of a Different Kind: Military Force and America's Search for Homeland Security.* Annapolis, MD: Naval Institute Press.

Eggen, Dan and Ellen Nakashima. 2008. "Spy Law Lapse Blamed for Lost Information." *The Washington Post* (February 23), A3.

Eggen, Dan and R. Jeffrey Smith. 2004. "FBI Agents Allege Abuse of Detainees at Guantanamo Bay." *The Washington Post* (December 21), A1.

Eggen, Dan and Joby Warrick. 2007. "CIA Destroyed Videos Showing Interrogations." *The Washington Post* (December 7), A1.

Electronic Privacy Information Center. 2017. "Foreign Intelligence Surveillance Act Court Orders 1979–2016." Available at: https://epic.org/privacy/surveillance/fisa/stats/default.html. Last accessed January 4, 2018.

"Electronic Surveillance under Bush and Obama." 2013. *The New York Times* (June 7), A18.

Ely, John Hart. 1993. *War and Responsibility: Constitutional Lessons of Vietnam and Its Aftermath*. Princeton, NJ: Princeton University Press.

Ewing, Philip. 2013. "Rand Paul Pulls Plug on Nearly 13-House Filibuster." Politico.com. (March 7).

Farley, Robert. 2009. "Colin Powell Overstates Bush-Cheney Differences on Closing Guantanamo." *Politifact*. Available at: http://www.politifact.com/truth-o-meter/statements/2009/may/26/colin-powell/colin-powell-bush-cheney-gitmo-differences/. Last accessed January 4, 2018.

Farrier, Jasmine. 2010. *Congressional Ambivalence: The Political Burdens of Constitutional Authority*. Lexington: University Press of Kentucky.

Federal Torture Statute, 18 U.S.C. Chapter 113C-Torture. Section 2340–2340A. Available at: https://www.law.cornell.edu/uscode/text/18/2340. Last accessed January 4, 2018.

Finn, Peter. 2009. "Key Democrats Would Let Guantanamo Detainees Be Tried in the U.S." *The Washington Post* (October 8), A7.

Finn, Peter. 2009. "Obama Set to Revive Military Commissions." *The Washington Post* (May 9), A1.

Finn, Peter and Aaron Blake. 2013. "John Brennan Confirmed as CIA Director, but Filibuster Brings Scrutiny of Drone Program." *The Washington Post* (March 7).

Finn, Peter and Anne Kornblut. 2011. "Guantanamo Bay: How the White House Lost the Fight to Close It." *The Washington Post* (April 23). Available at: https://www.washingtonpost.com/world/guantanamo-bay-how-the-white-house-lost-the-fight-to-close-it/2011/04/14/AFtxR5XE_story.html?utm_term=.f3db9462a6f4. Last accessed January 4, 2018.

The FISA Amendments Act of 2008. Public Law 100–261, 100th Congress (July 9).

Fisher, Louis. 2003. *Nazi Saboteurs on Trial*. Lawrence: University of Kansas Press.

Fisher, Louis. 2004. "Military Tribunals: Historical Patterns and Lessons." A Congressional Research Service Report for Congress (July 9).

Fisher, Louis. 2004. *Presidential War Power* (2nd ed.). Lawrence: University of Kansas Press.

Fisher, Louis. 2005. "Judicial Review of War Power." *Presidential Studies Quarterly* 35:3 (September), 466–495.

Fisher, Louis. 2005. *Military Tribunals and Presidential Power*. Lawrence: University of Kansas Press.

Bibliography

Fisher, Louis. 2008. *The Constitution and 9/11: Recurring Threats to America's Freedoms*. Lawrence: University of Kansas Press.

Flaherty, Martin S. 2015. "The Constitution Follows the Drone: Targeted Killings, Legal Constraints, and Judicial Safeguards." *Harvard Journal of Law & Public Policy* 38:1, 211–232.

Foreign Intelligence Surveillance Act (FISA). 1978. Public Law 95–511, 95th Congress (October 25).

Forsythe, David P. 2011. *The Politics of Prisoner Abuse*. Cambridge: Cambridge University Press.

Frieden, Terry and Chris Kokenes. 2009. "Accused 9/11 Plotter Khalid Sheikh Mohammed Faces New York Trial." (November 13). Available at: http://www.cnn.com/2009/CRIME/11/13/khalid.sheikh.mohammed/index.html. Last accessed January 4, 2018.

Funk, William. 2007. "Electronic Surveillance of Terrorism: The Intelligence/Law Enforcement Dilemma—A History." *Lewis & Clark Law Review* 11:4, 1099–1139.

Garcia, Michael John. 2009. "The War Crimes Act: Current Issues." Congressional Research Service Report for Congress (January 22).

Gellman, Barton and Jo Becker. 2007. "Angler: The Cheney Vice Presidency." *The Washington Post* (June 24–27), A1.

Gellman, Barton, Dafna Linzer, and Carol Leonnig. 2006. "Surveillance Net Yields Few Suspects; NSA's Hunt for Terrorists Scrutinizes Thousands of Americans, but Most Are Later Cleared." *The Washington Post* (February 5), A1.

Geneva Convention Relative to the Treatment of Prisoners of War 1949. Available at: https://www.icrc.org/eng/war-and-law/treaties-customary-law/geneva-conventions/overview-geneva-conventions.htm. Last accessed January 4, 2018.

Gertler, Jeremiah. 2012. "U.S. Unmanned Aerial Systems." Congressional Research Service (January 3).

Glazier, David. 2005. "Precedents Lost: The Neglected History of the Military Commission." *Virginia Journal of International Law* 46 (Fall), 5–81.

Global Security.org. n.d. "Abu Ghurayb Prison." Available at: https://www.globalsecurity.org/intell/world/iraq/abu-ghurayb-prison.htm. Last accessed January 4, 2018.

Golden, Tim. 2006. "For Guantanamo Review Boards, Limits Abound." *The New York Times* (December 31), A1.

Goldfarb, Ronald (ed.). 2015. *After Snowden: Privacy, Secrecy, and Security in the Information Age*. New York: Thomas Dunne Books.

Goldstein, Robert Justin. 1978. *Political Repression in Modern America, from 1870 to the Present*. Cambridge: Schenkman Publishing Company.

Gonzales, Alberto R. 2013. "Drones: The Power to Kill." *The George Washington Law Review* 82, 1–60.

Gonzales, Alberto and Michael Hayden. 2005. *Press Briefing on NSA Surveillance* (December 19). Available at: http://www.techlawjournal.com/cong109/bills/house/patriot/20051219.asp. Last accessed January 4, 2018.

Gordon, Donald. 2014. *Transparent Government: What It Means and How You Can Make It Happen.* Amherst, NY: Prometheus Books.

Greenberger, Michael. 2007. "You Ain't Seen Nothin' Yet: The Inevitable Post-Hamdan Conflict between the Supreme Court and the Political Branches." *Maryland Law Review* 66, 805–834.

Greenhouse, Linda. 2007. "Justices Ready to Answer Detainee Rights Question." *The New York Times* (December 6), A32.

Greenwald, Glenn. 2013. "NSA Collecting Phone Records of Millions of Verizon Customers Daily." *The Guardian* (June 5).

Greenwald, Glenn. 2013. "Three Key Lessons from the Obama Administration's Drone Lies." *The Guardian* (April 11).

Greenwald, Glenn. 2014. *No Place to Hide: Edward Snowden, the NSA, and the U.S. Surveillance State.* New York: Metropolitan Books.

Griffin, Stephen. 2013. *Long Wars and the Constitution.* Cambridge, MA: Harvard University Press.

Gusterson, Hugh. 2016. *Drone: Remote Control Warfare.* Cambridge, MA: MIT Press.

Haberman, Maggie, Matthew Rosenberg, and Glenn Thrush. 2017. "Trump, Offering No Evidence, Suggests Rice Committed a Crime." *The New York Times* (April 6), A15.

Hafez, Mohammed M. and Joseph M. Hattfield. 2006. "Do Targeted Assassinations Work? A Multivariate Analysis of Israeli Counter-Terrorism Effectiveness during Al-Aqsa Uprising." *Studies in Conflict & Terrorism* 29:4 (June), 359–382.

Hamilton, Alexander, James Madison, and John Jay. 1987. *The Federalist Papers.* Penguin Classics Reprint Edition. New York: Penguin Publishing.

Hansen, Victor and Lawrence Friedman. 2012. "The Value of the Military Commission Act as Nonjudicial Precedent in the Context of Litigation over National Security Policymaking." *South Texas Law Review* 53 (Fall), 1–28.

Harbury, Jennifer K. 2005. *Truth, Torture, and the American Way: The History and Consequences of U.S. Involvement in Torture.* Boston: Beacon Press.

Hardaway, Robert, Christopher Hardaway, and James Siegesmund. 2005. "Military Tribunals and Civil Liberties in Time of National Peril: A Legal and Historical Perspective." Chapter Eight in *Law in the War on International Terrorism*, Ned Vanda (ed.), 169–208. London: Transnational Publishing.

Harriger, Katy. 2003. "The Separation of Powers in the Modern Context." In *Separation of Powers: Documents and Commentary*, Katy Harriger (ed.), 15–26. Washington, DC: CQ Press.

Hattem, Julian. 2015. "Senate Approves Sweeping Reforms to NSA Spying Programs." *The Hill* (June 2). Available at: http://thehill.com/policy/national-security/243791-senate-approves-nsa-reforms. Last accessed January 4, 2018.

Bibliography

Hayden, Michael. 2016. "The Case for Drones." *The New York Times* (February 21), Opinion 1.

Haynes, William. 2002. "Counter-Resistance Techniques." Memo 21 in *The Torture Papers* (November 27), Karen Greenberg and Joshua Dratel (eds.), 237. Cambridge: Cambridge University Press.

Henkin, Louis. 1990. *Foreign Affairs and the US Constitution* (2nd ed.). Oxford: Clarendon Press.

Herman, Susan N. 2011. *Taking Liberties: The War on Terror and the Erosion of American Democracy*. Oxford: Oxford University Press.

Heymann, Philip B. and Juliette N. Kayyem. 2005. *Protecting Liberty in an Age of Terror*. Cambridge, MA: The MIT Press.

Hollywood, Dana. 2013. "Redemption Deferred: Military Commissions in the War on Terror and the Charge of Providing Material Support for Terrorism." *Hastings International and Comparative Law Review* 36 (Winter), 1–109.

Hood, Christopher and David Heald (eds.). 2006. *Transparency: The Key to Better Governance?* Oxford: Oxford University Press.

Howell, William G. 2003. *Power without Persuasion: The Politics of Direct Presidential Action*. Princeton, NJ: Princeton University Press.

Hulse, Carl and Edmund Andrews. 2007. "House Approves Changes in Eavesdropping Program." *The New York Times* (August 5), A1.

Hutcheson, Ron. 2005. "Furor over Revelations of Spying; Specter Vowed to Probe the Eavesdropping. Bush Said the Public and Liberties Were Being Protected." *The Philadelphia Inquirer* (December 17).

Hutcheson, Ron and James Kuhnhenn. 2005. "Call for Inquiry in Spying Program; Senators of Both Parties Questioned Its Legality. Cheney Rose in Defense." *The Philadelphia Inquirer* (December 21), A1.

Innes, Brian. 1998. *The History of Torture*. New York: St. Martin's Press.

International Committee of the Red Cross (ICRC). 2004. *Report of the International Committee of the Red Cross (ICRC) on the Treatment by the Coalition Forces of Prisoners of War and Other Protected Persons by the Geneva Conventions in Iraq during Arrest, Internment and Interrogation* (February). Available at: https://cryptome.org/icrc-report.htm. Last accessed January 4, 2018.

International Covenant on Civil and Political Rights. 1976. G.A. res. 2200A (XXI), 21 U.N. GAOR Supp. (No. 16) at 52, U.N. Doc. A/6316 (1966), 999 U.N.T.S. 171, entered into force March 23.

Jackson, David. 2012. "Obama Defends Drone Strikes." *The USA Today* (January 31).

Jacobs, Ben and Sabrina Siddiqui. 2015. "USA Freedom Act Fails as Senators Reject Bill to Scrap NSA Bulk Collection." *The Guardian* (May 23).

Jarnot, Charles. 2012. "History." In *Introduction to Unmanned Aircraft Systems*, Richard Barnhart et al. (eds.), 1–16. New York: CRC Press.

Johnson, Carrie. 2009. "Waterboarding Is Torture, Holder Tells Senators." *The Washington Post* (January 16), A2.

Johnson, Carrie and Ellen Nakashima. 2009. " 'Inappropriate' Secrecy Hurt Surveillance Effort, Report Says." *The Washington Post* (July 11), A3.

Johnson, Carrie and Julie Tate. 2009. "New Interrogation Details Emerge." *The Washington Post* (April 17), A1.

Johnson, Loch K. 1985. *A Season of Inquiry: The Senate Intelligence Investigation*. Lexington: University of Kentucky Press.

Johnson, Loch K. 2012. "Congress and Intelligence." In *Congress and the Politics of National Security*, David Auerswald and Colton Campbell (eds.), 121–143. Cambridge: Cambridge University Press.

Johnston, David and Charlie Savage. 2009. "Obama Signals His Reluctance to Investigate Bush Programs." *The New York Times* (January 12), A1.

Joint Chiefs of Staff, Joint Publication 3–60: Joint Targeting. 2013. Available at: http://cfr.org/content/publications/attachments/Joint_Chiefs_of_Staff-Joint_Targeting_31_January_2013.pdf. Last accessed January 4, 2018.

Jordan, Jenna. 2009. "When Heads Roll: Assessing the Effectiveness of Leadership Decapitation." *Security Studies* 18:4 (December), 719–755.

Joscelyn, Thomas. 2015. "Ex-Guantanamo Detainee Now an Al Qaeda Leader in Yemen." Foundation for the Defense of Democracies. Available at: https://www.longwarjournal.org/archives/2015/12/ex-guantanamo-detainee-now-an-al-qaeda-leader-in-yemen.php. Last accessed January 4, 2018.

Kaag, John and Sarah Kreps. 2014. *Drone Warfare*. Cambridge, UK: Polity Press.

Kane, Paul. 2009. "Top Pelosi Aide Learned of Waterboarding in 2003." *The Washington Post* (May 9), A1.

Kane, Paul and Joby Warrick. 2009. "Cheney Led Briefings of Lawmakers to Defend Interrogation Techniques." *The Washington Post* (June 3), A1.

Katyal, Neal and Lawrence Tribe. 2002. "Waging War, Deciding Guilt: Trying the Military Tribunals." *Yale Law Journal* 111:6 (April), 1259–1310.

Kelley, Christopher S. 2007. "Contextualizing the Signing Statement." *Presidential Studies Quarterly* 37:4 (December), 737–748.

Kitrosser, Heidi. 2015. *Reclaiming Accountability: Transparency, Executive Power, and the U.S. Constitution*. Chicago: University of Chicago Press.

Klaidman, Daniel. 2012. *Kill or Capture: The War on Terror and the Soul of the Obama Presidency*. Boston: Houghton Mifflin Harcourt.

Koh, Harold. 1990. *The National Security Constitution*. New Haven, CT: Yale University Press.

Koh, Harold. 2010. Speech at the Annual Meeting of the American Society of International Law (March 25).

Kuhnhenn, James. 2005. "Bush Says He Secretly Authorized U.S. Spying; It Happened More Than 30 Times, He Said. A Democratic Senator Called the Admission 'Shocking.'" *The Philadelphia Inquirer* (December 18), A1.

Kuhnhenn, James. 2005. "Republicans Fault Bush on Secret Spying." *The Philadelphia Inquirer* (December 19), A2.

Lancaster, John. 2001. "Hearings Reflect Some Unease with Ashcroft's Legal Approach." *The Washington Post* (December 2), A25.

Lancaster, John and Susan Schmidt. 2001. "U.S. Rethinks Strategy for Coping with Terrorists." *The Washington Post* (September 14), A9.

Landau, Susan. 2013. "Making Sense from Snowden." *IEEE Computer and Reliability Societies* (July/August), 54–63.

Lardner, George, Jr. 2001. "Democrats Blast Order on Tribunals; Senators Told Military Trials Fall under President's Power." *The Washington Post* (November 29), A22.

Leung, Rebecca. 2004. "His Year in Hell." *CBS News*. Available at: https://www.cbsnews.com/news/his-year-in-hell-21-01-2004/. Last accessed January 4, 2018.

Levi, William Ranny. 2009. "Interrogation's Law." *Yale Law Journal* 118:7, 1434–1483.

Lewis, Neil A. 2001. "A Nation Challenged: The Hearings; Justice Dept. and Senate Clash over Bush Actions." *The New York Times* (November 29), B7.

Lewis, Neil A. 2004. "Ashcroft Says the White House Never Authorized Tactics Breaking Laws on Torture." *The New York Times* (June 9), A8.

Lewis, Neil A. 2005. "U.S. Spells Out New Definition Curbing Torture." *The New York Times* (January 1), A1.

Lichtblau, Eric. 2006. "Republican Who Oversees N.S.A. Calls for Wiretap Inquiry." *The New York Times* (February 8), A12.

Lichtblau, Eric. 2006. "White House Rejects Senators' Request for Spying Documents." *The International Herald Tribune* (February 3), 5.

Lichtblau, Eric. 2008. "Deal Is Struck to Overhaul Wiretap Law." *The New York Times* (June 20), A1.

Lichtblau, Eric. 2008. "Senate Approves Bill to Broaden Wiretap Powers." *The New York Times* (July 10), A1.

Lichtblau, Eric. 2013. "In Secret, Court Vastly Broadens Powers of N.S.A." *The New York Times* (July 7), A1.

Lichtblau, Eric and David Johnston. 2007. "Court to Oversee U.S. Wiretapping in Terror Cases." *The New York Times* (January 18), A1.

Lichtblau, Eric and James Risen. 2009. "Officials Say U.S. Wiretaps Exceeded Law." *The New York Times* (April 16), A1.

Lichtblau, Eric and James Risen. 2009. "U.S. Wiretapping of Limited Value, Officials Report." *The New York Times* (July 11), A1.

Lichtblau, Eric and Scott Shane. 2006. "Bush Is Pressed over New Report on Surveillance." *The New York Times* (May 12), A1.

Lightle, Rebecca. 2014. "Balancing National Security Policy: Why Congress Must Assert Its Constitutional Check on Executives Power." *Florida State University Law Review* 42, 255–284.

Linfield, Michael. 1990. *Freedom under Fire: U.S. Civil Liberties in Times of War*. Boston: South End Press.

LoBianco, Tom. 2015. "Donald Trump on Terrorists: 'Take Out Their Families.'" CNN. Available at: http://www.cnn.com/2015/12/02/politics/donald-trump-terrorists-families/. Last accessed January 11, 2018.

Londono, Ernesto and Karen DeYoung. 2014. "Congress Cuts U.S. Military and Development Aid for Afghanistan." *The Washington Post* (January 24).

Available at: https://www.washingtonpost.com/world/national-security/congress-cuts-us-military-and-development-aid-for-afghanistan/2014/01/24/3d4cb818-8531-11e3-bbe5-6a2a3141e3a9_story.html?utm_term=.5b7197351e5b. Last accessed December 13, 2017.

Lowenthal, Mark M. 2015. *Intelligence: From Secrets to Policy* (6th ed.). Los Angeles: CQ Press.

Lue, Thomas. 2005. "Torture and Coercive Interrogations." In *Protecting Liberty in an Age of Terror*, Philip B. Heymann and Juliette N. Kayyem (eds.), 149–178. London: The MIT Press.

Lynch, Caroline and Lara Flint. 2017. "The USA Freedom Act Turns Two." Lawfare Blog (June 2). Available at: https://www.lawfareblog.com/usa-freedom-act-turns-two. Last accessed January 4, 2018.

Maass, Matthias. 2015. "From U-2s to Drones: U.S. Aerial Espionage and Targeted Killing during the Cold War and the War on Terror." *Comparative Strategy* 34:2 (May 16), 218–238.

Mannes, Aaron. 2008. "Testing the Snake Head Strategy: Does Killing or Capturing Its Leaders Reduce a Terrorist Group's Advocacy?" *Journal of International Policy Solutions* 9 (Spring), 40–49.

Marguilies, Joseph. 2006. *Guantanamo and the Abuse of Presidential Power*. New York: Simon & Schuster.

Markon, Jerry. 2010. "September 11 Trials Still in Search of a Venue." *The Washington Post* (July 4), A-3.

Mason, Jeff and Ayesha Rascoe. 2016. "Obama Makes Last Attempt to Persuade Congress to Close Guantanamo." *Reuters* (February 23).

Mayer, Jane. 2005. "Outsourcing Torture." *The New Yorker* (February 14).

Mazzetti, Mark. 2007. "Key Lawmakers Getting Files about Surveillance Program." *The New York Times* (February 1), A12.

Mazzetti, Mark. 2007. "Pentagon Revises Its Rules on Prosecution of Terrorists." *The New York Times* (January 19), A18.

Mazzetti, Mark. 2013. "U.S. Drone War Began with a Secret Pact; 2004 Killing of Militant in Pakistan Marked Shift in CIA's Terrorism Fight." *The New York Times* (April 8), News 1.

Mazzetti, Mark and Matt Apuzzo. 2015. "Deep Support in Washington for C.I.A.'s Drone Missions." *The New York Times* (April 26), A-1.

Mazzetti, Mark, Matthew Rosenberg, and Charlie Savage. 2017. "Trump Administration Returns Copies of Report on C.I.A. Torture to Congress." *The New York Times* (June 3), A1.

Mazzetti, Mark and Jonathan Weisman. 2014. "Conflict Erupts in Public Rebuke on C.I.A. Inquiry." *The New York Times* (March 12), A1.

McCain, John. 2005. "McCain Statement on Detainee Amendments." Available at: https://www.mccain.senate.gov/public/index.cfm/speeches?ID=0effe15d-0a29-4940-b052-74206536325a. Last accessed January 4, 2018.

McCaul, Michael T. and Ronald J. Sievert. 2011. "Congress's Consistent Intent to Utilize Military Commissions in the War against Al-Qaeda and Its Adoption of the Commission Rules That Fully Comply with Due Process." *St. Mary's Law Journal* 42, 595–644.

Bibliography

McCoy, Alfred W. 2006. *A Question of Torture: CIA Interrogation, from the Cold War to the War on Terror*. New York: Metropolitan Books.

McKelvey, Benjamin. 2011. "Due Process Rights and Targeted Killing of Suspected Terrorists: The Unconstitutional Scope of Executive Killing Power." *Vanderbilt Journal of Transnational Law* 44, 1353–1384.

Mehta, Aaron. 2016. "White House Rolls Out Armed Drone Declaration." Defense News. Available at: http://www.defensenews.com/articles/white-house-rolls-out-armed-drone-declaration. Last accessed January 4, 2018.

Michel, Arthur Holland. 2013. "Drones in Bosnia." Center for the Study of the Drone. Available at: http://dronecenter.bard.edu/drones-in-bosnia/. Last accessed January 4, 2018.

Mikolashek, Paul. 2004. *Detainee Operations Inspection*. United States Army, The Inspector General (July 21).

The Military Commissions Act. 2006. Public Law 109–366 (October 17).

Moe, Terry M. and William G. Howell. 1999. "The Presidential Power of Unilateral Action." *Journal of Law, Economics, and Organization* 15 (April), 132–179.

Monmouth University Poll. 2016. Attitudes on Terrorism (September 22–25). Available at: http://pollingreport.com/terror.htm. Last accessed January 11, 2018.

Myers, Steven Lee. 2008. "Bush Decides to Keep Guantanamo Open." *The New York Times* (October 20).

Nakashima, Ellen. 2007. "Bush Wants Phone Firms Immune to Privacy Suits." *The Washington Post* (May 4), A14.

Nakashima, Ellen. 2015. "Congressional Action on NSA Is a Milestone in the Post-9/11 World." *Washington Post* Blogs (June 2). Available at: https://www.washingtonpost.com/world/national-security/congressional-action-on-nsa-is-a-milestone-in-the-post-911-world/2015/06/02/f46330a2-0944-11e5-95fd-d580f1c5d44e_story.html?noredirect=on&utm_term=.9f10f786c20. Last accessed May 14, 2018.

Nakashima, Ellen. 2015. "Two Years after Snowden's Leaks, Law Marks a Milestone." *The Washington Post* (June 3), A2.

Nakashima, Ellen, Devlin Barrett, and Adam Entous. 2017. "Court Let FBI Monitor an Advisor to Trump." *The Washington Post* (April 12), A1.

Nakashima, Ellen and Spencer Hsu. 2007. "Democrats Offer Compromise Plan on Surveillance; Proposal Would Involve FISA Court in Warrants." *The Washington Post* (August 2), A3.

Nakashima, Ellen and Ed O'Keefe. 2014. "Senate Fails to Advance Legislation on NSA Reform." *The Washington Post* (November 18).

National Defense Authorization Act for Fiscal Year 2016. Public Law 114–92. 114th Congress (November 25).

NBC News/*Wall Street Journal* Poll. 2016. Attitudes on Terrorism (June 19–23). Available at: http://pollingreport.com/terror.htm. Last accessed January 11, 2018.

The New America Foundation. 2016. "International Security." Available at: http://securitydata.newamerica.net/drones/pakistan-analysis.html. Last accessed January 4, 2018.

Newcome, Laurence R. 2004. *Unmanned Aviation: A Brief History of Unmanned Aerial Vehicles.* Reston, VA: American Institute of Aeronautics and Astronautics, Inc.

Obama, Barack. 2009. "Ensuring Lawful Interrogations." Executive Order 13491 (January 22). Available at: http://www.federalregister.gov/articles/2009/01/27/E9-1885/ensuring-lawful-interrogations. Accessed January 4, 2018.

Obama, Barack. 2009. "Review and Disposition of Individuals Detained at the Guantanamo Bay Naval Base and Closure of Detention Facilities." Executive Order 13492 (January 22). Available at: http://www.federalregister.gov/articles/2009/01/27/E9-1893/review-and-disposition-of-individuals-detained-at-the-guantaacutenamo-bay-naval-base-and-closure-of. Accessed January 4, 2018.

Obama, Barack. 2009. "Review of Detention Policy Options." Executive Order 13493 (January 22). Available at: http://www.federalregister.gov/articles/2009/01/27/E9-1895/review-of-detention-policy-options. Accessed January 4, 2018.

Obama, Barack. 2009. "Transparency and Open Government." Memorandum for the Heads of Departments and Agencies (January 21). Available at: https://obamawhitehouse.archives.gov/the-press-office/transparency-and-open-government. Last accessed January 4, 2018.

Obama, Barack. 2011. "Statement on Signing the National Defense Authorization Act for Fiscal Year 2012" (December 31).

Obama, Barack. 2013. Remarks by the President at the National Defense University (May 23). Available at: https://obamawhitehouse.archives.gov/the-press-office/2013/05/23/remarks-president-national-defense-university. Last accessed January 4, 2018.

Obama, Barack. 2016. "Remarks by the President on Plan to Close the Prison at Guantanamo Bay" (February 23).

Obama, Barack. 2016. "United States Policy on Pre- and Post-Strike Measures to Address Civilian Casualties in U.S. Operations Involving the Use of Force." Executive Order 13, 732 (July 1).

Obama Administration White Paper. 2013. *Bulk Collection of Telephony Metadata under Section 215 of the USA Patriot Act* (August 9).

Office of the Director of National Intelligence. 2016. *Summary of Information Regarding U.S. Counterterrorism Strikes Outside Areas of Active Hostilities* (July 1).

Offices of Inspectors General. 2009. *Unclassified Report on the President's Surveillance Program* (July 10).

O'Keefe, Ed and Aaron Blake. 2013. "Rand Paul Conducts Filibuster in Opposition to John Brennan, Obama's Drone Policy." *The Washington Post* (March 7). Available at https://www.washingtonpost.com/politics/rand-paul-conducts-filibuster-in-opposition-to-john-brennan-obamas-drone-policy/2013/03/06/1367b1b4-868c-11e2-9d71-f0feafdd1394_story.html?utm_term=.4c647a33a2b3. Last accessed June 28, 2018.

Bibliography

Omnibus Crime Control and Safe Streets Act of 1968. Public Law 90–35, 90th Congress (June 19).

Orin, Deborah and Brian Blomquist. 2004. "W. 'Disgusted' by Latest Pics—Weighs Release of New Abu Ghraib Photos." *The New York Post* (May 11), Sports 7.

Otterman, Michael. 2007. *American Torture: From the Cold War to Abu Ghraib and Beyond*. Ann Arbor, MI: Pluto Press.

Pallitto, Robert M. and William G. Weaver. 2007. *Presidential Secrecy and the Law*. Baltimore: Johns Hopkins University Press.

Parry, John T. 2009. "Torture Nation, Torture Law." *Georgetown Law Journal* 97 (April), 1001–1053.

Parry, John T. and Welsh S. White. 2002. "Interrogating Suspected Terrorists: Should Torture Be an Option?" *University of Pittsburgh Law Review* 63(4), 743–766.

Paust, Jordan. 2007. *Beyond the Law: The Bush Administration's Unlawful Responses in the "War" on Terror*. New York: Cambridge University Press.

Perine, Keith and Edward Epstein. 2009. "Purchase of Ill. Prison for Guantanamo Detainees Meets Swift GOP Backlash." *Congressional Quarterly Today* (December 15).

Philbin, Patrick F. 2001. "Legality of the Use of Military Commissions to Try Terrorists." Memorandum for Alberto R. Gonzales, Counsel for the President (November 6).

Phillip, Abby. 2011. "Holder Transfers KSM Case" (April 4). Available at: http://www.politico.com/story/2011/04/holder-transfers-ksm-case-052509. Last accessed January 4, 2018.

Pincus, Walter. 2006. "Spying Necessary, Democrats Say: But Harman, Daschle Question President's Legal Reach." *The Washington Post* (February 13), A3.

Pincus, Walter. 2009. "Intelligence Pick Calls Torture Immoral, Ineffective." *The Washington Post* (January 23), A2.

Pious, Richard M. 2006. *The War on Terrorism and the Rule of Law*. Los Angeles: Roxbury Publishing Company.

Pious, Richard M. 2007. "Inherent War and Executive Powers and Prerogative Politics." *Presidential Studies Quarterly* 37:1 (March), 66–84.

Plaw, Avery, Matthew S. Fricker, and Carlos R. Colon. 2016. *The Drone Debate: A Primer on the U.S. Use of Unmanned Aircraft Outside Conventional Battlefields*. New York: Rowman & Littlefield.

Port, Bob. 2001. "Congress Challenges W on Tribunal Rules." *The New York Daily News* (December 5), NEWS 32.

Powell, Colin L. 2002. "Draft Decision Memorandum for the President on the Applicability of the Geneva Convention to the Conflict in Afghanistan." Memo 8 in *The Torture Papers* (January 26), Karen Greenberg and Joshua Dratel (eds.), 122–126. Cambridge: Cambridge University Press.

Priest, Dana. 2004. "CIA Puts Harsh Tactics on Hold." *The Washington Post* (June 27), A1.

Priest, Dana. 2005. "Senate Urged to Probe CIA Practices." *The Washington Post* (April 22), A2.

Protect America Act. 2007. Public Law 110–55, 110th Congress (August 5).

"Q&A: Guantanamo Bay, US Detentions, and the Trump Administration." 2017. Human Rights Watch (May 4). Available at: https://www.hrw.org/news/2017/05/04/qa-guantanamo-bay-us-detentions-and-trump-administration. Last accessed January 4, 2018.

Quinnipiac University Poll. 2014. Attitudes on Terrorism (January 4–7). Available at: http://pollingreport.com/terror.htm. Last accessed January 11, 2018.

Radsan, Afsheen and Richard Murphy. 2012. "The Evolution of Law and Policy for CIA Targeted Killing." *Journal of National Security Law & Policy* 5, 439–463.

Ransom, Harry H. 1975. *The Intelligence Establishment*. Cambridge, MA: Harvard University Press.

Ratner, Michael and Ellen Ray. 2004. *Guantanamo: What the World Should Know*. White River Junction, VT: Chelsea Green Pub.

Richey, Warren. 2009. "Obama Endorses Military Commissions for Guantanamo Detainees." *The Christian Science Monitor* (October 29). Available at: https://www.csmonitor.com/USA/Justice/2011/0404/In-abrupt-reversal-9-11-suspects-to-get-Guantanamo-military-tribunals. Last accessed May 14, 2018.

Richey, Warren. 2011. "In Abrupt Reversal, 9/11 Suspects to Get Guantanamo Military Tribunals." *The Christian Science Monitor* (April 4). Available at: https://www.csmonitor.com/USA/Justice/2011/0404/In-abrupt-reversal-9-11-suspects-to-get-Guantanamo-military-tribunals. Last accessed May 14, 2018.

Risen, James and David Johnston. 2002. "Bush Has Widened Authority of C.I.A. to Kill Terrorists." *The New York Times* (December 14), A1.

Risen, James and Eric Lichtblau. 2005. "Bush Lets U.S. Spy on Callers without Courts." *New York Times* (December 16), A1.

Risen, James and Eric Lichtblau. 2009. "Court Affirms Wiretapping without Warrants." *The New York Times* (January 16), A13.

Risen, James and Eric Lichtblau. 2009. "E-Mail Surveillance Renews Concerns in Congress." *The New York Times* (June 17), A1.

Roberts, Dan. 2013. "Patriot Act Author Prepares Bill to Put NSA Bulk Collection 'Out of Business.'" *The Guardian* (October 10). Available at: https://www.theguardian.com/world/2013/oct/10/nsa-surveillance-patriot-act-author-bill. Last accessed May 14, 2018.

Roberts, Dan. 2013. "U.S. Drone Strikes Being Employed as Alternative to Guantanamo, Lawyer Says." *The Guardian* (May 2). Available at: https://www.theguardian.com/world/2013/may/02/us-drone-strikes-guantanamo. Last accessed May 14, 2018.

Robinson, Gwen. 2001. "Lawmakers Criticise Military Tribunals." *Financial Times* (December 5), The Americas 14.

Rockefeller, John D. 2003. *Letter to Vice-President Cheney* (July 17).

Rosenberg, Carol. 2006. "Gitmo Defense Whiz Forced Out; Navy Lawyer Passed Over, Must Retire." *The Seattle Times* (October 8), A7.

Bibliography

Rosenberg, Carol. 2016. "Federal Judge Preserves CIA 'Torture Report' after Guantanamo War Court Wouldn't Do It." *The Miami Herald* (December 30). Available at: http://www.miamiherald.com/news/nation-world/world/americas/guantanamo/article123591209.html. Last accessed May 14, 2018.

Rosenthal, Andrew (ed.). 2012. "Tortured Logic." *The New York Times* (May 3). Available at: https://takingnote.blogs.nytimes.com/2012/05/03/tortured-logic/. Last accessed January 4, 2018.

Rossiter, Clinton. 1960. *The American Presidency* (rev. ed.). New York: Harcourt, Brace.

Rossiter, Clinton and Richard Longaker. 1976. *The Supreme Court and the Commander in Chief.* Ithaca, NY: Cornell University Press.

Ruane, Michael E. 1995. "Setbacks Leave Pilotless Plane with Uncharted Course the Spy Aircraft Worked Well in the Persian Gulf, but Not in Bosnia." *The Philadelphia Inquirer* (August 28), A2.

Rudalevige, Andrew. 2005. *The New Imperial Presidency.* Ann Arbor: The University of Michigan Press.

Rumsfeld v. Padilla. 2004. *Oyez* (April 28). Available at: www.oyez.org/cases/2003/03-1027. Last accessed January 4, 2018.

Savage, Charlie. 2005. *Takeover: The Return of the Imperial Presidency and the Subversion of American Democracy.* Boston: Little, Brown and Company.

Savage, Charlie. 2011. "In a Reversal, Military Trials for 9/11 Cases." *The New York Times* (April 4), A5.

Savage, Charlie. 2011. "Senators Say Patriot Act Is Being Misinterpreted." *The New York Times* (May 27), A17.

Savage, Charlie. 2012. "At Guantanamo, Trial for 9/11 Defendants, and a Revamped Tribunal." *The New York Times* (May 5), A13.

Savage, Charlie. 2015. "Guantanamo Detainee's Conviction Is Thrown Out on Appeal." *The New York Times* (June 13), A12.

Savage, Charlie. 2015. *Power Wars: Inside Obama's Post-9/11 Presidency.* New York: Little, Brown & Company.

Savage, Charlie. 2016. "Guantanamo Detainee's Conspiracy Conviction Upheld, but Legal Issue Lingers." *The New York Times* (October 21), A3.

Savage, Charlie. 2016. "Trump Backs Guantanamo for Trials of Americans." *The New York Times* (August 13), A11.

Savage, Charlie. 2017. "White House Backs Off Reviving C.I.A. Prisons." *The New York Times* (February 5), A13.

Savage, Charlie and Adam Goldman. 2017. "Sessions, Seeking Guantanamo Prison, Echoes Trump's Pledge to Keep It Open." *The New York Times* (July 8), A14.

Schlesinger, James R. 2005. *The Schlesinger Report: An Investigation of Abu Ghraib.* United States Department of Defense Report (November 15).

Schoenfeld, Gabriel. 2010. *Necessary Secrets: National Security, the Media and the Rule of Law.* New York: W.W. Norton Company.

Schubert, Glendon. 1957. *The Presidency in the Courts.* Minneapolis: University of Minnesota Press.

Schwarz, Frederick and Aziz Z. Huq. 2007. *Unchecked and Unbalanced: Presidential Power in a Time of Terror.* New York: The New Press.

Scigliano, Robert. 1971. *The Supreme Court and the Presidency.* New York: Free Press.

Serwer, Adam. 2017. "Can Trump Bring Back Torture?" *The Atlantic Online* (January 26). Available at: https://www.theatlantic.com/politics/archive/2017/01/trump-torture/514463/. Last accessed May 14, 2018.

Setty, Sudha. 2015. "Surveillance, Secrecy, and the Search for Meaningful Accountability." *Stanford Journal of International Law* 51 (Winter), 69–102.

Shane, Scott. 2015. "Ghosts in the Cross Hairs." *The New York Times* (April 24), A-1.

Shane, Scott and Mark Mazzetti. 2009. "In Adopting Harsh Tactics, No Inquiry into Past Use." *The New York Times* (April 22), A1.

Shaw, Ian. 2016. *Predator Empire: Drone Warfare and Full Spectrum Dominance.* Minneapolis: University of Minnesota Press.

Shear, Michael D. and Peter Finn. 2009. "Obama to Revamp Military Tribunals." *The Washington Post* (May 16), A1.

Sherman, Jerome L. 2007. "Senate Defeats Bill on Detainee Trial Rights." *Pittsburgh Post-Gazette* (September 20), A1.

Simon, Richard and Elizabeth Shogren. 2004. "Iraq Prison Scandal." *The Los Angeles Times* (May 8), A11.

Sink, Justin. 2017. "Comey Hits Trump Credibility." *The Gazette* (Montreal) (March 21), World, N1.

"A Small but Fast-Growing Club: Countries with Killer Drones." 2016. *The Toronto Star* (March 6), IN 3.

Smist, Frank J., Jr. 1994. *Congress Oversees the United States Intelligence Community 1949–1994* (2nd ed.). Knoxville: University of Tennessee Press.

Smith, R. Jeffrey. 2004. "Senators Fault Pentagon as New Photos Emerge." *The Washington Post* (May 10), A1.

Solomon, John. 2007. "FBI Provided Inaccurate Data for Surveillance Warrants." *The Washington Post* (March 27), A5.

Sorkin, Amy Davidson. 2013. "The N.S.A.-Verizon Scandal." *The New Yorker* (June 6). Available at: https://www.newyorker.com/news/amy-davidson/the-n-s-a-verizon-scandal. Last accessed May 14, 2018.

The Stimson Group. 2014. *Recommendations and Report of the Task Force on U.S. Drone Policy* (2nd ed.) Dallas, Texas. (June 14).

Stolberg, Sheryl. 2017. "Senate Rejects Bipartisan Effort to End 9/11 Military Force Declaration." *The New York Times* (September 14), A15.

Sugiyama, Tara M. and Marisa Perry. 2006. "The NSA Domestic Surveillance Program: An Analysis of Congressional Oversight during an Era of One-Party Rule." *University of Michigan Journal of Law Reform* 40 (Fall), 149–189.

Sweeney, Joseph. 2007. "Guantanamo and U.S. Law." *Fordham International Law Journal* 30 (February), 673–779.

Szoldra, Paul. 2016. "This Is Everything Edward Snowden Revealed in One Year of Unprecedented Top-Secret Leaks." *Business Insider* (September 16).

Bibliography

Available at: http://www.businessinsider.com/snowden-leaks-timeline-2016-9. Last accessed May 14, 2018.

Taylor, Stuart, Jr., and Benjamin Wittes. 2009. "Looking Forward, Not Backward: Refining U.S. Interrogation Law." In *Legislating the War on Terror: An Agenda for Reform*, Benjamin Wittes (ed.), 289–345. Washington, DC: Brookings Institution Press.

Tigar, Michael E. 2014. "The National Security State: The End of Separation of Powers." *Monthly Review* 66(3), 136–159.

Tiron, Roxana. 2006. "Human-Rights Groups Back Dems' Detainee Law Overhaul." *The Hill* (November 21), 10.

Uniform Code of Military Justice. 10 U.S. Code, 836.

United States Constitution. *The Avalon Project*. Available at: www.avalon.law.yale.edu/18th_century/usconst.asp. Last accessed June 27, 2018.

United States Department of Defense. 2007. Salim Hamdan Charge Sheets. Available at: http://www.mc.mil/CASES/MilitaryCommissions.aspx. Last accessed January 4, 2018.

United States Department of Defense. 2017. Office of Military Commissions. Available at: http://www.mc.mil/ABOUTUS.aspx. Last accessed January 4, 2018.

United States Department of Justice. 2006. *Legal Authorities Supporting the Activities of the National Security Agency Described by the President* (January 19).

United States Department of Justice. 2006. *Transcript of Attorney General Alberto R. Gonzales and Federal Trade Commission Chairman Deborah Platt Majoras at Press Conference Announcing Identity Theft Task Force Interim Recommendations* (September 19).

United States Department of Justice White Paper. 2011. *Lawfulness of a Lethal Operation Directed against a U.S. Citizen Who Is a Senior/Operational Leader of Al-Qa'ida or An Associated Force* (November 8).

United States Senate Committee on Armed Services. 2008. *Inquiry into the Treatment of Detainees in U.S. Custody*. 110th Congress, 2nd session (November 20).

United States Senate Select Committee on Intelligence. 2014. Committee Study of the Central Intelligence Agency's Detention and Interrogation Program [Executive Summary]. S. Report 113–288 (December 9).

United States Senate Committee on the Judiciary. Subcommittee on the Constitution, Civil Rights, and Human Rights. 2013. *Drone Wars: The Constitutional and Counterterrorism Implications of Targeted Killing* (April 23).

United States Senate Select Committee on Intelligence. 2014. Committee Study of the Central Intelligence Agency's Detention and Interrogation Program [Executive Summary]. S. Report 113–288 (December 9).

Uniting and Strengthening America by Providing Appropriate Tools Required to Intercept and Obstruct Terrorism (USA PATRIOT ACT) Act of 2001, Pub. L. No. 107–56, 115 Stat. 272 (2001).

Universal Declaration of Human Rights. 1948. U.N. General Assembly, 217 (III). Paris.

USA Freedom Act of 2015. Public Law 114–23, 114th Congress (June 2).

Vagts, Detlev. 2007. "Military Commissions: A Concise History." *American Journal of International Law* 101 (January), 35–48.

Verble, Joseph. 2014. "The NSA and Edward Snowden: Surveillance in the 21st Century." *Computers & Society* 44:3, 14–20.

Vladeck, Stephen I. 2014. "Targeted Killing and Judicial Review." *George Washington Law Review* 82 (January), 11–29.

Wagner, William. 1982. *Lightning Bugs and Other Reconnaissance Drones*. Fallbrook, CA: Aero Publishers.

Wald, Matthew. 2013. "Current Laws May Offer Little Protection against Prying Drones, Senators Are Told." *The New York Times* (March 21), A-20.

Walquist, John. 2009. "Enhancing Interrogation: Advancing a New Agenda." *Parameters* 39:2 (Summer), 38–51.

Walters, Joanna. 2017. "Will Accused 9/11 Architect Khalid Sheikh Mohammed Ever Come to Trial?" *The Guardian* (September 11), US News 1.

War Crimes Act of 1996. United States Code. Title 18, Part I, Chapter 118—War Crimes, Section 2441.

Warrick, Joby. 2009. "Senate Panel to Examine CIA Detainee Handling." *The Washington Post* (February 27), A4.

Warrick, Joby and Walter Pincus. 2007. "How the Fight for Vast New Spying Powers Was Won." *The Washington Post* (August 12), A1.

Weiser, Benjamin. 2010. "Detainee Acquitted on Most Counts in '98 Bombings." *The New York Times* (November 17), A-1.

Weisman, Jonathan. 2006. "Battle Looms in Congress over Military Tribunals." *The Washington Post* (July 13), A6.

Weisman, Jonathan and Dan Eggen. 2008. "Surveillance Law Set to Expire Today; Both Sides Weigh Political Effects." *The Washington Post* (February 16), A2.

Wheeler, Darren. 2009. "Checking Presidential Detention Power in the War on Terror: What Should We Expect from the Judiciary?" *Presidential Studies Quarterly* 39:4, 677–700.

The White House. 2017. *Detention and Interrogation of Enemy Combatants*. Draft Executive Order (January).

Whittington, Keith. 2003. "The Separation of Powers at the Founding." In *Separation of Powers: Documents and Commentary*, Katy Harriger (ed.), 1–14. Washington, DC: CQ Press.

The Wickersham Commission Report on Alcohol Prohibition. 1931. Available at: https://www.alcoholproblemsandsolutions.org/wickersham-commission-pro-or-anti-repeal/. Last accessed May 14, 2018.

Wittes, Benjamin. 2008. *Law and the Long War: The Future of Justice in the Age of Terror*. New York: Penguin Press.

Wolf, Richard and Mimi Hall. 2009. "Obama's Anti-Terrorism Policies Hit Walls." *The USA Today* (May 21), NEWS 5A.

Wolf, Z. Byron. 2013. "Rand Paul Launches Filibuster—the Talking Kind—against John Brennan." ABC News.com. Available at: http://abcnews.go.com/Politics/rand-paul-launches-filibuster-the-talking-kind-against-john-brennan/blogEntry?id=18668622. Last accessed January 5, 2018.

Wood, Gordon S. 1969. *The Creation of the American Republic*. New York: W.W. Norton.

Woods, Chris. 2015. *Sudden Justice: America's Secret Drone Wars*. Oxford: Oxford University Press.
Woodward, Bob. 2002. *Bush at War*. New York: Simon & Schuster.
Wright, Austin. 2017. "Mattis, Pompeo Stunned by CIA 'Black Sites' Report." *Politico* (January 25). Available at: https://www.politico.com/story/2017/01/torture-mattis-pompeo-defense-234180. Last accessed November 8, 2017.
Wright, Lawrence. 2008. "The Spymaster." *The New Yorker* (January 21). Available at: https://www.newyorker.com/magazine/2008/01/21/the-spymaster. Last accessed May 14, 2018.
Wright, Robin. 2004. "Top U.S. Officials Apologize to Arabs for Prisoner Abuse." *The Washington Post* (May 5), A19.
Yoo, John. 2006. *War by Other Means*. New York: Atlantic Monthly Press.
Yoo, John. 2001. "The President's Constitutional Authority to Conduct Military Operations against Terrorists and Nations Supporting Them." Memo 1 (September 25) in *The Torture Papers*, Karen J. Greenberg and Joshua Dratel (eds.), 3–24. New York: Cambridge University Press.
Yoo, John. 2002. "Application of Treaties and Laws to al Qaeda and Taliban Detainees." Memo 4 (January 9) in *The Torture Papers*, Karen Greenberg and Joshua Dratel (eds.), 38–79. New York: Cambridge University Press.
Yoo, John. 2005. *The Powers of War and Peace*. Chicago: The University of Chicago Press.
Zakaria, Tabassum. 2013. "Nominee for CIA Chief Says Casualties from Drone Strikes Should Be Public." *Reuters* (February 15). Available at: http://www.reuters.com/article/us-obama-nominations-brennan-drones-idUSBRE91E18N20130215. Last accessed January 5, 2018.
Zenko, Micah and Sarah Kreps. 2015. "Limiting Armed Drone Proliferation." In *Drones and Targeted Killings: Ethics, Law and Politics*, Sarah Knuckey (ed.), 124–136. New York: International Debate Education Association.
Zernike, Kate. 2005. "Newly Released Reports Show Early Concern on Prison Abuse." *The New York Times* (January 6), A1.
Zernike, Kate. 2006. "Military Lawyers Urge Protections for Detainees." *The New York Times* (July 14), A1.
Zernike, Kate. 2006. "Senate Passes Detainee Bill Sought by Bush." *The New York Times* (September 28). Available at: https://www.nytimes.com/2006/09/28/washington/29detaincnd.html. Last accessed May 14, 2018.
Zernike, Kate. 2006. "A Top Senate Republican Is Uncertain on Legislation for Military Tribunals for Terror Suspects." *The New York Times* (July 1), A1.
Zernike, Kate. 2008. "McCain and Obama Split on Justices' Ruling." *The New York Times* (June 13), A23.

Cases

ACLU v. Clapper, 785 F.3d 787 (2nd Cir. 2015).
ACLU v. Clapper, 959 F.Supp. 2d 724 (S.D. NY 2013).

ACLU v. Department of Justice, 109 F.Supp. 3d 220 (D.C. Dist. 2015).
ACLU v. Department of Justice, 710 F.3d 422 (D.C. Cir. 2013).
ACLU v. Department of Justice, 2016 U.S. App. LEXIS 7308 (D.C. Cir. 2016).
ACLU v. National Security Agency, 438 F.Supp. 2d 754 (E.D. Mich. 2006).
ACLU v. National Security Agency, 493 F.3d 644 (6th Cir. 2007).
ACLU v. National Security Agency, 552 U.S. 1179 (2008).
Al-Aulaqi v. Obama, 727 F.Supp. 2d 1 (D.D.C. 2010).
Al-Aulaqi v. Panetta, 35 F.Supp. 3d (D.D.C. 2014).
Al-Bahlul v. United States, 767 F.3d 1 (D.C. Cir. 2014).
Al-Haramain Islamic Foundation, Inc. v. Bush, 451 F.Supp. 2d 1215 (D. Or. 2006).
American Civil Liberties Union v. Department of Justice, 808 F.Supp. 2d 280 (D.C. Dist. 2011).
Arar v. Ashcroft, 414 F.Supp 2d 250 (E.D.N.Y. 2006).
Arar v. Ashcroft, 532 F.3d 157 (2nd Cir. 2008).
Arar v. Ashcroft, 585 F.3d 555 (2nd Cir. 2009).
Ashcraft v. Tennessee, 322 U.S. 143 (1944).
Ashcroft v. Iqbal, 556 U.S. 662 (2009).
Boumediene v. Bush, 553 U.S. 723 (2008).
Brown v. Mississippi, 297 U.S. 298 (1936).
Camara v. Municipal Court, 387 U.S. 523 (1967).
Clapper v. Amnesty International, 568 U.S. 398 (2013).
Culombe v. Connecticut, 367 U.S. 581 (1961).
Duncan v. Kahanamoku, 324 U.S. 833 (1945).
Ex Parte McCardle, 74 U.S. 506 (1868).
Ex Parte Milligan, 71 U.S. 2 (1866).
Ex Parte Quirin, 317 U.S. 1 (1942).
Ex Parte White, 66 F.Supp. 982 (1944).
Hamdan v. Rumsfeld, 548 U.S. 557 (2006).
Homma v. Patterson, 327 U.S. 759 (1946).
In re NSA Telecommunications Records Litigation, 2009 U.S. Dist. LEXIS 48313.
In Re Yamashita, 327 U.S. 1 (1946).
Johnson v. Eisentrager, 339 U.S. 763 (1950).
Katz v. U.S., 389 U.S. 358 (1967).
Klayman v. Obama, 957 F.Supp. 2d 1 (D.C.C. 2013).
Korematsu v. U.S., 323 U.S. 214 (1944).
Miranda v. Arizona, 384 U.S. 436 (1966).
Olmstead v. U.S., 277 U.S. 438 (1928).
Nardone v. U.S., 302 U.S. 379 (1937).
Nardone v. U.S., 308 U.S. 338 (1939).
The New York Times et al. v. U.S. Department of Justice, 752 F.3d 123 (2nd Cir. 2014).
The New York Times et al. v. U.S. Department of Justice, 758 F.3d 436 (2nd Cir. 2014).
The New York Times et al. v. U.S. Department of Justice, 915 F.Supp. 2d 508 (D.C.C. 2013).
Padilla v. Yoo, 633 F.Supp. 2d 1005 (N.D. Cal. 2009).

Padilla v. Yoo, 678 F.3d 748 (9th Cir. 2012).
The Paquette Habana, 175 U.S. 677 (1900).
Rasul v. Bush, 542 U.S. 466 (2004).
Rhodes v. Chapman, 452 U.S. 337 (1981).
Rochin v. California, 342 U.S. 165 (1952).
Smith v. Maryland, 442 U.S. 735 (1979).
State of Washington v. Trump, No. 17–35105 (9th Cir. 2017).
Talbot v. Seeman, 5 U.S. 1 (1801).
Terkel v. AT&T, 441 F.Supp. 2d 899 (N.D. Ill. 2006).
U.S. v. Curtiss-Wright, 299 U.S. 304 (1936).
U.S. v. U.S. District Court, 407 U.S. 297 (1972) [cited as the Keith Case]
Youngstown Sheet & Tube Co. v. Sawyer, 343 U.S. 579 (1952).

Index

Abu Ghraib, 19, 77–79, 163
Accountability in government, 17–18, 166–67
ACLU v. Clapper, 48–49
Addington, David, 104, 110
Afghanistan, 164
Al-Aulaqi, Anwar, 145–46
Alexander, Keith, 48, 49
Al-Haramain Foundation, 38, 40
Al Qaeda, 1, 6, 71–72, 132, 142
Al Qaeda Arabian Peninsula (AQAP), 135
Amash, Justin, 49
Arar, Maher, 75–76
Ashcroft, John, 84, 103, 105, 106
Authorization to Use Military Force (AUMF), 3, 8, 34, 109, 141, 152–53, 163, 170

Bahlul, Ali al, 119
Bentham, Jeremy, 14
Bill of Rights, 63, 64, 69, 144
Blunt, Roy, 3
Boehner, John, 116
Bosnian conflict, 129–30
Boumediene v. Bush, 112–13
Brandeis, Louis, 15
Brennan, John, 87, 139–40
Burr, Richard, 87
Burton, Dan, 30
Bush, George H. W., 63

Bush, George W., 1, 163; drones and, 130–33; electronic surveillance, 21, 29–41; interrogation, 65, 71–81; military tribunals, 103–8, 110–14. *See also* Terrorist Surveillance Program (TSP)
Bybee, Jay, 30, 72, 73

Casey, William, 28
Central Intelligence Agency (CIA), 16, 28, 67–68, 74–77, 87–88, 121, 129, 135, 138, 145
Checks and balances, 11–14
Cheney, Dick, 32, 34, 44, 60, 75, 80, 81, 82, 104, 105, 110
Church Committee, 25–26, 27, 138
Civil War, 98–99, 129
Clapper, James, 45, 136
Clapper v. Amnesty International, 44–45
Clifford, Clark, 24
Cold War, 6, 67–68
Comey, James, 53
Congress: drones and, 137–41; interrogation, 88–91; military tribunals, 105–6; oversight, 28, 31–32, 54–55, 79–81, 137–39, 162, 168; Trump presidency and, 168–70; War on Terror and, 2–4; war powers, 6–9, 162–64

Convention against Torture (CAT), 62–63
Conyers, John, 49
Corwin, Edward, 12

Detainee Treatment Act 2005, 3, 80–81, 108, 109, 112–13
Drones, 19, 161, 166; Bush administration and, 130–33; casualties, 136–37; domestic issues, 151–52; history of, 128–30; international law and, 143–44; Obama administration and, 133–37 (legal defense, 141–44); signature strikes and, 132–33; targeting, 143, 152–53, 155; technology, proliferation of, 149–51. *See also* Targeted killing
Dunleavy, Michael, 74

Electronic surveillance, 18, 161; Bush administration and, 21, 29–41; Cold War era, 23–24, 28; lawsuits and, 37–38; Obama administration and, 21, 42–51; Trump administration and, 52–53. *See also* Terrorist Surveillance Program (TSP)
Ex Parte Quirin, 100

Federal Bureau of Investigation (FBI), 23, 73
Federal Communications Act of 1934, 23
Federalist Papers, 1, 13, 22
Federal Torture Statute, 65
Feingold, Russ, 34, 35, 106
Feinstein, Dianne, 47, 83, 83, 87, 154
FISA Amendments Act of 2008, 39–41, 43, 44, 47
Flynn, Michael, 53
Ford, Gerald, 25
Foreign Intelligence Surveillance Act (FISA), 165; creation and content, 26–27; reforms, 56–57; Terrorist Surveillance Program and, 32–35; warrants, 26–27, 36–37, 43, 52
Foreign Intelligence Surveillance Court (FISC), 26–27, 30, 36, 43, 47, 50–51, 56
Foreign Intelligence Surveillance Court of Review (FISCR), 26–27, 42, 51, 56
Fourth Amendment, 21
Frist, Bill, 36, 78, 110

Gang of 8, 32
Geneva Conventions, 63, 64, 71–72, 161
Ghailani, Ahmed, 121
Gonzales, Alberto, 31, 32–34, 75, 103
Graham, Lindsey, 34, 78, 121, 140, 170
Guantanamo Bay, 19, 71–74, 91, 107, 121, 122, 123, 164, 168; closing, 60, 81, 85–86, 117

Hagel, Chuck, 3
Hamdan, Salim, 120
Hamdan v. Rumsfeld, 108–10
Hatch, Orrin, 79, 106
Hayden, Michael, 29, 31, 133
Henry, Patrick, 14–15
Hersh, Seymour, 25
Hicks, David, 120
Hoekstra, Peter, 31, 36
Holder, Eric, 82, 116, 140

International Covenant on Civil and Political Rights (ICCPR), 63, 101
Interrogation, 19, 161; Bush administration and, 65, 71–81; civil suits and, 83–85; criminal justice model, 61–62; history in U.S., 66–70; military model, 61–62; Obama administration and, 81–88
Iqbal, Javaid, 83–84
Iraq, 164

Jackson, Andrew, 97
Jackson, Robert, 9, 10, 23

Index

Jay, John, 22
Jefferson, Thomas, 13
Johnson v. Eisentrager, 100
Judiciary: drones and, 144–46, 154–55; electronic surveillance and, 37–38; military tribunals and, 122–23; war powers, 9–11. *See also* United States Supreme Court

Kant, Immanuel, 14
Katz v. U.S., 24
Kennedy, Ted, 30
Khadr, Omar, 119
Khalid Sheikh Mohammed, 75
Klayman v. Obama, 48
Kollar-Kotelly, Colleen, 30, 43
Korematsu v. U.S., 10

LaHood, Ray, 8
Lamberth, Royce, 27, 30
Leahy, Pat, 40, 76, 82, 103, 105, 106, 112, 139, 154
Lieber Code, 67
Lincoln, Abraham, 6, 18, 98
Locke, John, 13
The Long War, 2, 159
Lott, Trent, 30, 162

Madison, James, 1, 7, 13–14
Marshall, John, 7
McCain, John, 80, 83, 89, 113, 140, 170
McConnell, Mike, 60
McConnell, Mitch, 50, 106, 116, 117, 140
MERRIMAC, 24
Military commissions. *See* Military tribunals
Military Commissions Act (MCA) of 2006, 3, 110–13, 114, 160
Military Commissions Act (MCA) of 2009, 115
Military tribunals: alternatives to, 115–17; Bush administration and, 103–8, 110–14; Congress and, 105–6; defined, 95–96; history of, 97–101; Obama administration and, 114–17; post 9/11, 118–21; Trump administration and, 121–22
MINARET, 24
Mohammed, Khalid Sheikh, 116, 118–19
Montesquieu, 13
Moussaoui, Zacarias, 120–21

Nashiri, Abd al, 88, 118
National Security Agency (NSA), 16, 21, 30, 45–48, 160; bulk metadata collection, 48–49. *See also* Snowden, Edward
New York Times, 21, 25, 30, 31, 134, 145, 166
9/11, 1
Nunes, Devin, 53

Obama, Barack, 40, 113, 135; accountability in government and, 17; closing Guantanamo, 85–86; drones and, 133–37, 141–44; executive orders, 114; military tribunals and, 114–17; transparency in government and, 15
Obey, David, 3
Office of Legal Counsel (OLC), 29–30, 74–75, 103–4, 153
Office of Military Commissions, 118
Olmstead v. U.S., 22
Omnibus Crime Control and Safe Streets Act of 1968, 25, 26

Padilla, Jose, 77, 84–85
Pakistan, 132, 135, 155
Panetta, Leon, 145
Patriot Act, 3, 26, 47, 50, 160, 163
Paul, Rand, 50, 139–40, 170
Pelosi, Nancy, 31, 39, 79
Philbin, Patrick, 103–4
Powell, Lewis, 25
Predator drones, 131

Presidential war powers, 5–6
Protect American Act of 2007, 39, 42

Rasul v. Bush, 107–8
Reagan, Ronald, 63, 129
Reid, Harry, 32, 140
Revolutionary War, 22, 66, 97
Roberts, Pat, 31, 35
Rockefeller, Jay, 32, 40, 76
Roosevelt, Franklin D., 99–100, 107
Rumsfeld, Donald, 59, 71, 73, 78

Schumer, Chuck, 111, 117
Scott, Winfield, 97–98
Senate Select Committee on Intelligence, 86–88
Separation of powers, 11–14, 160–62, 165–66
SHAMROCK, 24
Signature strikes, 132–33
Signing statements, 80, 117
Snowden, Edward, 21, 45–48, 55, 167
Specter, Arlen, 30, 33, 105, 111, 112
State secrets privilege, 37–38, 40, 57, 76, 167
Sutherland, George, 10

Taft, William Howard, 22
Taliban, 71
Targeted killing: effectiveness, 147–49. *See also* Drones
Taylor, Anna Diggs, 38
Telecommunications companies, 36, 37–39
Tenet, George, 29, 131
Terkel v. AT&T, 37–38
Terrorist Surveillance Program (TSP), 43–45; Congress and, 31–32, 34–35; legal defense, 32–33; origins, 29–30
Torture, 73; international law and, 62–64; Senate "Torture Report," 86–87; U.S. law and, 64–65

Transparency in government, 14–15, 167–68; drones and, 134, 136, 145, 152–53; national security and, 14–17
Trump, Donald: Congress and, 168–70; drones and, 155–56; electronic surveillance and, 52–53; interrogation and, 88–89; military tribunals and, 121–22; travel ban, 169

Udall, Mark, 45
Uniform Code of Military Justice (UCMJ), 100–101, 109
United States Supreme Court: electronic surveillance and, 44–45; interrogation and, 69–70; military tribunals and, 108–10
Universal Declaration of Human Rights (UDHR), 63
Unmanned Aerial Vehicles (UAVs). *See* Drones
USA Freedom Act, 3, 50–51, 54–55, 56, 167
U.S. v. Curtiss-Wright, 10
U.S. v. U.S. District Court, 24–25

Walker, Vaughn, 40
War Crimes Act (WCA), 65
War on Terror (WOT), 1, 18–19
Waterboarding, 75, 76, 82
Whistleblowers, 166
Wickersham Report, 69
Wilson, Heather, 32, 36
Wittes, Benjamin, 3
Wyden, Ron, 45, 140

Yemen, 132, 135, 155, 169
Yoo, John, 5, 30, 43–44, 84–85, 104, 106, 108, 112
Youngstown Sheet & Tube v. Sawyer, 9, 10–11

About the Author

Darren A. Wheeler, PhD, is an associate professor and chair of the Political Science Department at Ball State University, Muncie, Indiana. He is the author of *Presidential Power in Action: Implementing Supreme Court Detainee Decisions.*